STOP!

This is the back of the book.
You wouldn't want to spoil a great ending!

This book is printed "manga-style," in the authentic Japanese right-to-left format. Since none of the artwork has been flipped or altered, readers get to experience the story just as the creator intended. You've been asking for it, so TOKYOPOP® delivered: authentic, hot-off-the-press, and far more fun!

DIRECTIONS

If this is your first time reading manga-style, here's a quick guide to help you understand how it works.

It's easy... just start in the top right panel and follow the numbers. Have fun, and look for more 100% authentic manga from TOKYOPOP®!

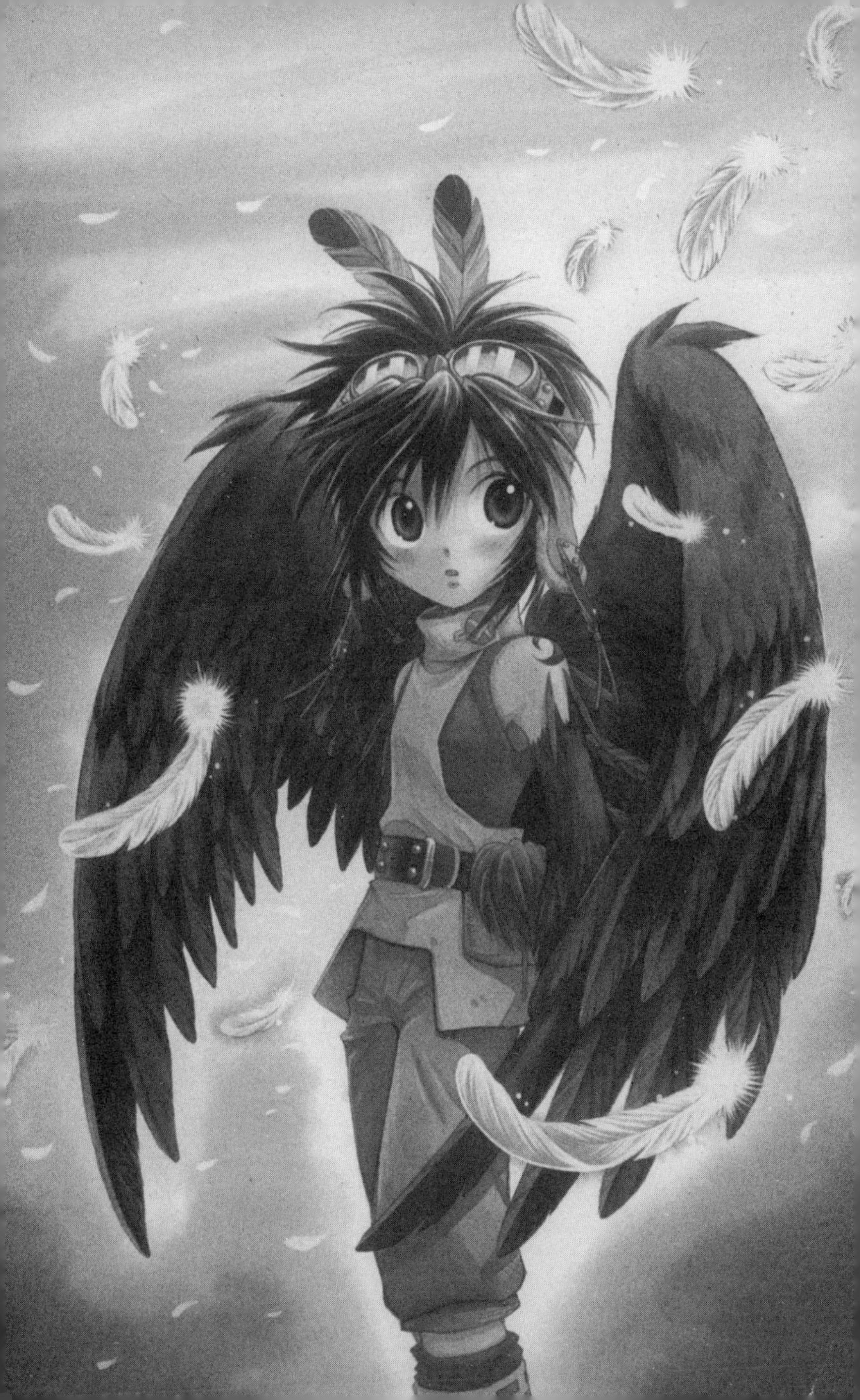

+ *Anima Vol.3*
Created By Natsumi Mukai

Translation - Alethea and Athena Nibley
English Adaption - Karen Ahlstrom
Copy Editor - Stephanie Duchin
Layout and Lettering - Star Print Brokers
Cover Layout - James Lee

Editor - Troy Lewter
Digital Imaging Manager - Chris Buford
Pre-Press Supervisor - Erika Terriquez
Art Director - Anne-Marie Horne
Managing Editor - Vy Nguyen
Production Manager - Elisabeth Brizzi
VP of Production - Ron Klamert
Editor-in-Chief - Rob Tokar
Publisher - Mike Kiley
President and C.O.O. - John Parker
C.E.O. and Chief Creative Officer - Stuart Levy

A  Manga

TOKYOPOP Inc.
5900 Wilshire Blvd. Suite 2000
Los Angeles, CA 90036

E-mail: info@TOKYOPOP.com
Come visit us online at www.TOKYOPOP.com

ISBN: 978-1-59816-349-0

First TOKYOPOP printing: January 2007
10 9 8 7 6 5
Printed in the USA

Volume 3
by Natsumi Mukai

HAMBURG // LONDON // LOS ANGELES // TOKYO

+ANIMA

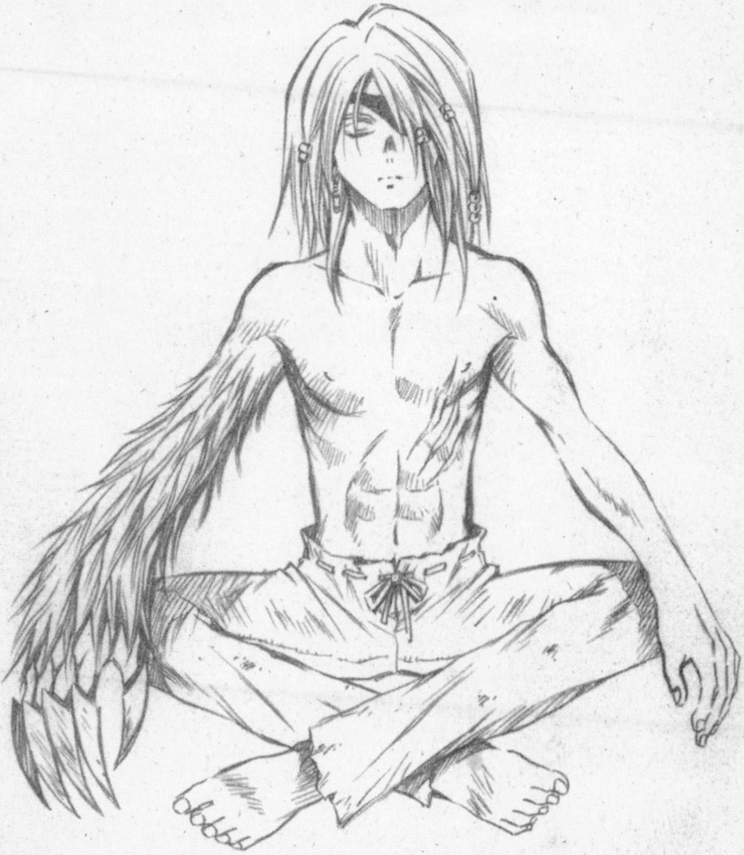

プラスアニマ
+ANIMA

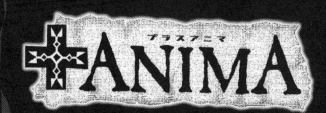

迎夏生

NATSUMI MUKAI

STORY & CHARACTERS

The +Anima are beings that possess animal-like powers. Cooro, a crow +Anima, peeks in at a circus during his travels and meets Husky, a fish +Anima who is playing a mermaid princess in the show. Though Cooro invites Husky to run away from the circus and join him on his travels, he refuses. Husky is tired of the circus life, though, and waiting for the ringmaster to fall asleep, he plans to leave Cooro and run away himself. However, the ringmaster is one step ahead of them. He captures Husky and forces him to continue playing the mermaid princess, with Cooro added to the show as the angel of death. Thanks to Cooro's quick thinking, the two soon get their chance to escape. Though circus people surround them, Cooro uses his +Anima power to carry Husky into the sky, and the two leave the circus far behind them.

クーロ [Cooro]

**Crow +Anima.
When he spreads his pitch-black wings, he can fly freely in the sky.
He is a bit of a glutton!**

ハスキー [Husky]

**Fish +Anima. He can swim freely through water like a merman.
He's a little stubborn, and he hates girls.**

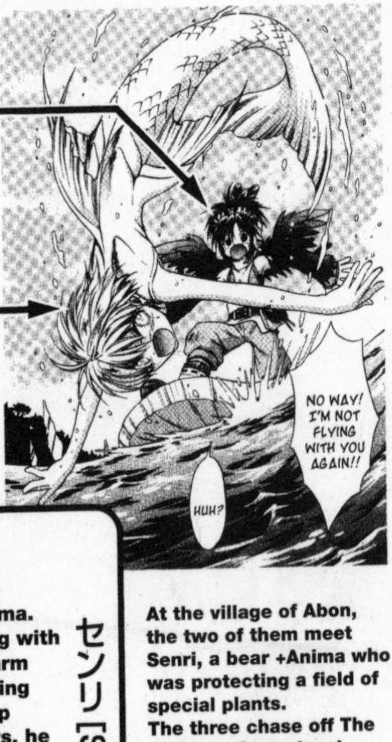
NO WAY! I'M NOT FLYING WITH YOU AGAIN!!
HUH?

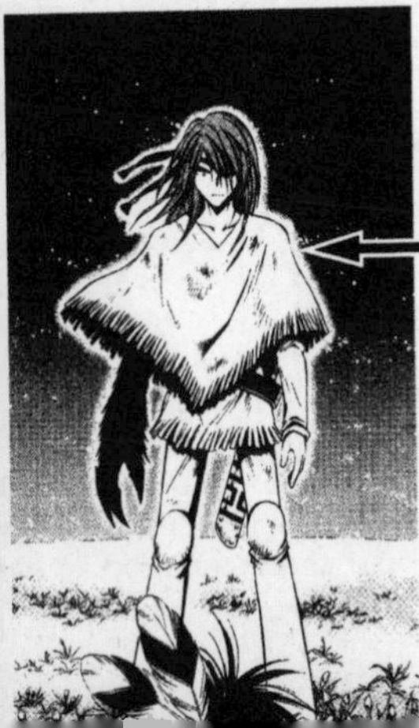

センリ [Senri]

**Bear +Anima.
Along with his arm bearing sharp claws, he also has amazing strength.
He doesn't talk very much.**

**At the village of Abon, the two of them meet Senri, a bear +Anima who was protecting a field of special plants.
The three chase off The Garrison Gang, local thugs who thought there was a gold mine under the field. As peace returns to the village, Senri's duties as a bodyguard have come to an end, so he joins Cooro and Husky as they travel onward.**

In the underground ruins beneath the metropolis Octopus, Husky's pearls are stolen, and Cooro and the others meet the bat +Anima, Nana. They soon solve the crime and move on. Nana wants to travel with the party, but Husky, who hates girls for some reason, refuses to let Nana join them, and leaves the party himself. Nana goe after Husky, and tells him the story of how she was awakened as a +Anima, and he finally accepts her as one of the group.
And thus the journey begins...

LIKE ME... SEE?

ナナ [Nana]
Bat +Anima. She can fly and use an ultrasonic screech. A fashion-conscious girl, she is scared of forests at night.

ローズ [Rose]
Cat +Anima. A girl Cooro and the others met on their journey. She works by herself to make and sell accessories. She has a little brother who is almost eight years old.

フライ [Fly]

イグナス [Igneous]

......

IT MUST BE COORO ...!
AND TO THINK HE'S STILL AROUND, AFTER ALL THIS TIME...!

During their travels, the party meets the peddler Rose, and crosses the mountain pass with her. It seems the journey will g smoothly, but then they encounter Igneou a commander of the Astarian Military. Igneous hates the mountain people Kim-un-kur (Senri's clan), and the narrow mountain pathway is thrown into confusi Working together with Rose, Cooro and th others manage to settle things and arrive in town. The party says goodbye to Rose and continues its journey.
And who is the mysterious Researcher wh seems to knows an awful lot about Cooro What awaits the four young +Anima at the end of their journey?

C O N T E N T S

Chapter 9: Wings of the Wind — Part 1

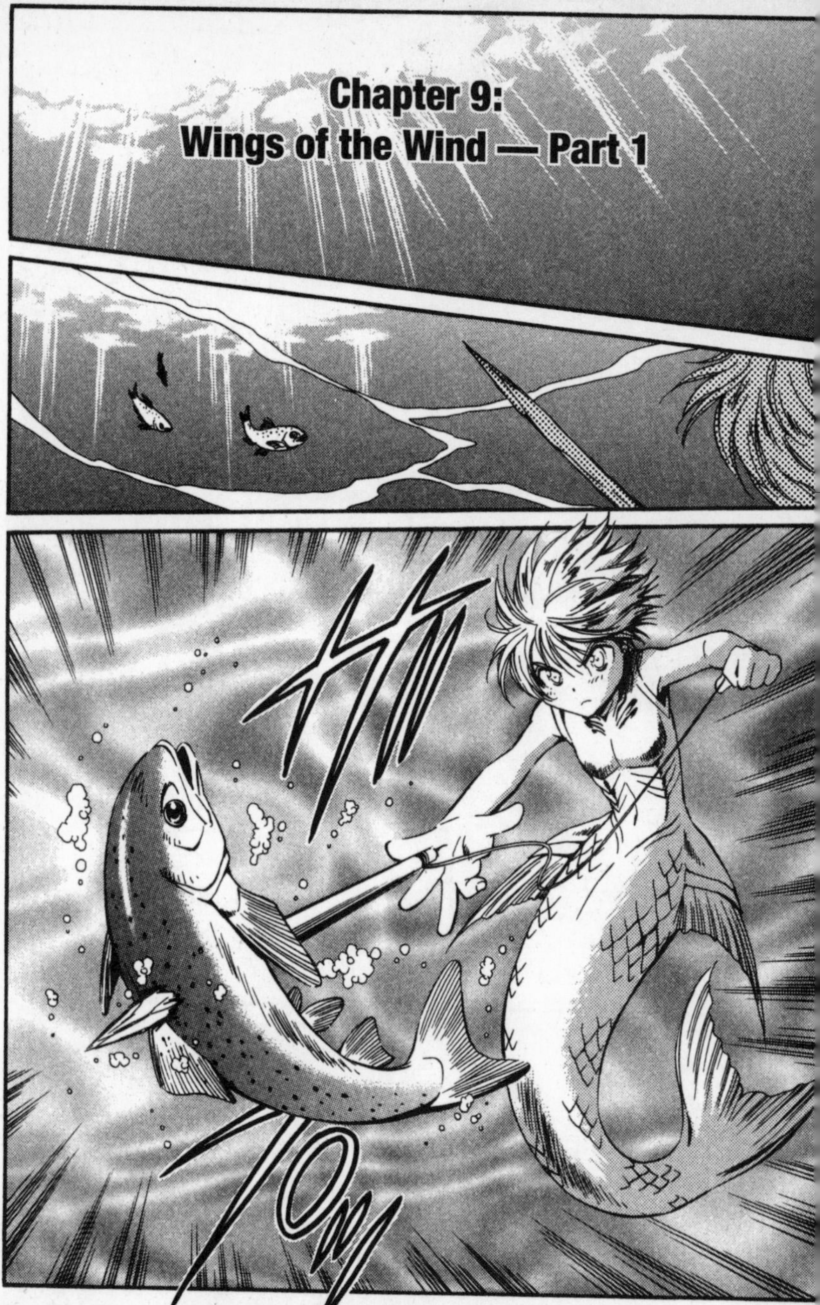

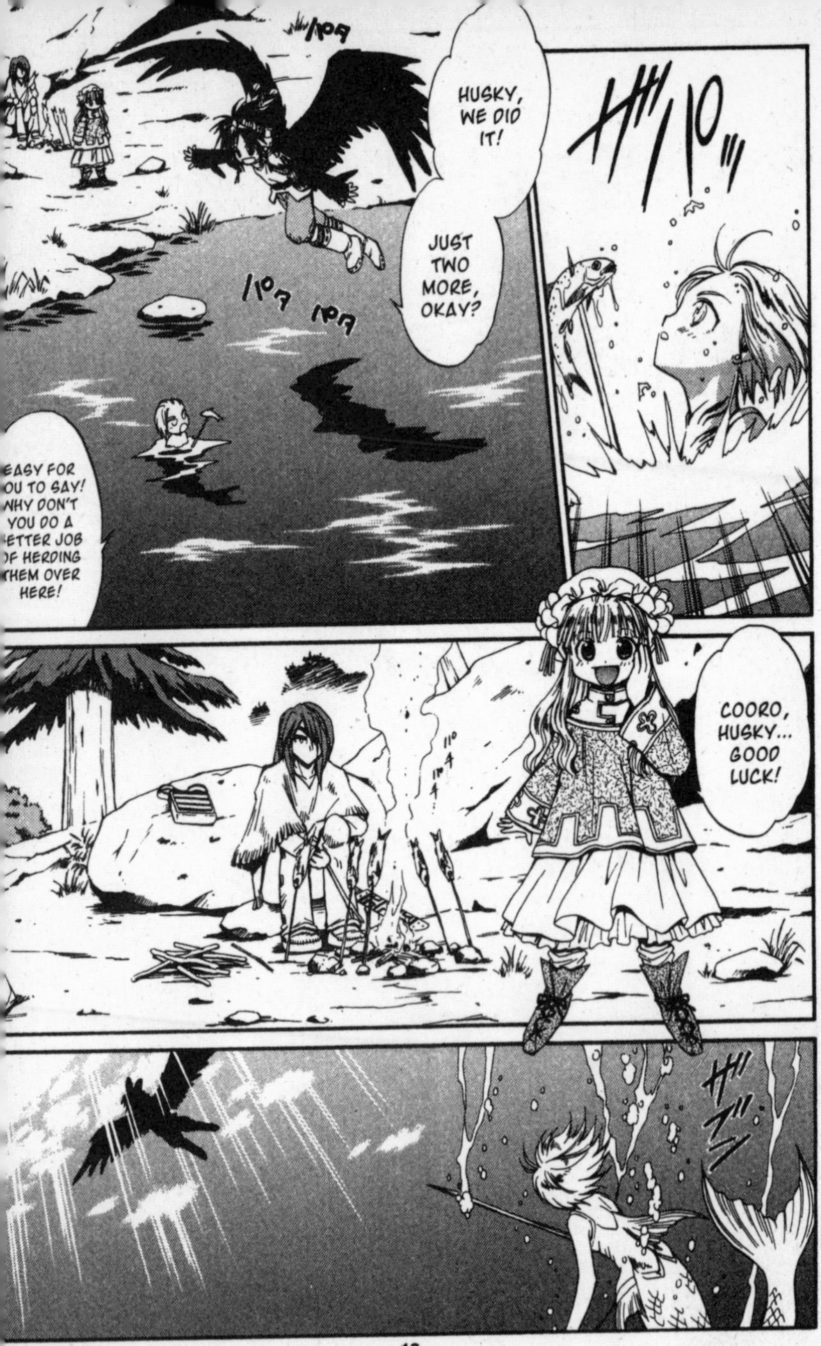
HUSKY, WE DID IT!
JUST TWO MORE, OKAY?
EASY FOR OU TO SAY! WHY DON'T YOU DO A ETTER JOB OF HERDING THEM OVER HERE!
COORO, HUSKY... GOOD LUCK!

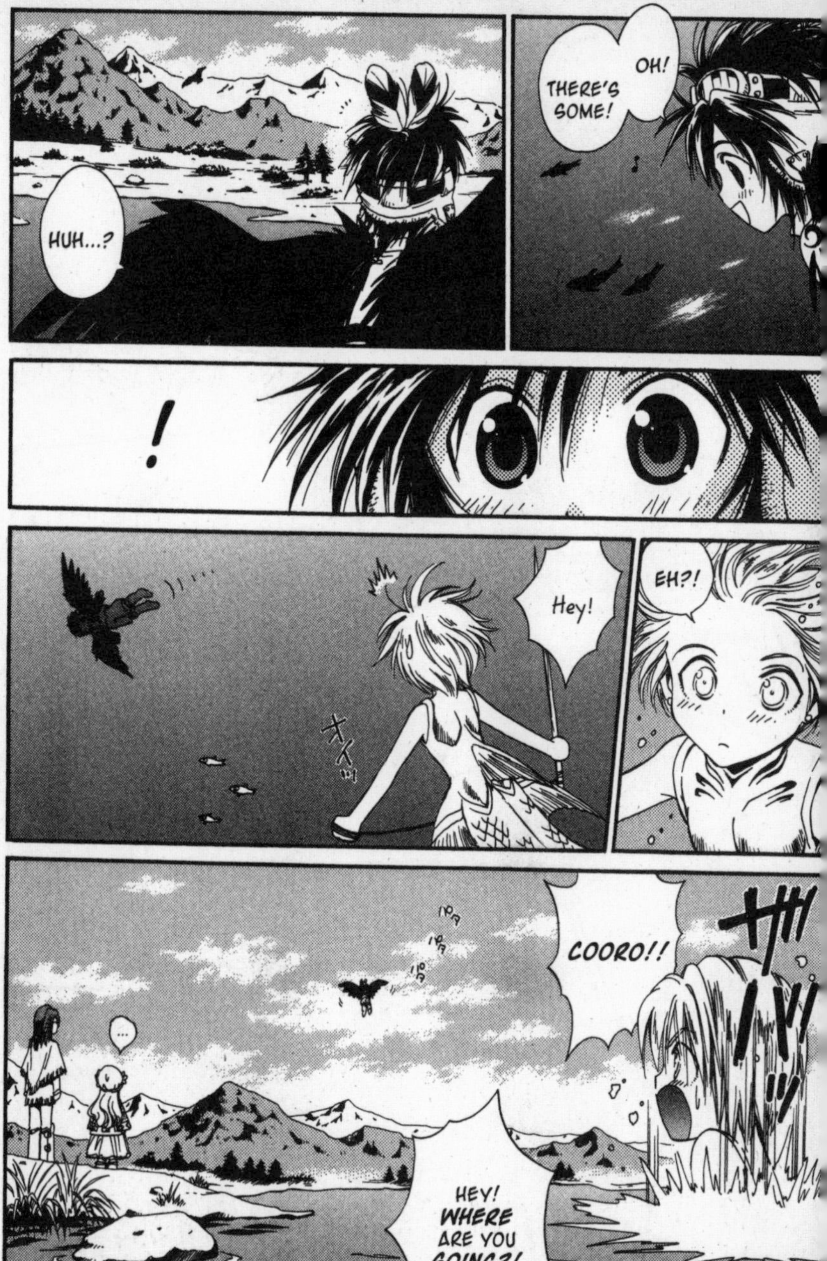
OH! THERE'S SOME!
HUH...?
!
EH?!
Hey!
COORO!!
HEY! WHERE ARE YOU GOING?!
...

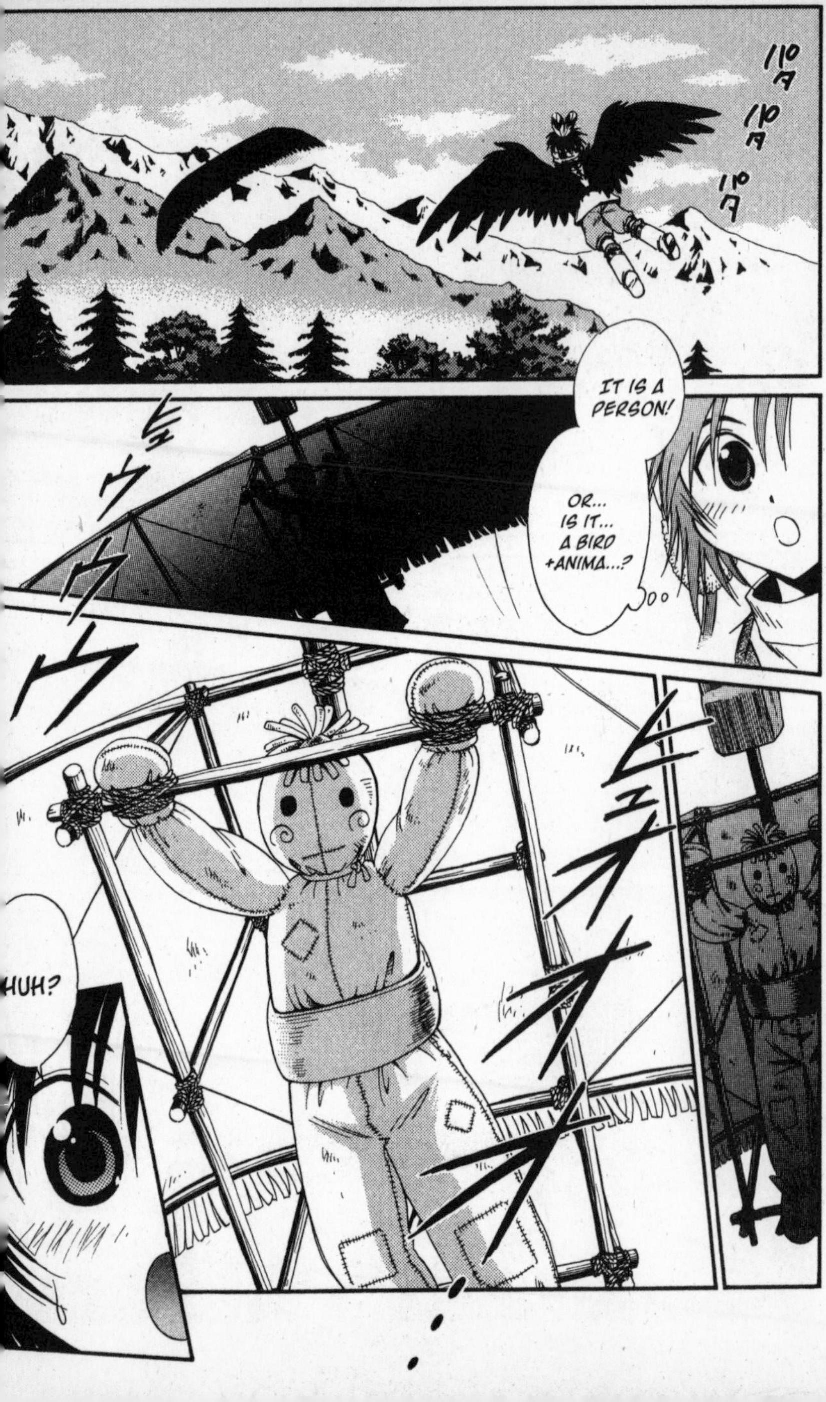

パタ
パタ
パタ
IT IS A PERSON!
OR... IS IT... A BIRD +ANIMA...?
HUH?

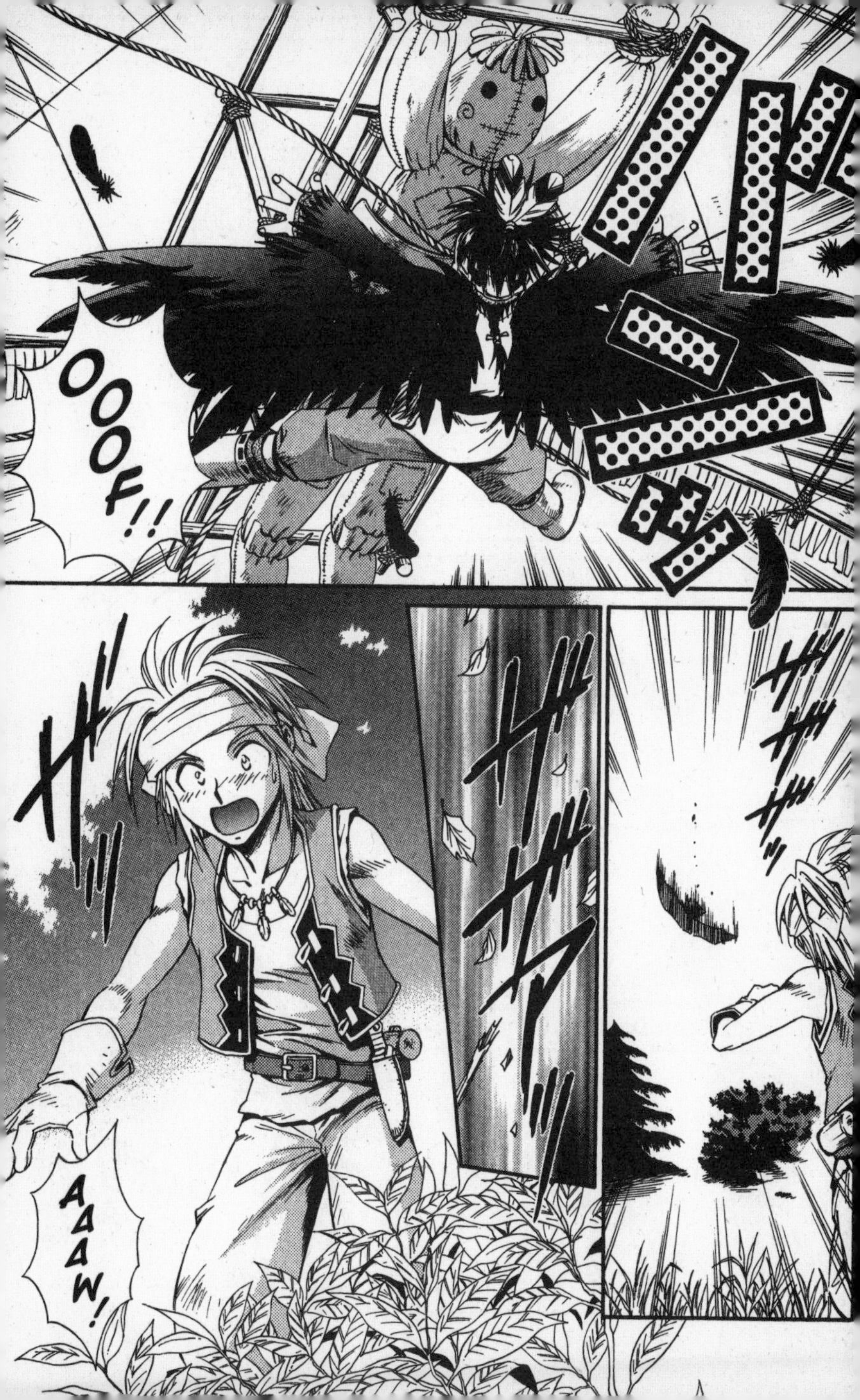
OOOF!!
AAAW!

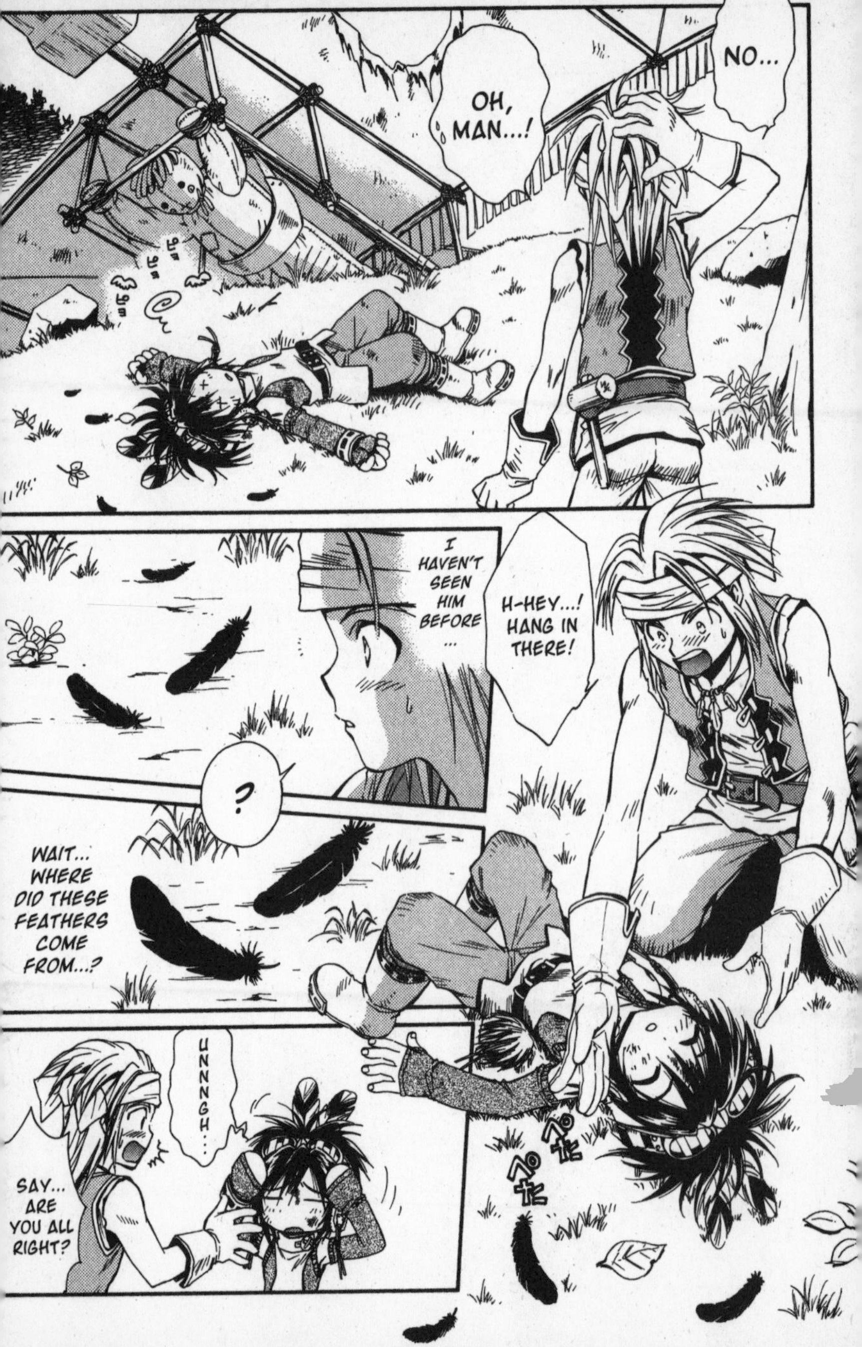
NO...
OH, MAN...!
H-HEY...! HANG IN THERE!
I HAVEN'T SEEN HIM BEFORE...
?
WAIT... WHERE DID THESE FEATHERS COME FROM...?
UNNNGH...
SAY... ARE YOU ALL RIGHT?

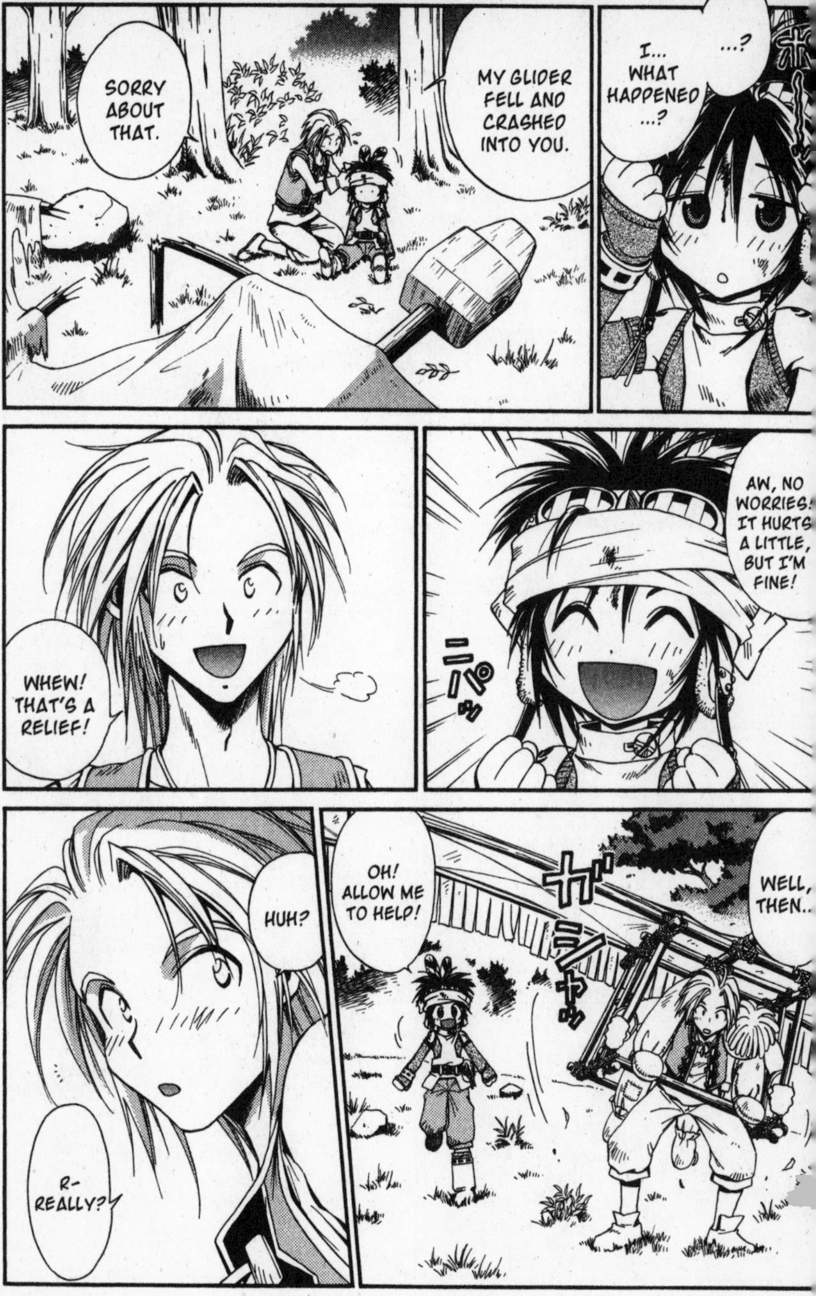

...?
I... WHAT HAPPENED ...?
MY GLIDER FELL AND CRASHED INTO YOU.
SORRY ABOUT THAT.
AW, NO WORRIES! IT HURTS A LITTLE, BUT I'M FINE!
ニパッ
WHEW! THAT'S A RELIEF!
WELL, THEN...
ガシャッ
OH! ALLOW ME TO HELP!
HUH?
R-REALLY?

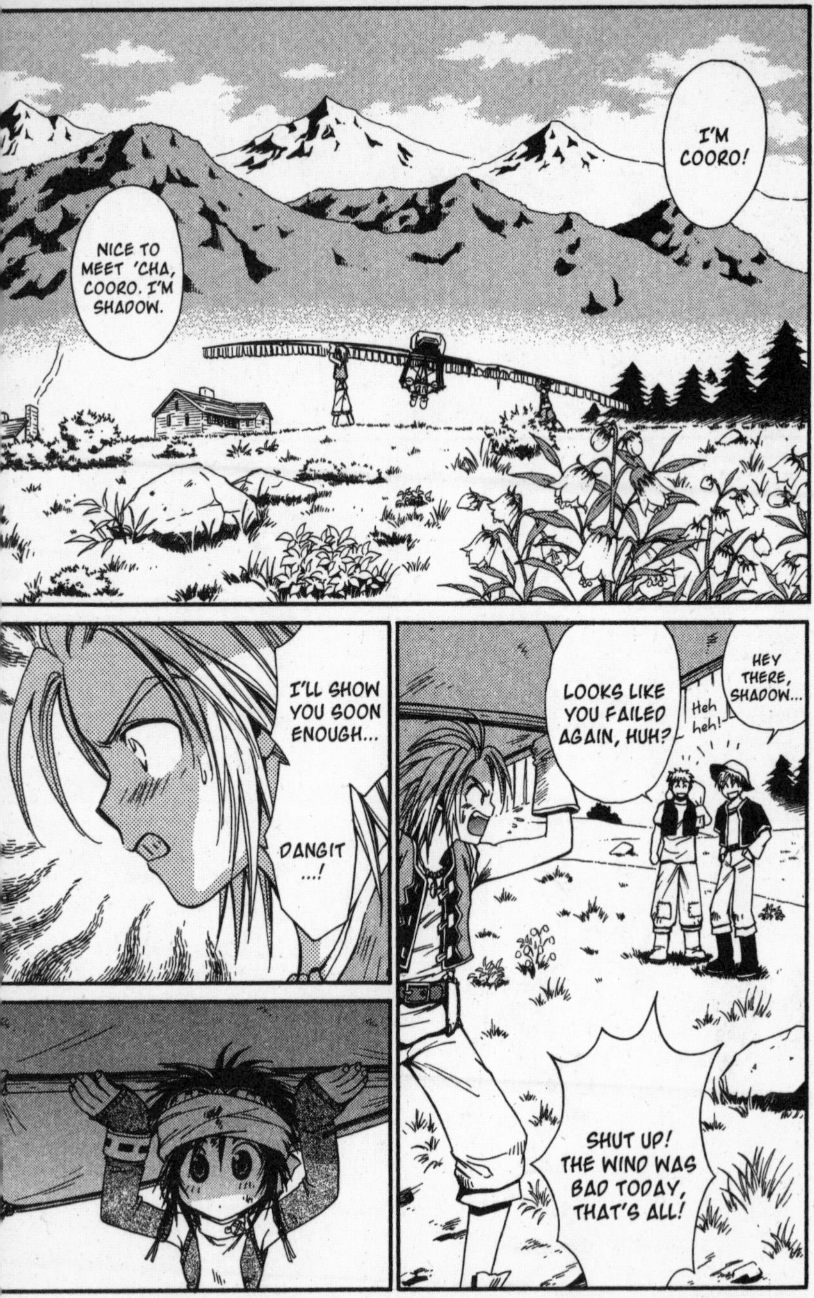
I'M COORO!
NICE TO MEET 'CHA, COORO. I'M SHADOW.
HEY THERE, SHADOW...
Heh heh!
LOOKS LIKE YOU FAILED AGAIN, HUH?
SHUT UP! THE WIND WAS BAD TODAY, THAT'S ALL!
I'LL SHOW YOU SOON ENOUGH...
DANGIT ...!

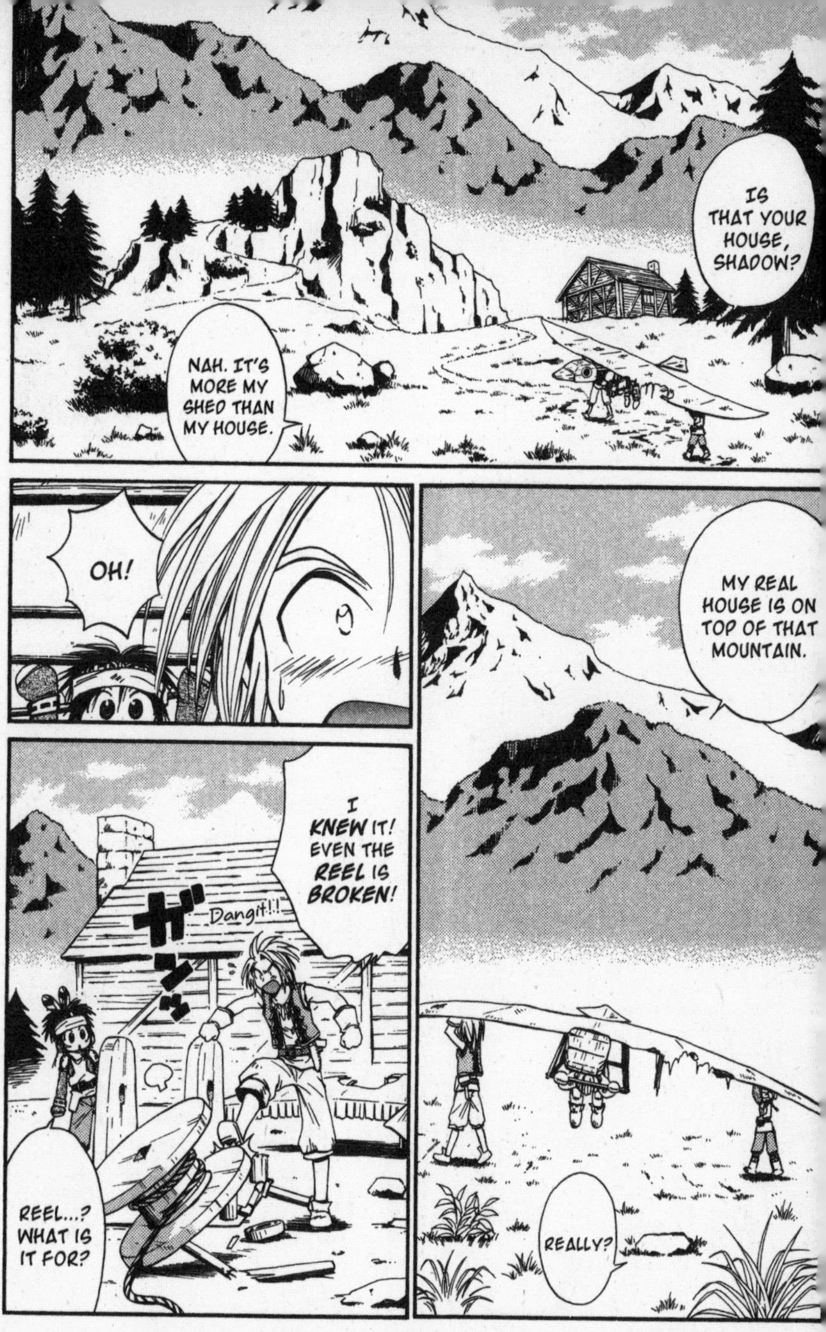
IS THAT YOUR HOUSE, SHADOW?
NAH. IT'S MORE MY SHED THAN MY HOUSE.
MY REAL HOUSE IS ON TOP OF THAT MOUNTAIN.
REALLY?
OH!
I KNEW IT! EVEN THE REEL IS BROKEN!
Dangit!!!
REEL...? WHAT IS IT FOR?

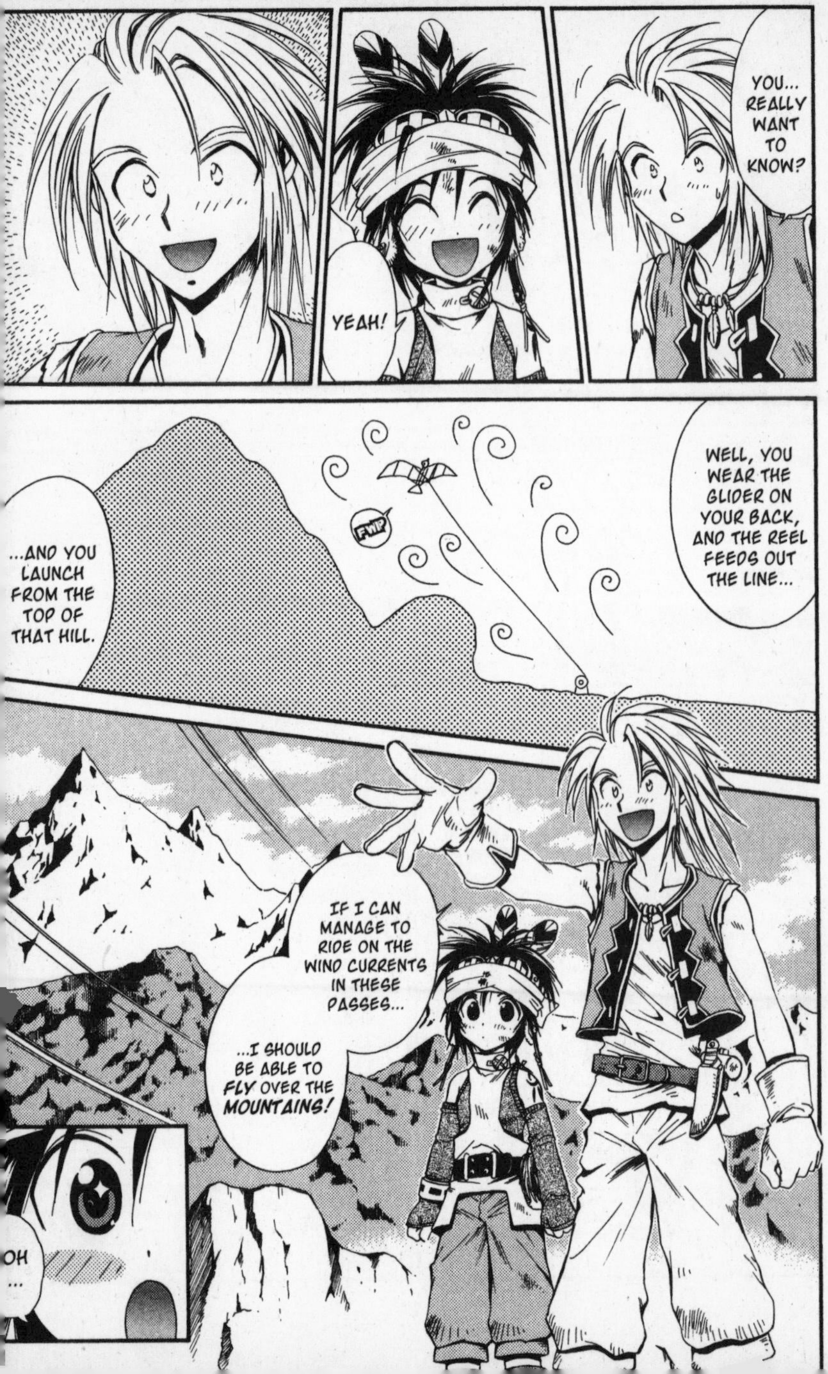
YOU... REALLY WANT TO KNOW?
YEAH!
WELL, YOU WEAR THE GLIDER ON YOUR BACK, AND THE REEL FEEDS OUT THE LINE...
FWP
...AND YOU LAUNCH FROM THE TOP OF THAT HILL.
IF I CAN MANAGE TO RIDE ON THE WIND CURRENTS IN THESE PASSES...
...I SHOULD BE ABLE TO FLY OVER THE MOUNTAINS!
OH...

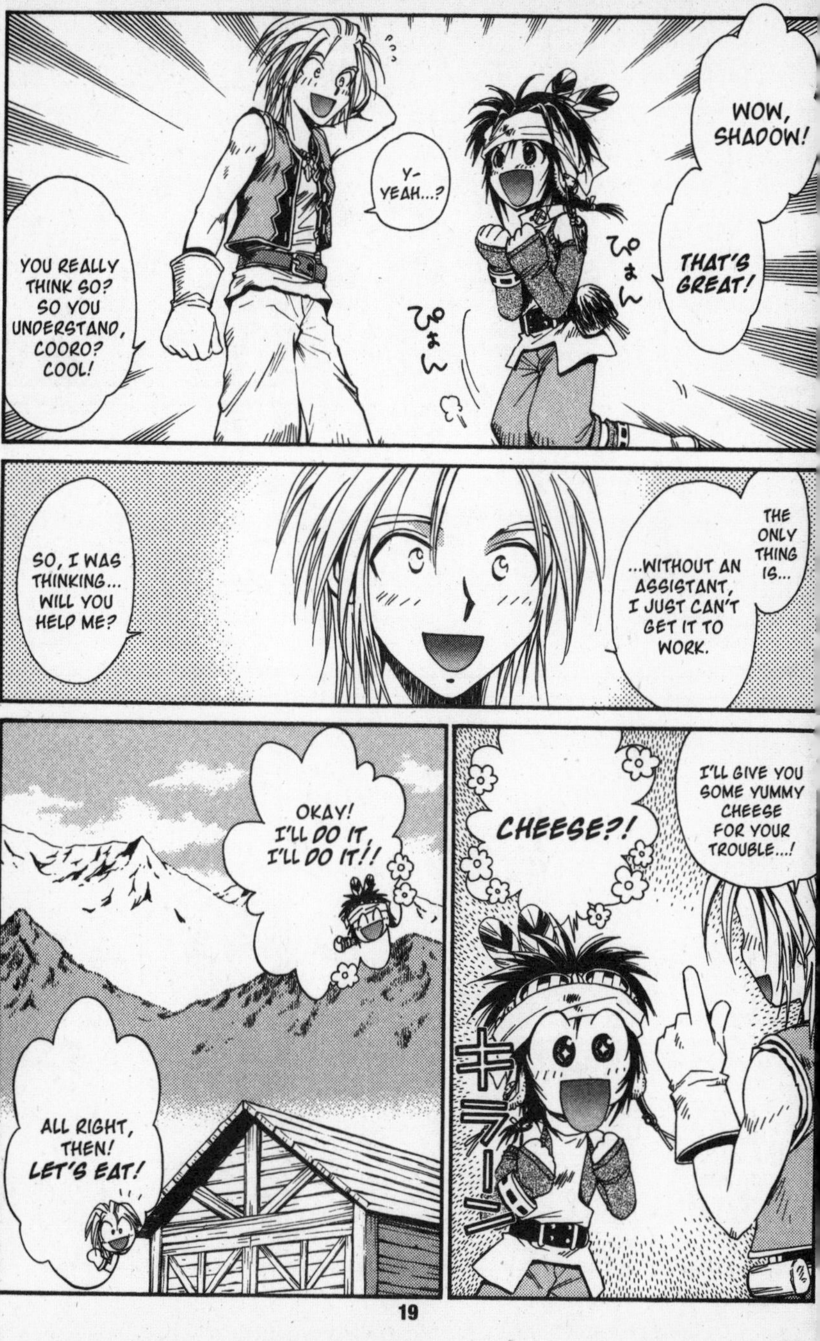
WOW, SHADOW! THAT'S GREAT!
ぴょん
ぴょん
Y-YEAH...?
YOU REALLY THINK SO? SO YOU UNDERSTAND, COORO? COOL!
THE ONLY THING IS...
...WITHOUT AN ASSISTANT, I JUST CAN'T GET IT TO WORK.
SO, I WAS THINKING... WILL YOU HELP ME?
I'LL GIVE YOU SOME YUMMY CHEESE FOR YOUR TROUBLE...!
CHEESE?!
キラーン
OKAY! I'LL DO IT, I'LL DO IT!!
ALL RIGHT, THEN! LET'S EAT!

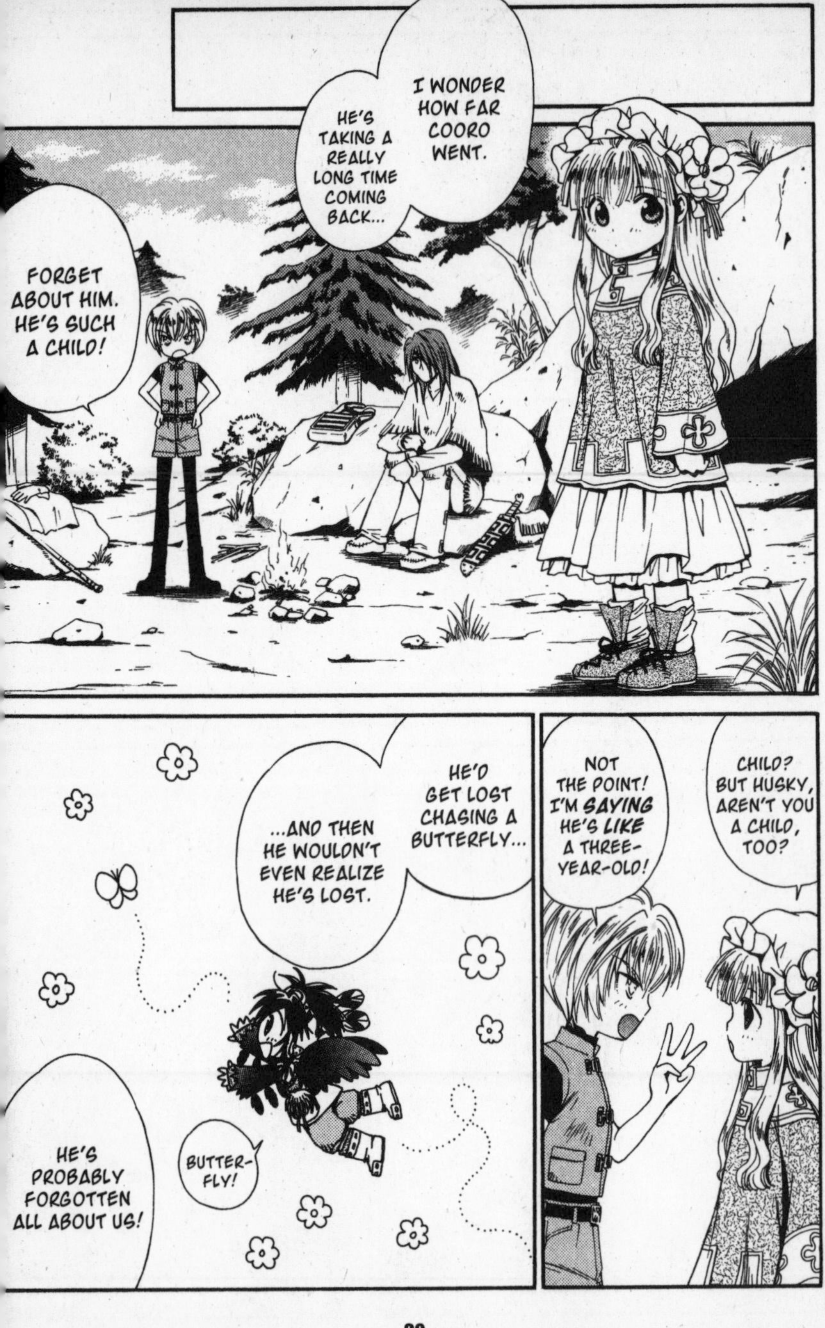
I WONDER HOW FAR COORO WENT.
HE'S TAKING A REALLY LONG TIME COMING BACK...
FORGET ABOUT HIM. HE'S SUCH A CHILD!
CHILD? BUT HUSKY, AREN'T YOU A CHILD, TOO?
NOT THE POINT! I'M *SAYING* HE'S *LIKE* A THREE-YEAR-OLD!
HE'D GET LOST CHASING A BUTTERFLY...
...AND THEN HE WOULDN'T EVEN REALIZE HE'S LOST.
BUTTER-FLY!
HE'S PROBABLY FORGOTTEN ALL ABOUT US!

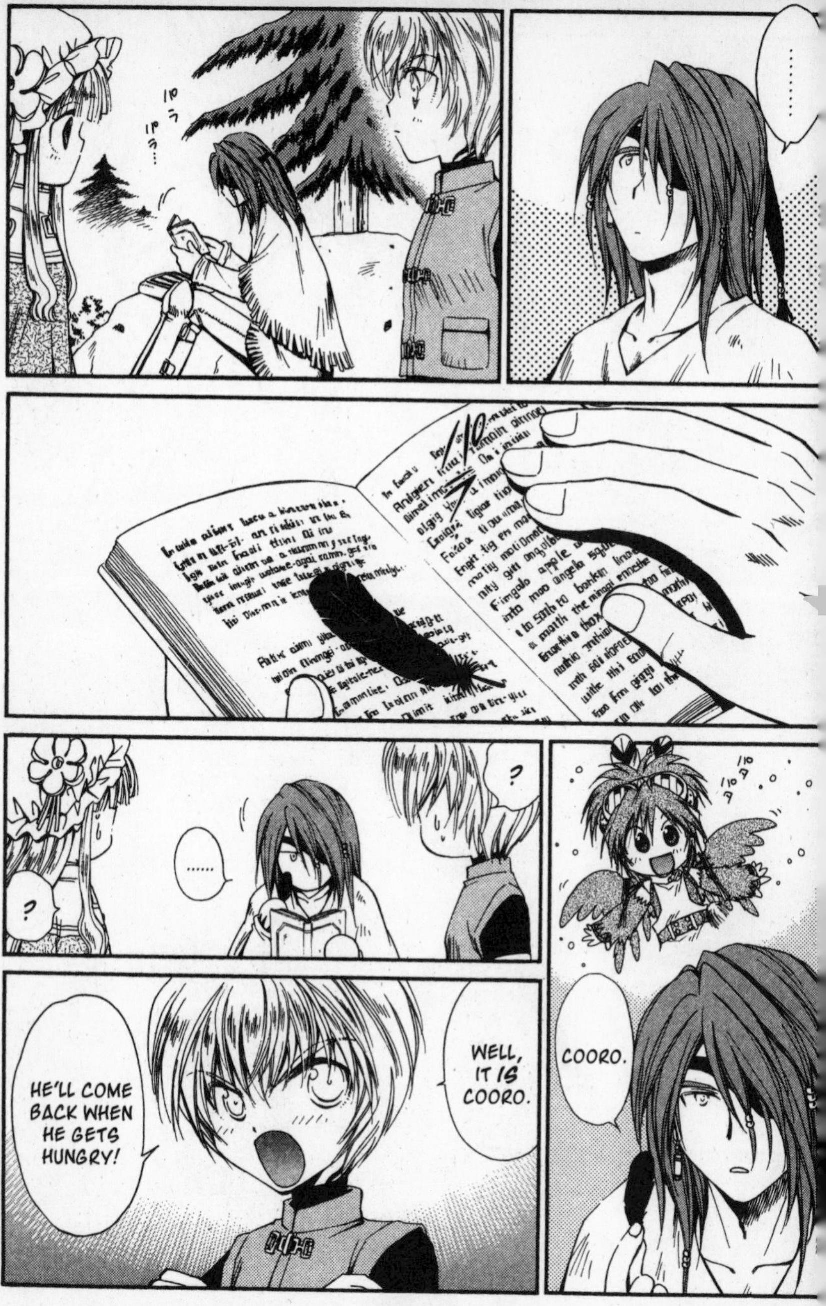
......
COORO.
?
......
?
WELL, IT IS COORO.
HE'LL COME BACK WHEN HE GETS HUNGRY!

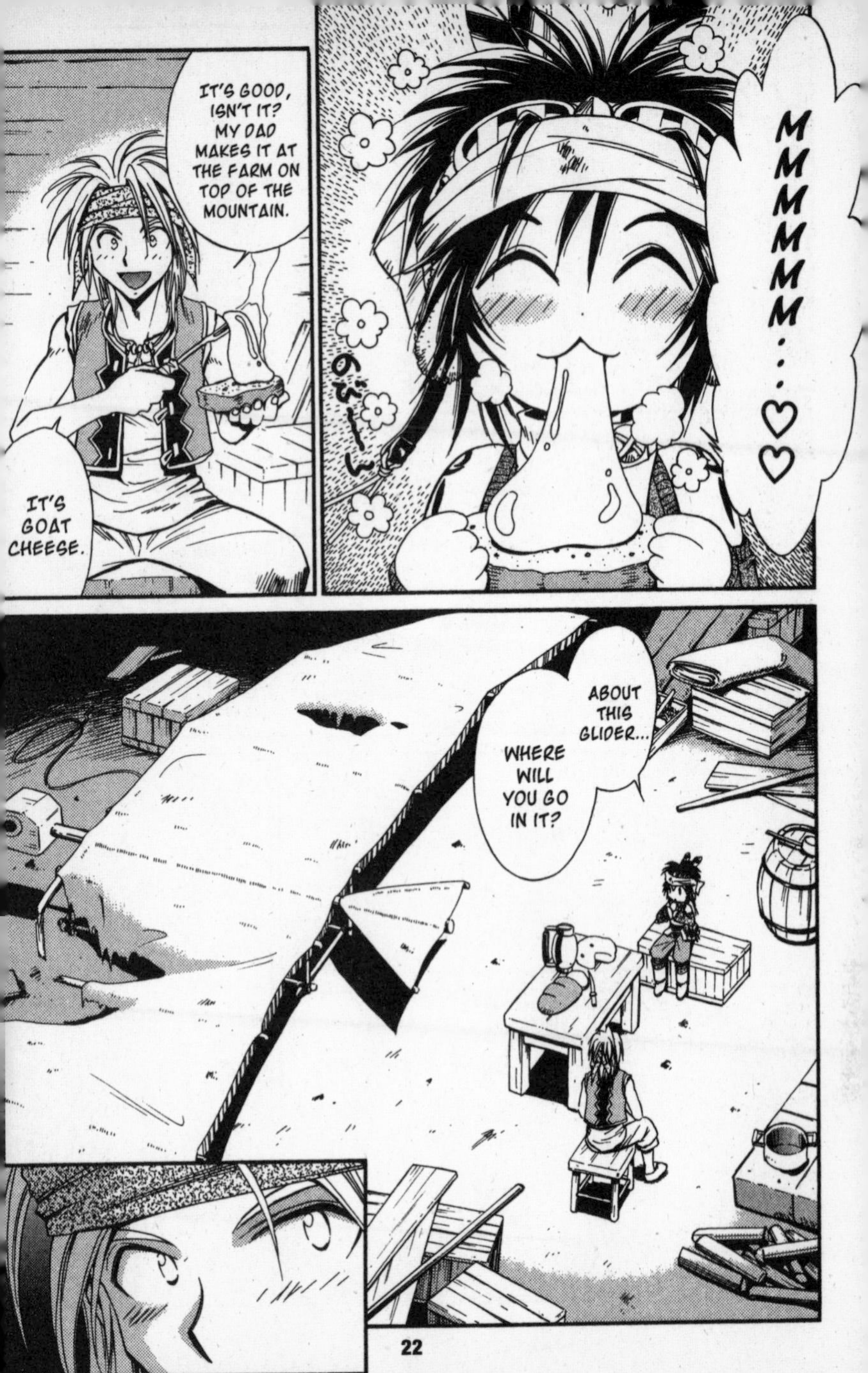
MMMMMMM...♡♡
のびーん
IT'S GOOD, ISN'T IT? MY DAD MAKES IT AT THE FARM ON TOP OF THE MOUNTAIN.
IT'S GOAT CHEESE.
ABOUT THIS GLIDER...
WHERE WILL YOU GO IN IT?

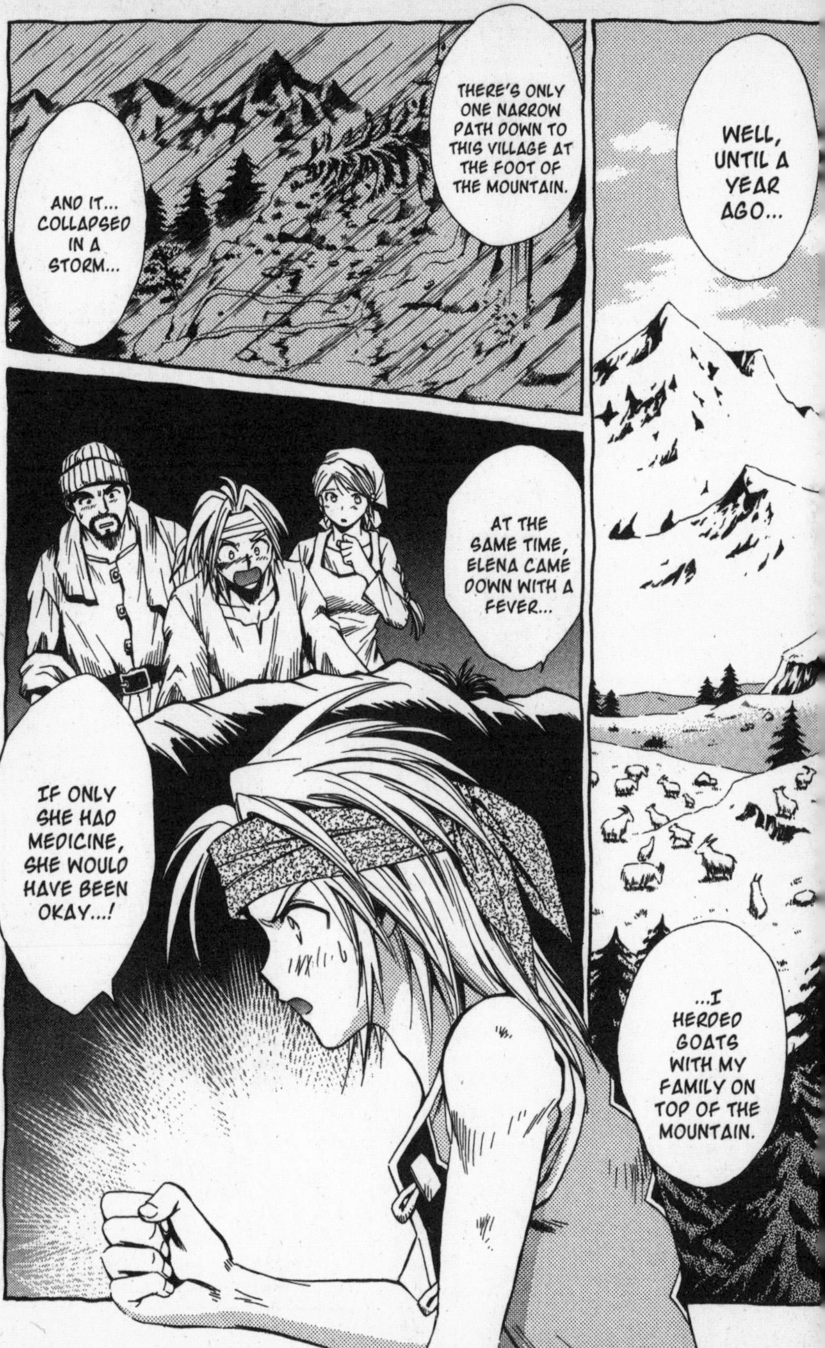
WELL, UNTIL A YEAR AGO...
...I HERDED GOATS WITH MY FAMILY ON TOP OF THE MOUNTAIN.
THERE'S ONLY ONE NARROW PATH DOWN TO THIS VILLAGE AT THE FOOT OF THE MOUNTAIN.
AND IT... COLLAPSED IN A STORM...
AT THE SAME TIME, ELENA CAME DOWN WITH A FEVER...
IF ONLY SHE HAD MEDICINE, SHE WOULD HAVE BEEN OKAY...!

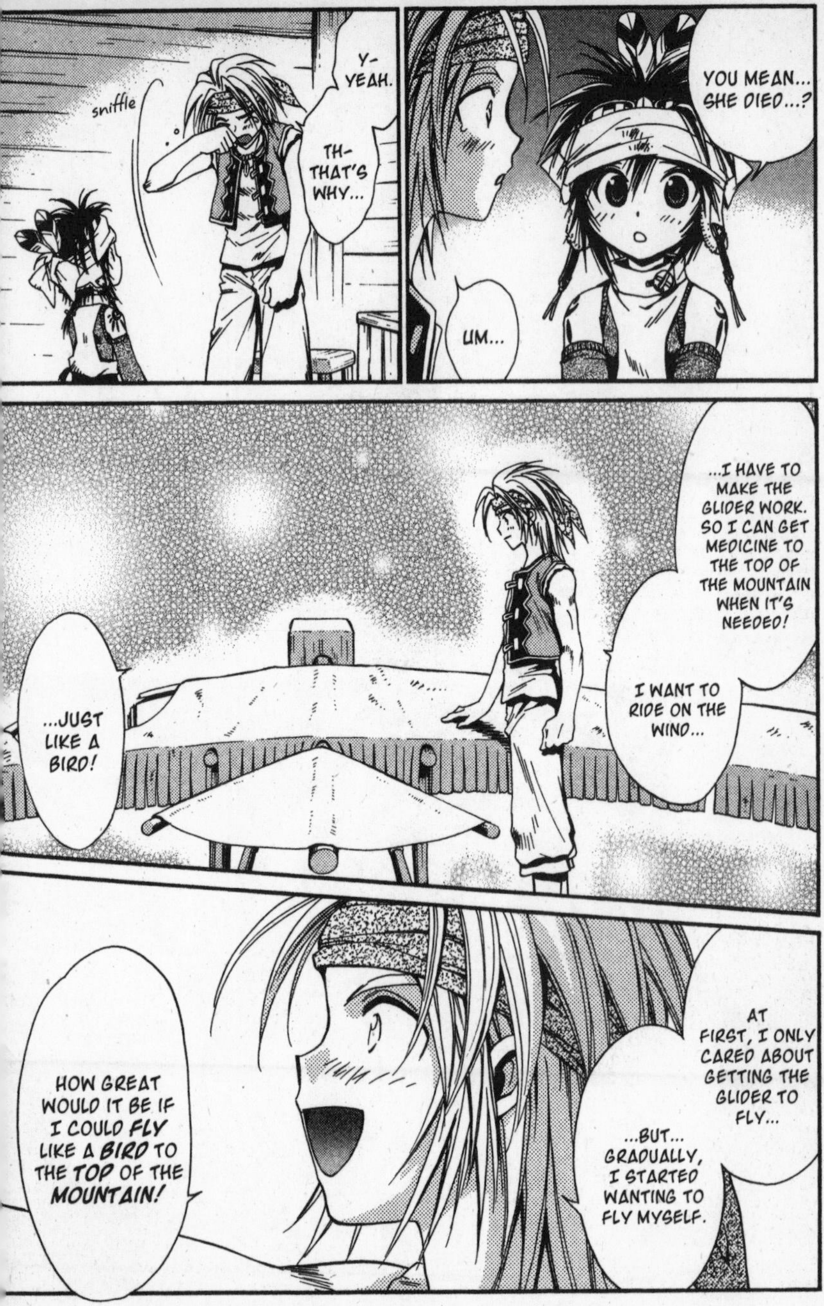
YOU MEAN... SHE DIED...?
UM...
Y-YEAH.
TH-THAT'S WHY...
sniffle
...I HAVE TO MAKE THE GLIDER WORK. SO I CAN GET MEDICINE TO THE TOP OF THE MOUNTAIN WHEN IT'S NEEDED!
I WANT TO RIDE ON THE WIND...
...JUST LIKE A BIRD!
AT FIRST, I ONLY CARED ABOUT GETTING THE GLIDER TO FLY...
...BUT... GRADUALLY, I STARTED WANTING TO FLY MYSELF.
HOW GREAT WOULD IT BE IF I COULD FLY LIKE A BIRD TO THE TOP OF THE MOUNTAIN!

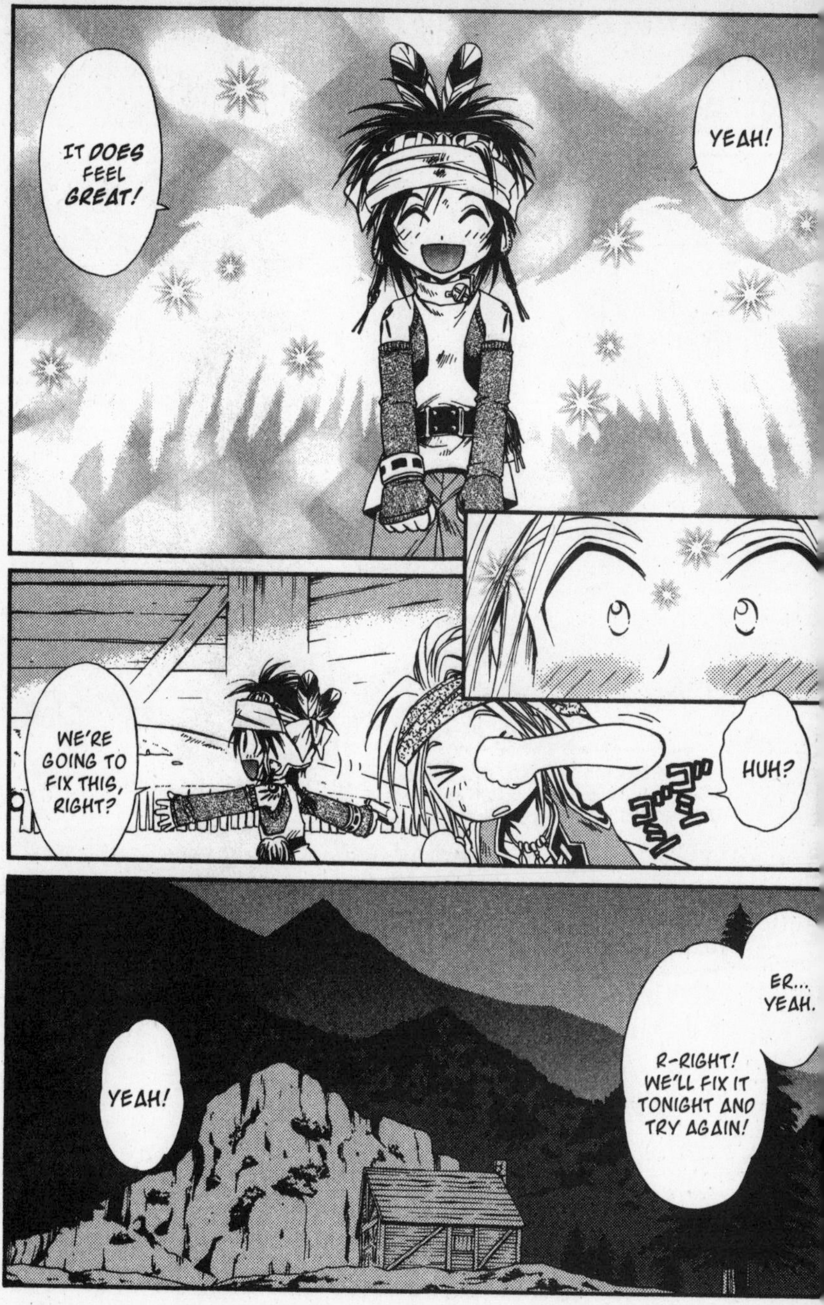
YEAH!
IT DOES FEEL GREAT!
HUH?
WE'RE GOING TO FIX THIS, RIGHT?
ER... YEAH.
R-RIGHT! WE'LL FIX IT TONIGHT AND TRY AGAIN!
YEAH!

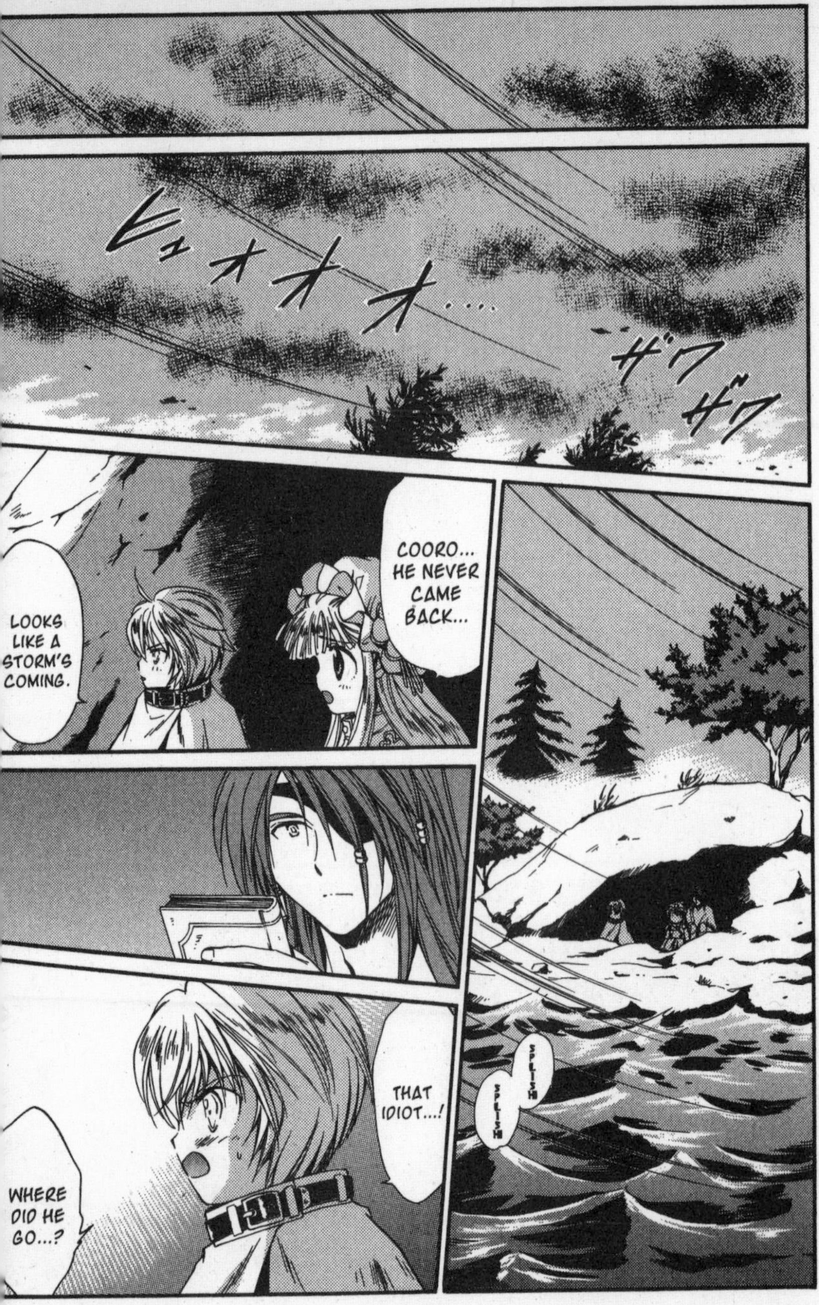
ヒュオオオ…
ザワザワ
SPLISH
SPLISH
COORO... HE NEVER CAME BACK...
LOOKS LIKE A STORM'S COMING.
THAT IDIOT...!
WHERE DID HE GO...?

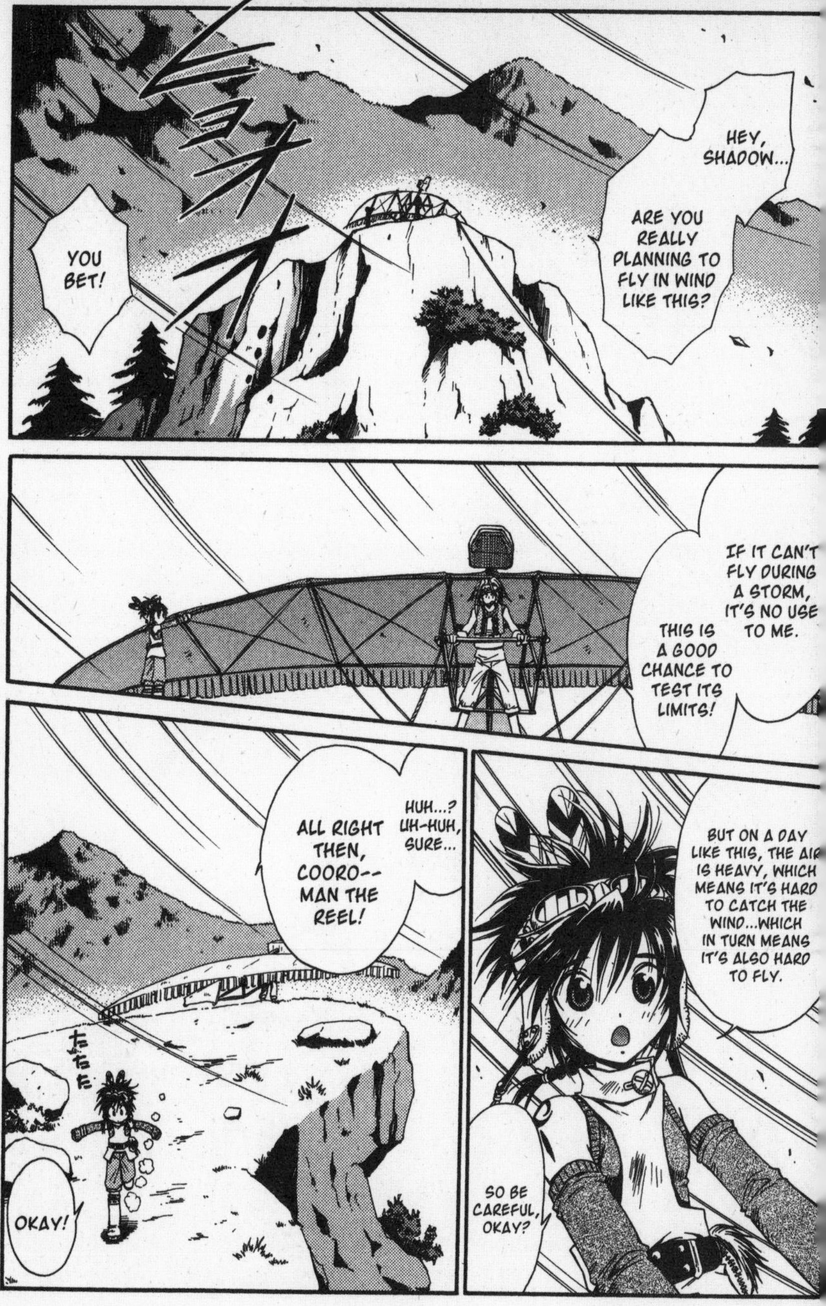
HEY, SHADOW...
ARE YOU REALLY PLANNING TO FLY IN WIND LIKE THIS?
YOU BET!
IF IT CAN'T FLY DURING A STORM, IT'S NO USE TO ME.
THIS IS A GOOD CHANCE TO TEST ITS LIMITS!
BUT ON A DAY LIKE THIS, THE AIR IS HEAVY, WHICH MEANS IT'S HARD TO CATCH THE WIND...WHICH IN TURN MEANS IT'S ALSO HARD TO FLY.
SO BE CAREFUL, OKAY?
HUH...? UH-HUH, SURE...
ALL RIGHT THEN, COORO-- MAN THE REEL!
たたた
OKAY!

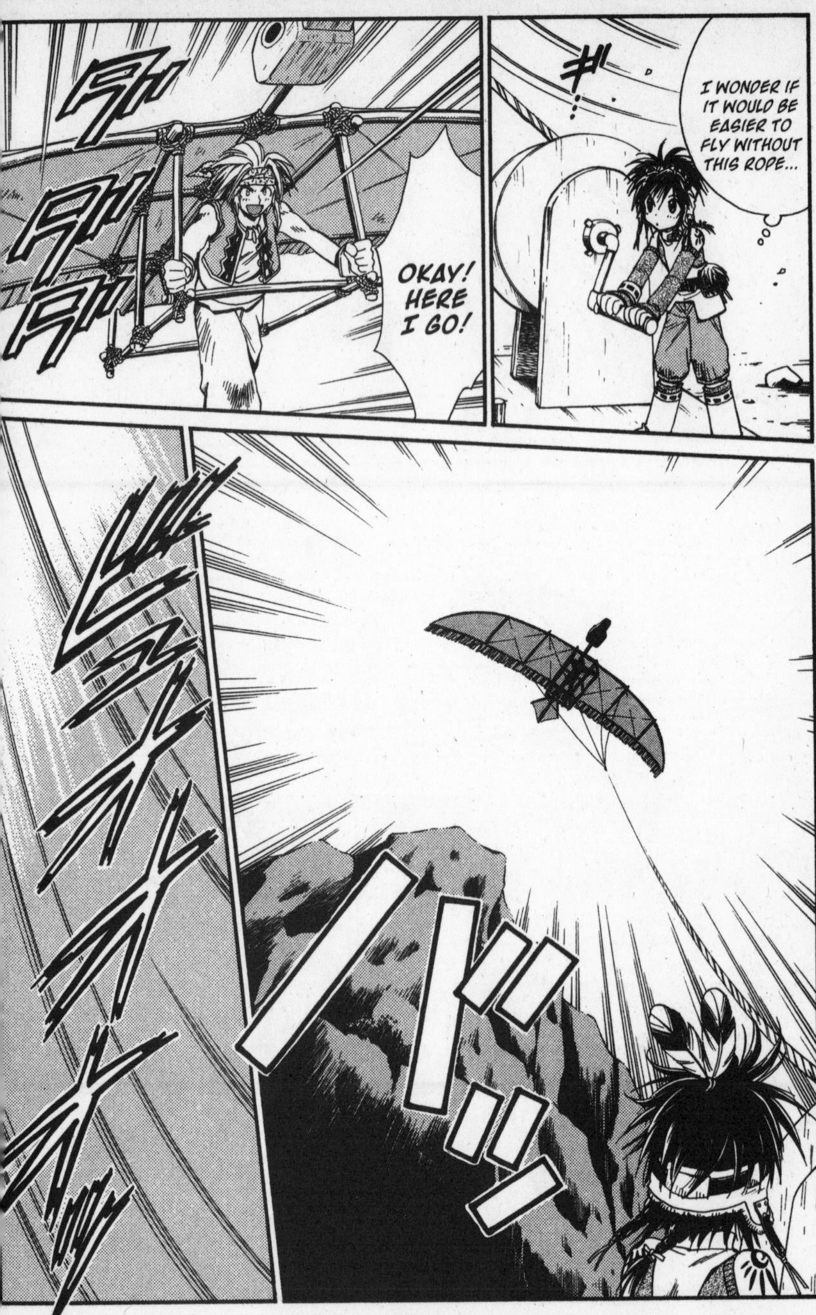
I WONDER IF IT WOULD BE EASIER TO FLY WITHOUT THIS ROPE...
OKAY! HERE I GO!

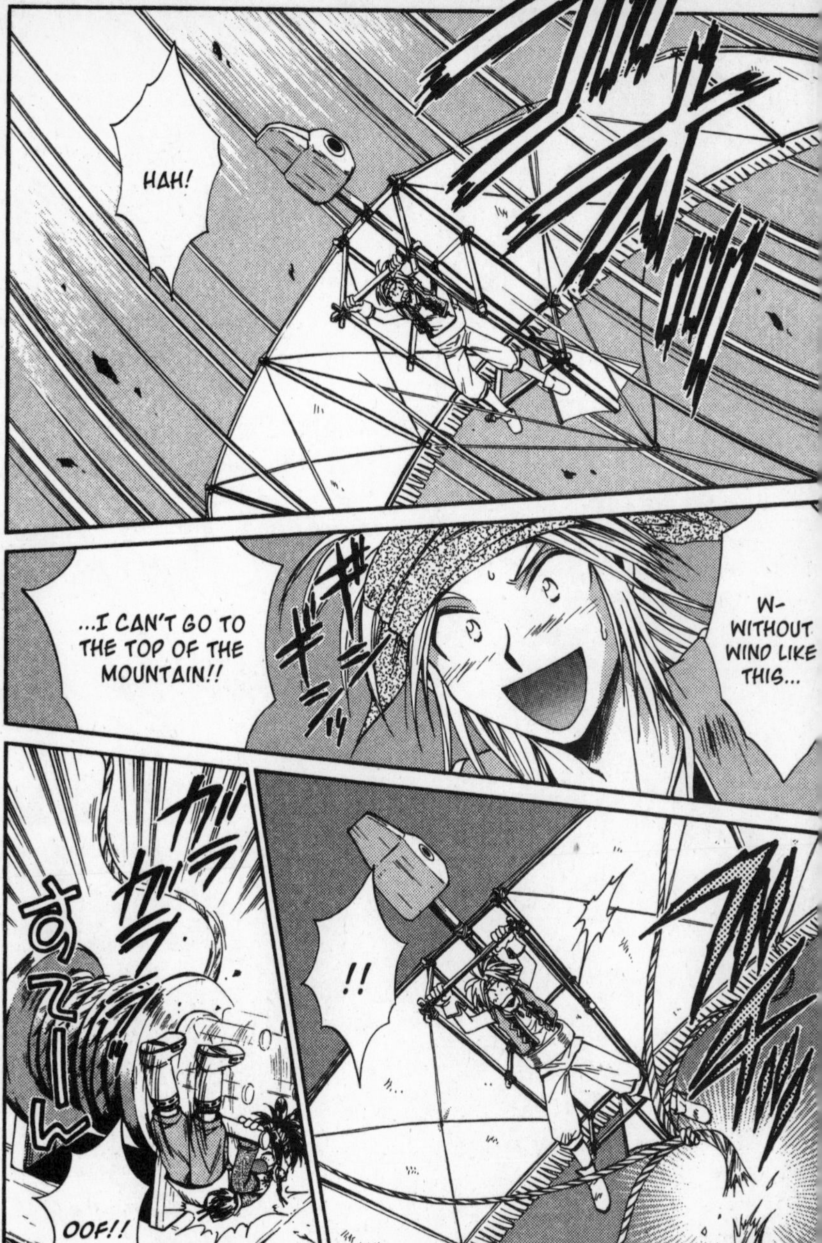
HAH!
W- WITHOUT WIND LIKE THIS...
...I CAN'T GO TO THE TOP OF THE MOUNTAIN!!
!!
OOF!!

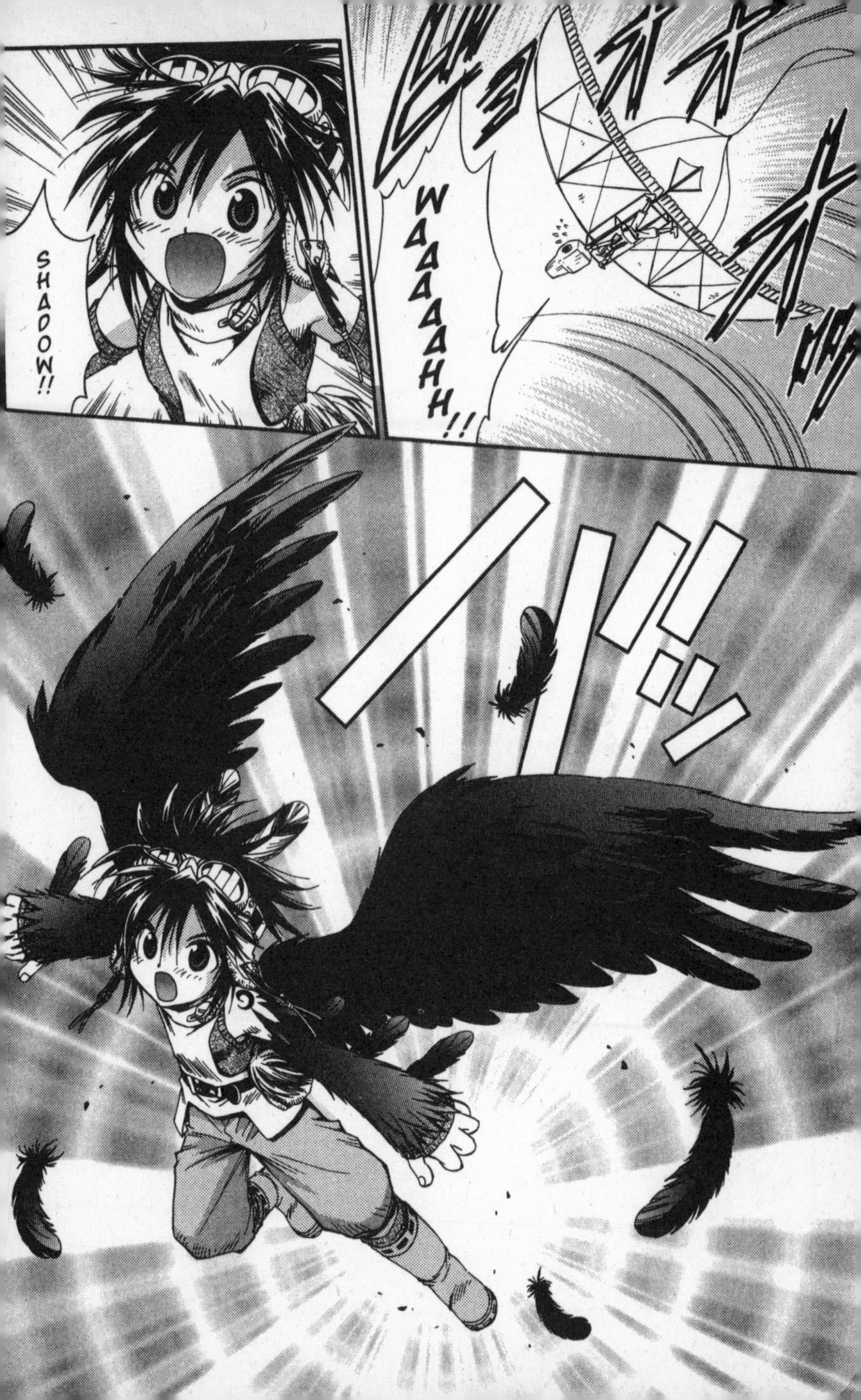
WAAAAAAHH!!
SHADOOW!!

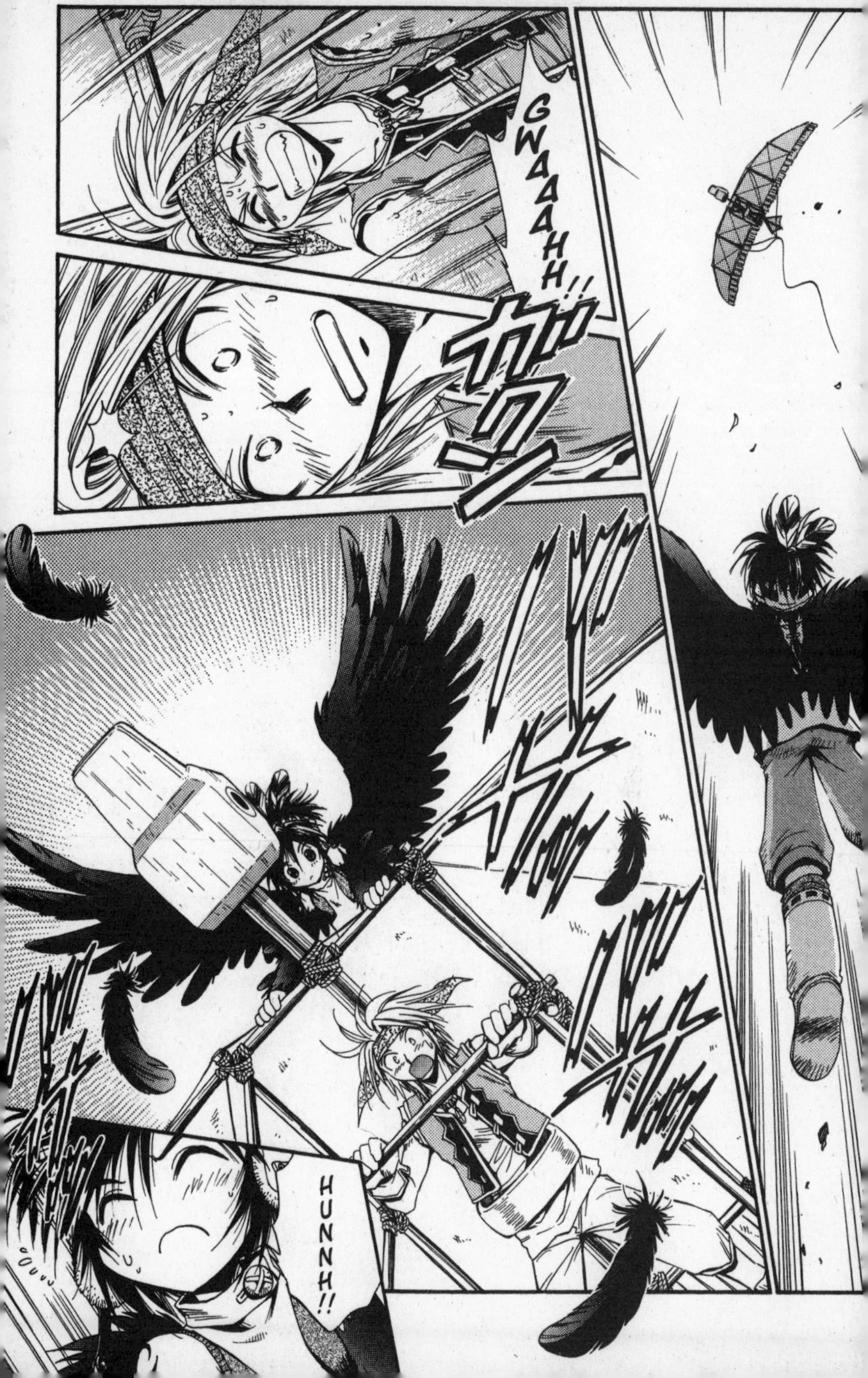
GWAAAAHH!!
HUNNH!!

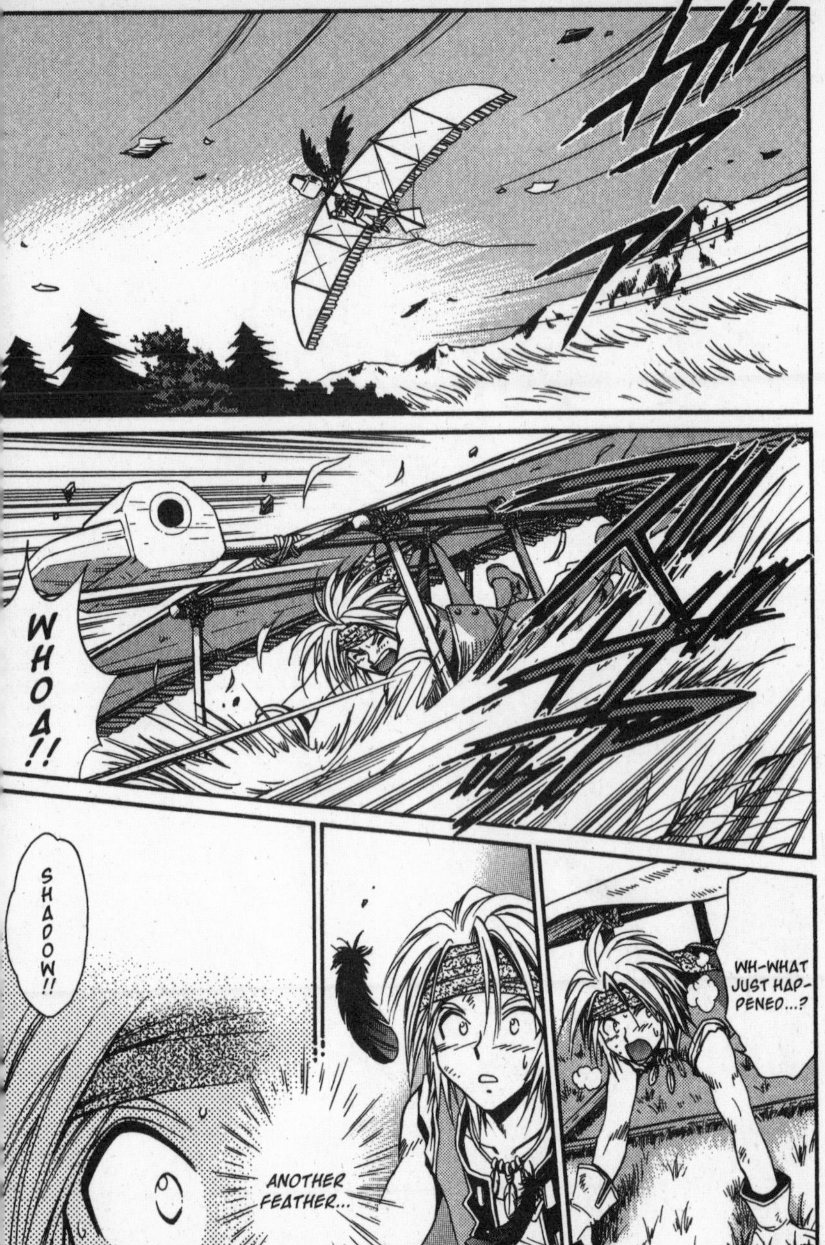
WHOA!!
WH-WHAT JUST HAP-PENED...?
ANOTHER FEATHER...
SHADOW!!

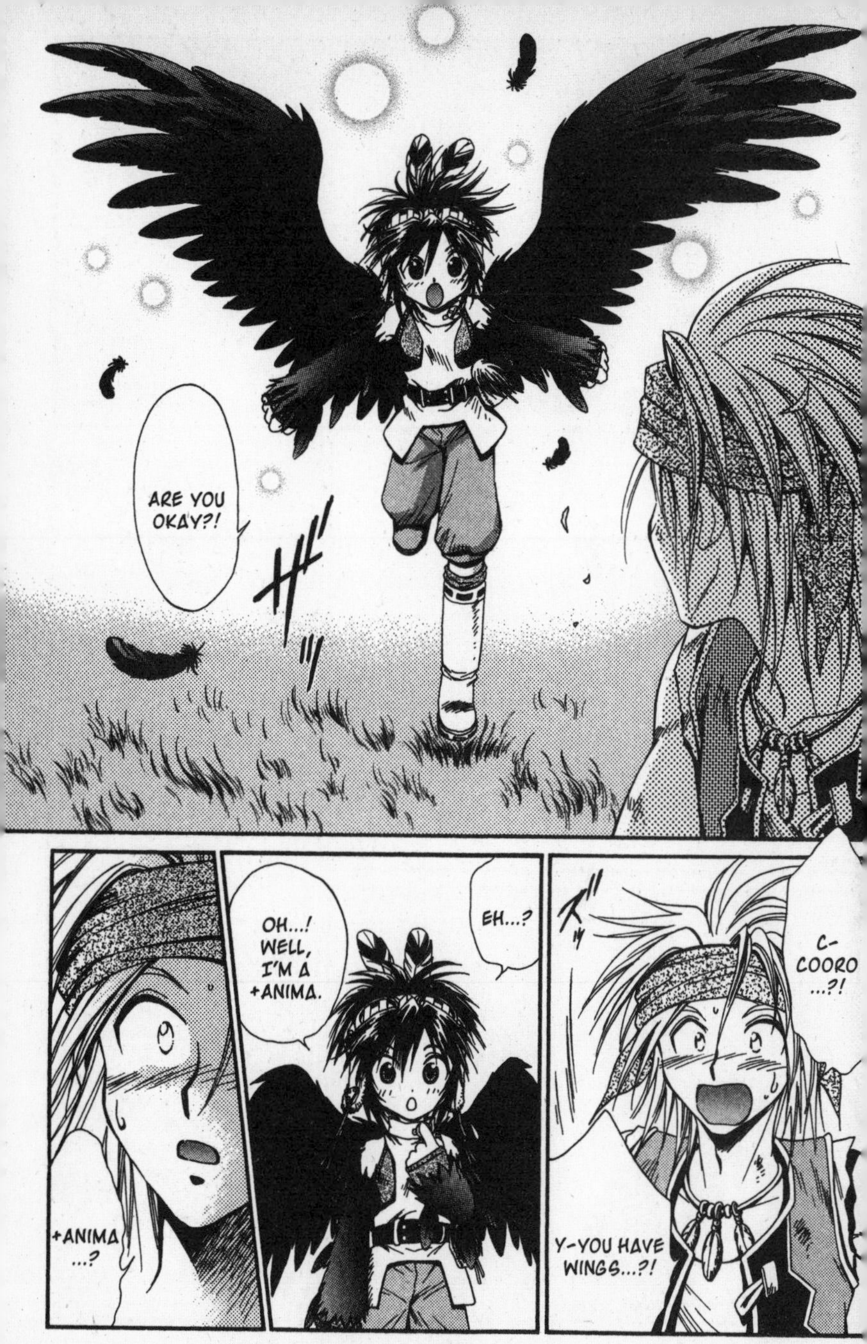
ARE YOU OKAY?!
C-COORO ...?!
Y-YOU HAVE WINGS...?!
EH...?
OH...! WELL, I'M A +ANIMA.
+ANIMA ...?

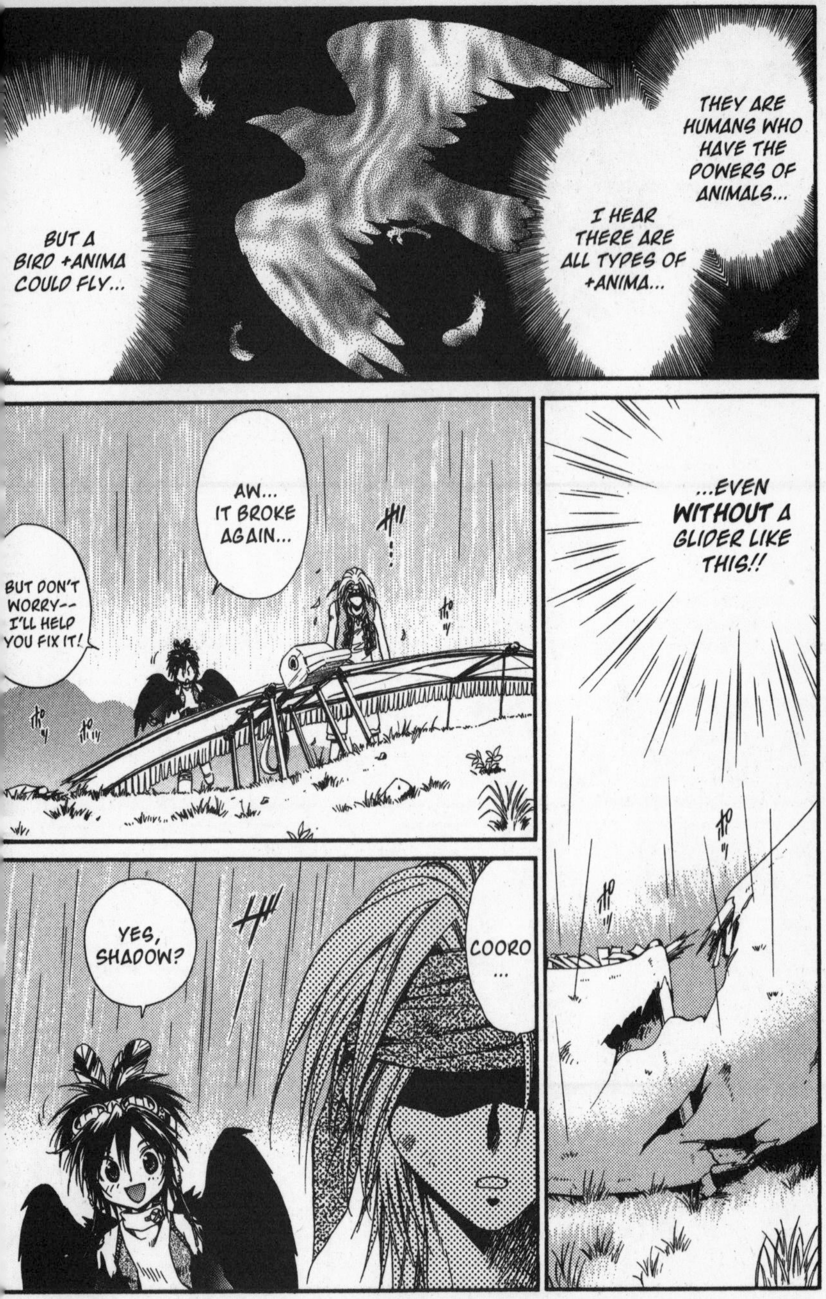
THEY ARE HUMANS WHO HAVE THE POWERS OF ANIMALS...
I HEAR THERE ARE ALL TYPES OF +ANIMA...
BUT A BIRD +ANIMA COULD FLY...
...EVEN WITHOUT A GLIDER LIKE THIS!!
AW... IT BROKE AGAIN...
BUT DON'T WORRY-- I'LL HELP YOU FIX IT!
COORO ...
YES, SHADOW?

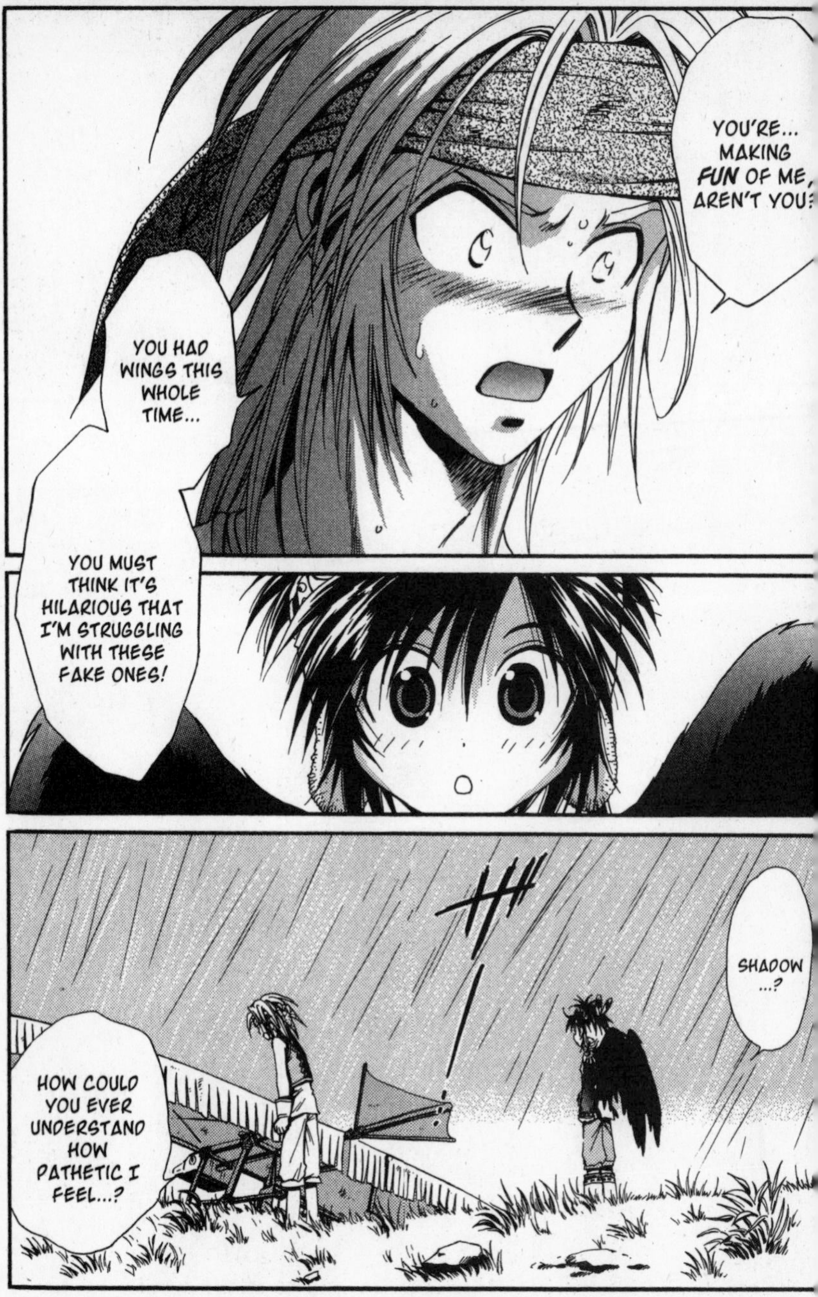
YOU'RE... MAKING FUN OF ME, AREN'T YOU?
YOU HAD WINGS THIS WHOLE TIME...
YOU MUST THINK IT'S HILARIOUS THAT I'M STRUGGLING WITH THESE FAKE ONES!
SHADOW ...?
HOW COULD YOU EVER UNDERSTAND HOW PATHETIC I FEEL...?

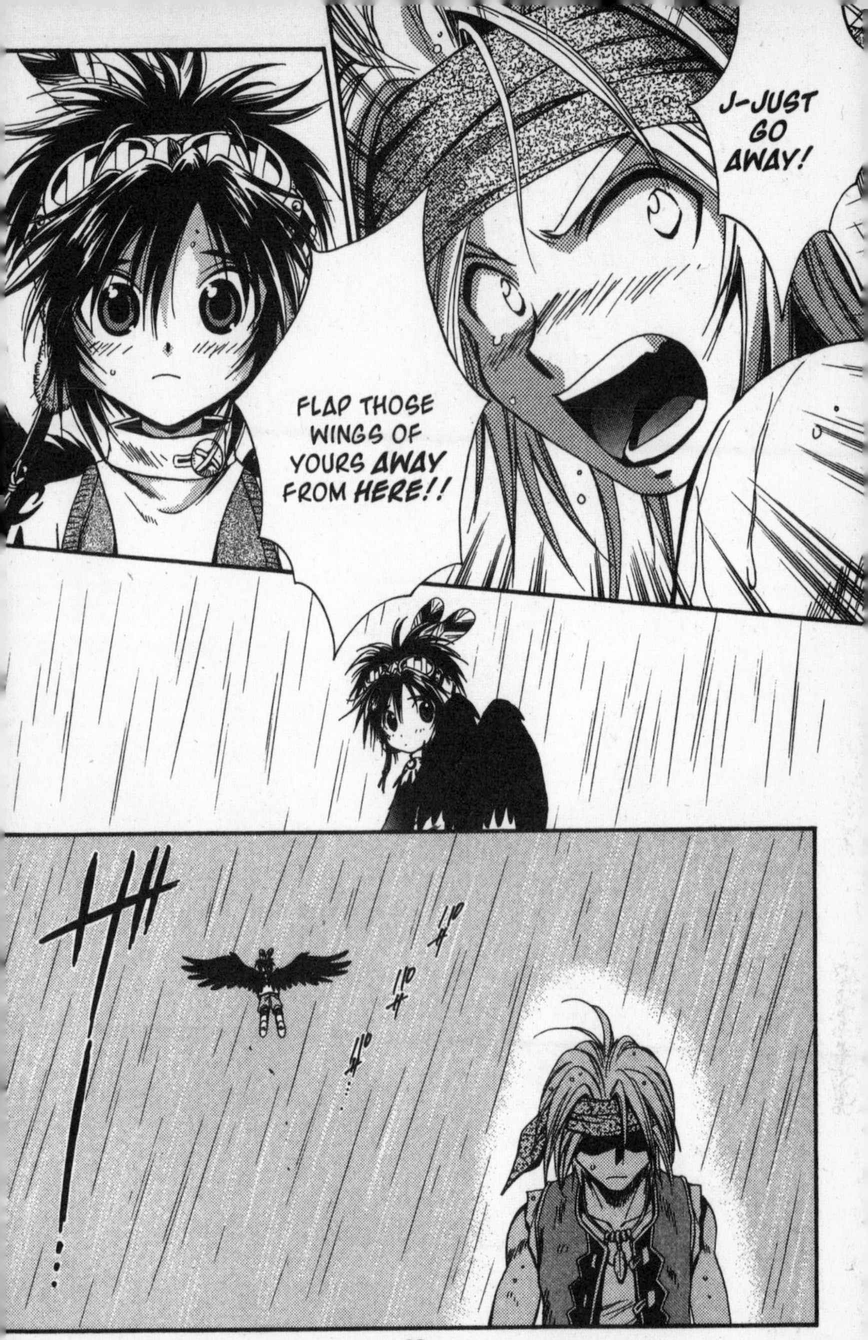
J-JUST GO AWAY!
FLAP THOSE WINGS OF YOURS AWAY FROM HERE!!

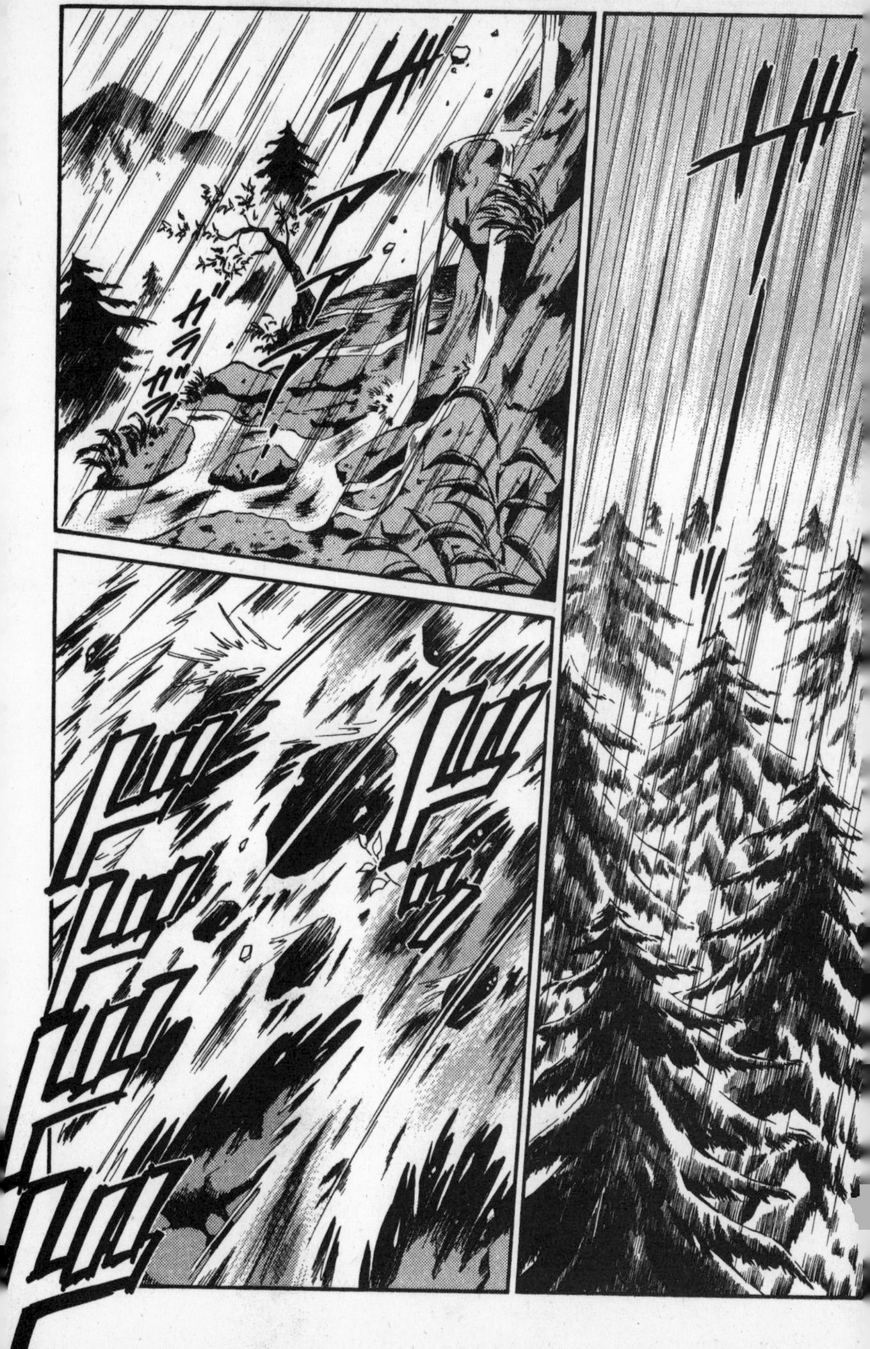
ザー
ザアアアーー!
ガラガラ

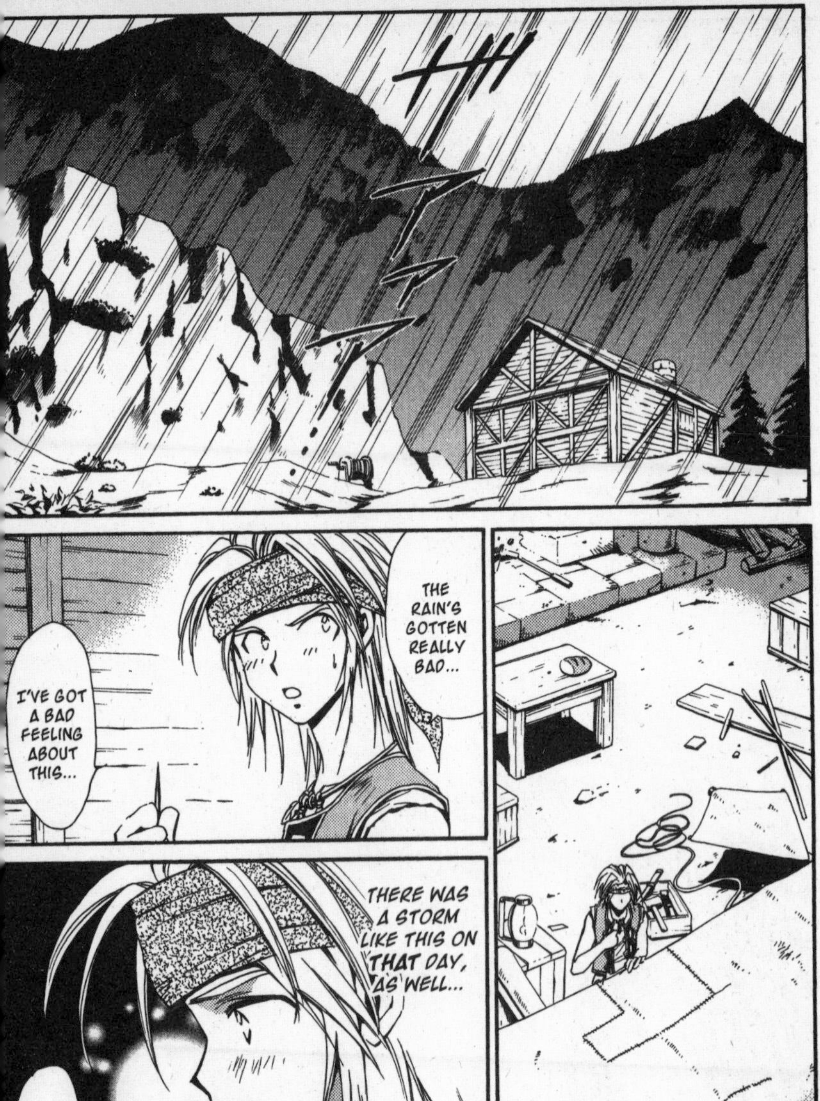
THE RAIN'S GOTTEN REALLY BAD...
I'VE GOT A BAD FEELING ABOUT THIS...
THERE WAS A STORM LIKE THIS ON THAT DAY, AS WELL...
ELENA ...

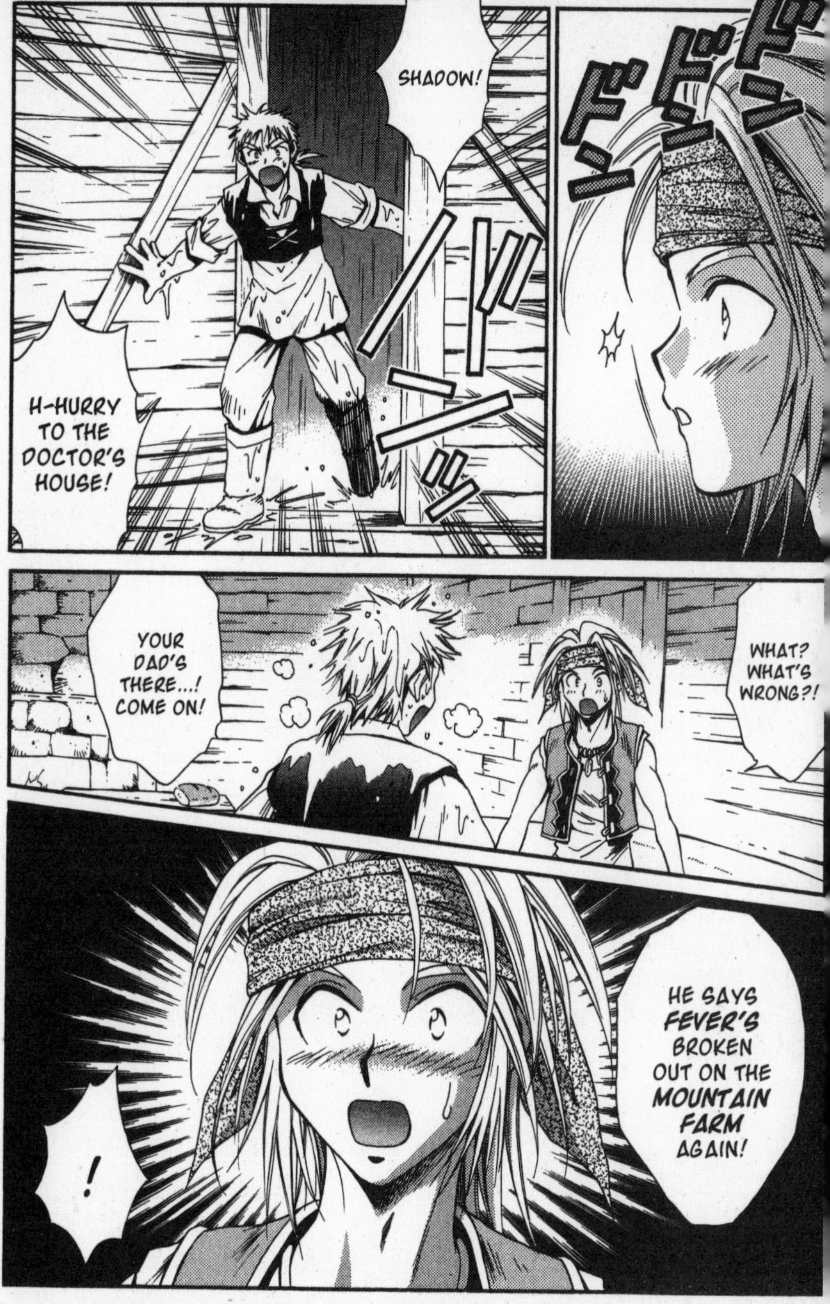
SHADOW!
H-HURRY TO THE DOCTOR'S HOUSE!
WHAT? WHAT'S WRONG?!
YOUR DAD'S THERE...! COME ON!
HE SAYS FEVER'S BROKEN OUT ON THE MOUNTAIN FARM AGAIN!
!

He is downhearted with shock.

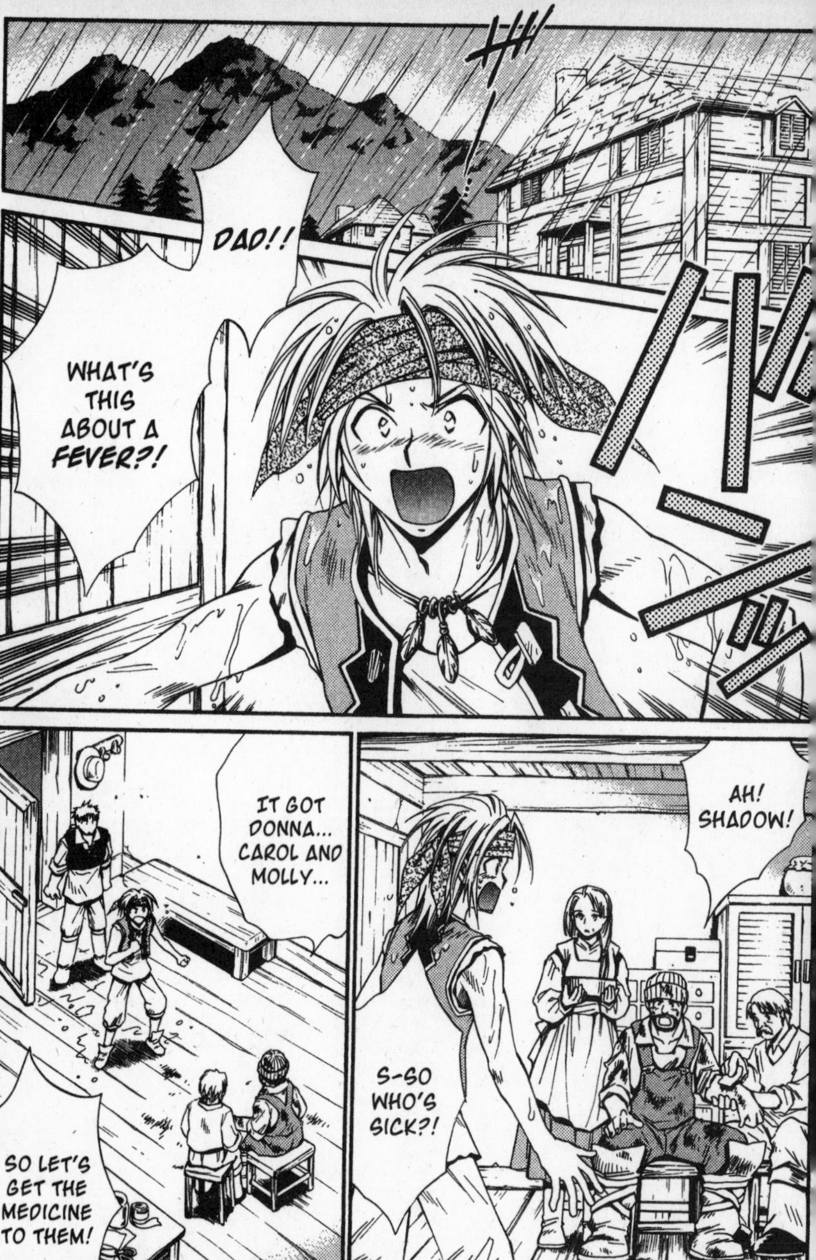
DAD!!
WHAT'S THIS ABOUT A FEVER?!
AH! SHADOW!
S-SO WHO'S SICK?!
IT GOT DONNA... CAROL AND MOLLY...
SO LET'S GET THE MEDICINE TO THEM!

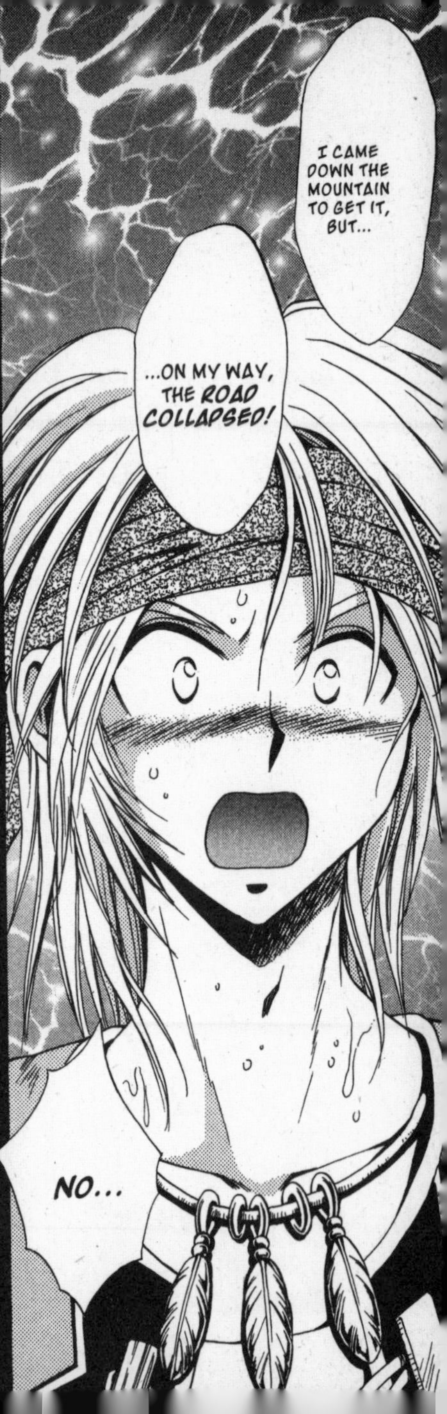
I CAME DOWN THE MOUNTAIN TO GET IT, BUT...
...ON MY WAY, THE ROAD COLLAPSED!
NO...
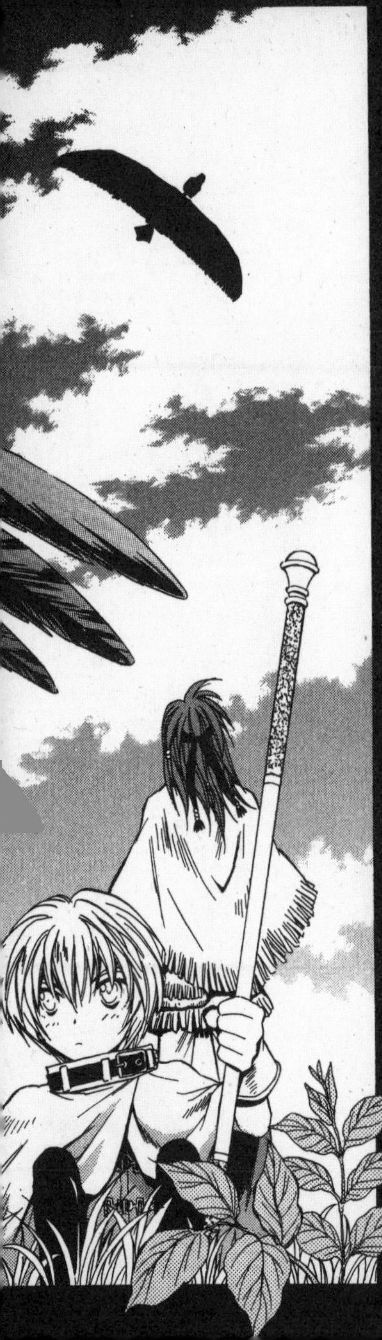

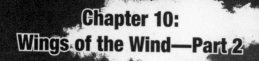

Chapter 10:
Wings of the Wind—Part 2

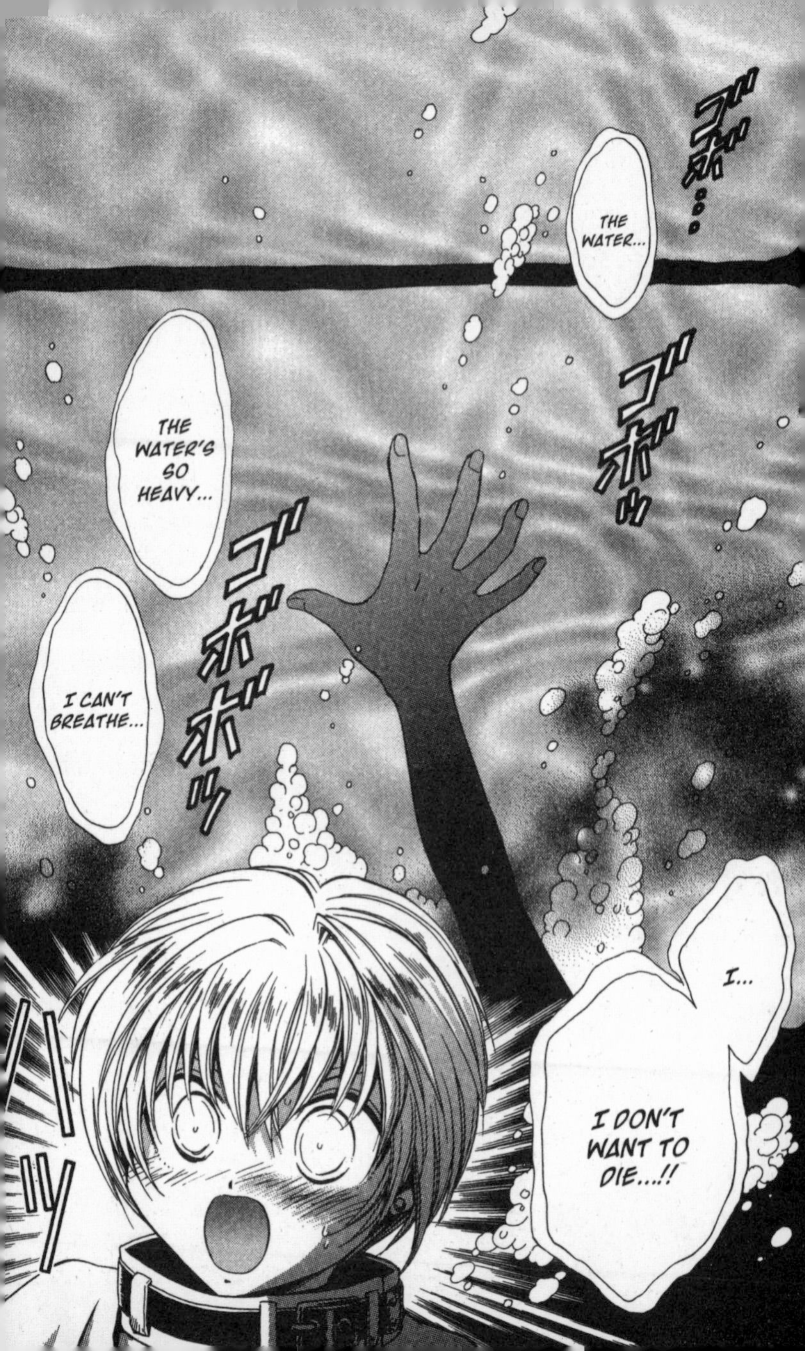
ゴボ…
THE WATER...
ゴボッ
THE WATER'S SO HEAVY...
ゴボボッ
I CAN'T BREATHE...
I...
I DON'T WANT TO DIE...!!
ハッ

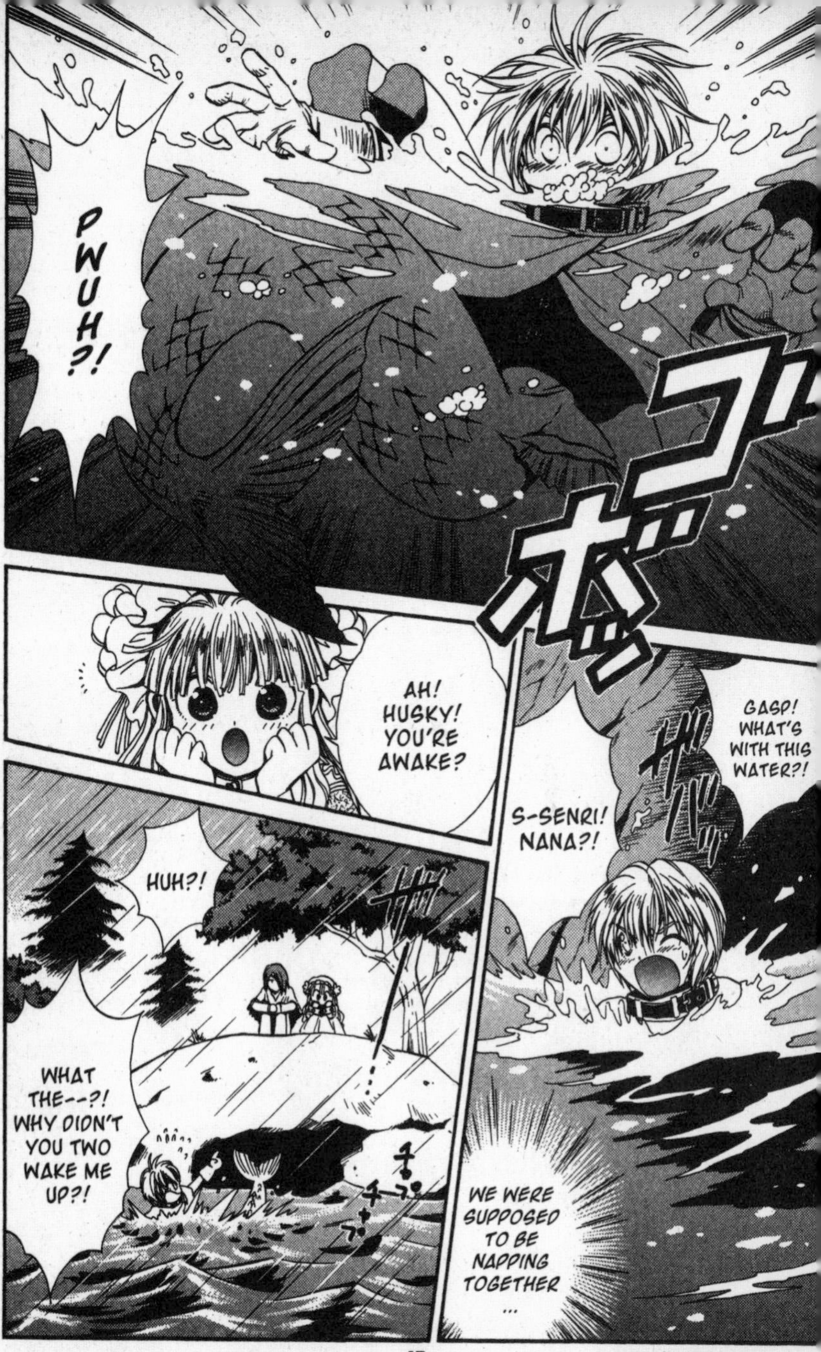
PWUH?!
AH! HUSKY! YOU'RE AWAKE?
GASP! WHAT'S WITH THIS WATER?!
S-SENRI! NANA?!
HUH?!
WE WERE SUPPOSED TO BE NAPPING TOGETHER ...
WHAT THE--?! WHY DIDN'T YOU TWO WAKE ME UP?!

THE POND FLOODED BECAUSE OF THE RAIN...

...BUT WE THOUGHT SINCE YOU'RE PART FISH, YOU'D BE FINE.

THAT'S NOT THE PROBLEM!!

FLAP

FLAP FLAP

FLAP

!

SENRI! DON'T JUST SIT THERE! HELP ME EXPLAIN IT TO HER!!

WHAT...?

COORO ....?!

I HEARD WINGS!

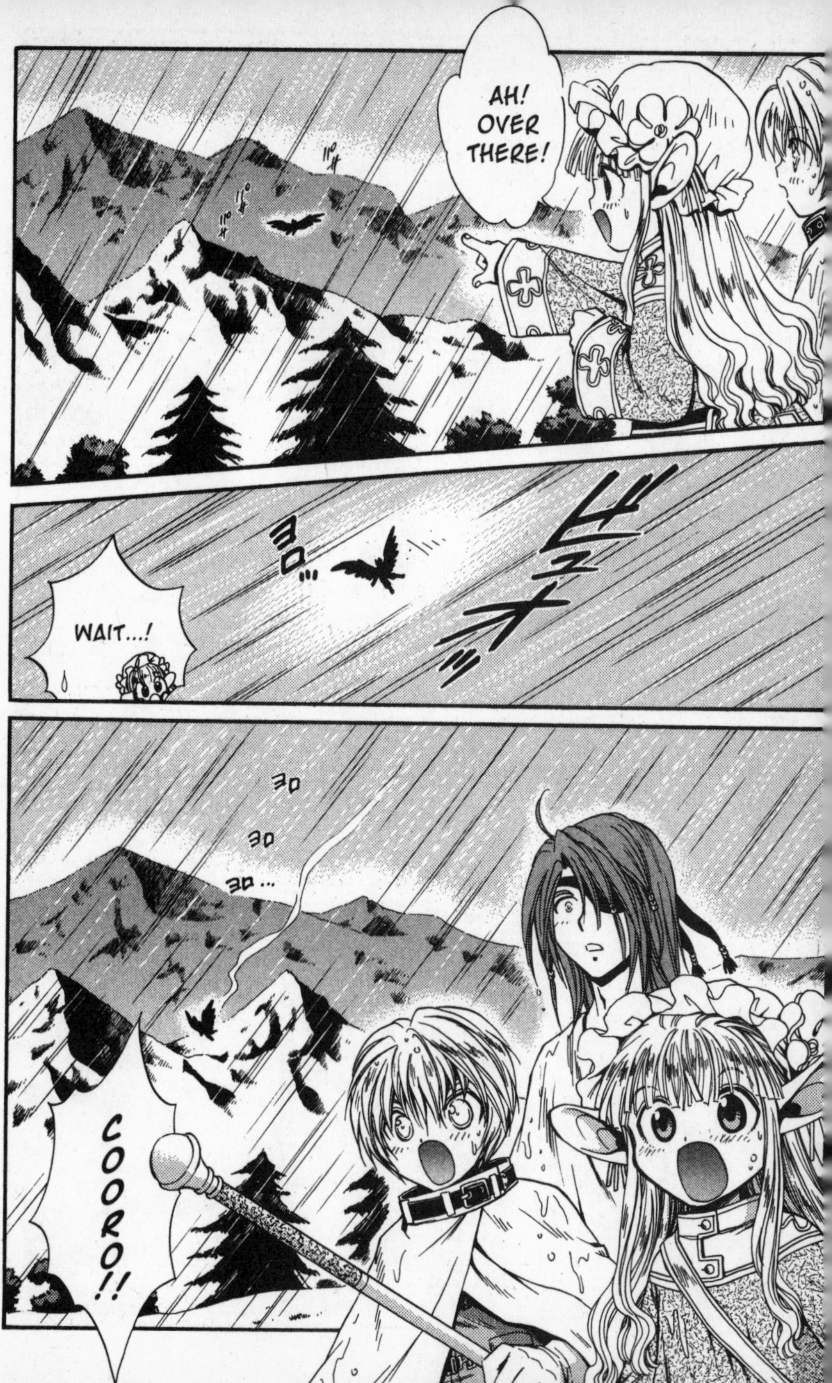
AH! OVER THERE!
WAIT...!
COOORO!!

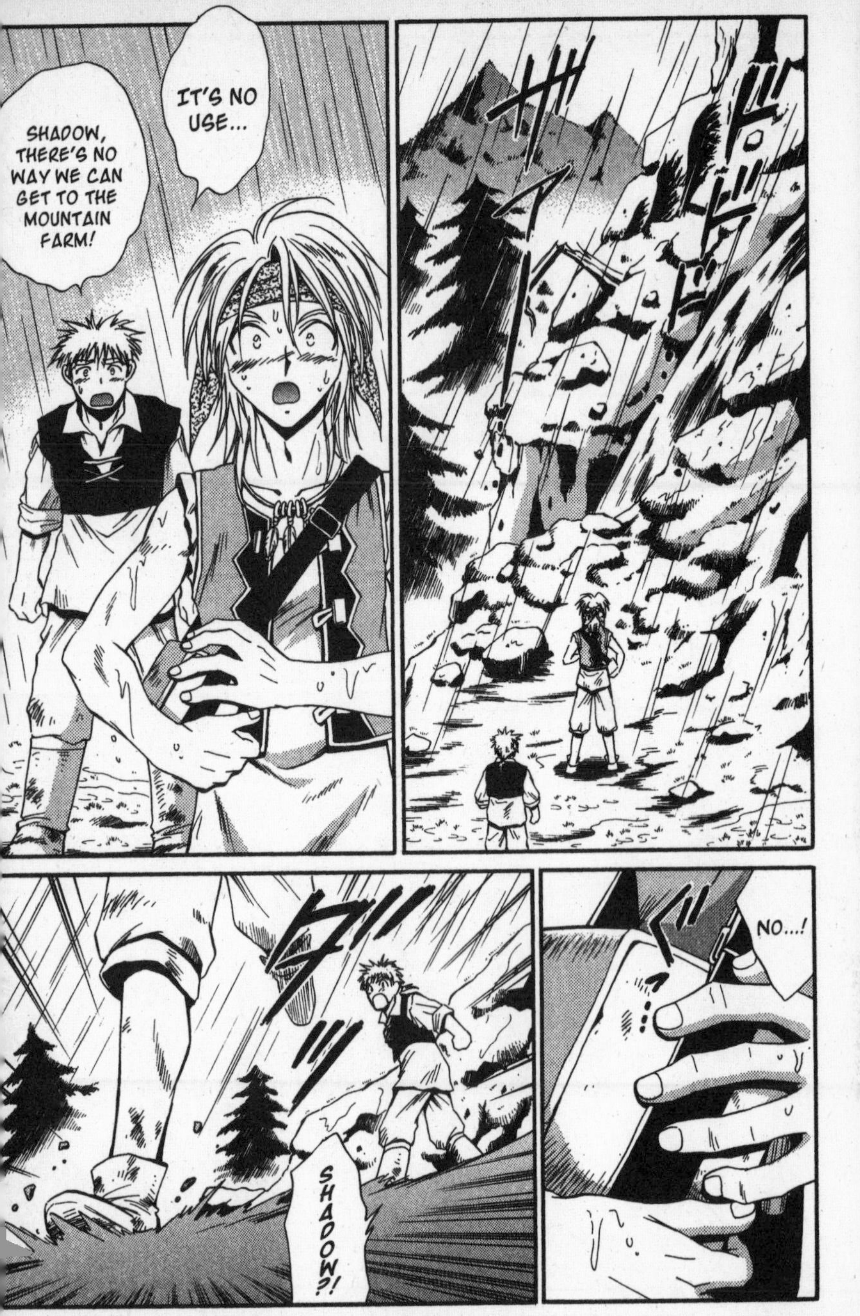
IT'S NO USE...
SHADOW, THERE'S NO WAY WE CAN GET TO THE MOUNTAIN FARM!
NO...!
SHADOW?!

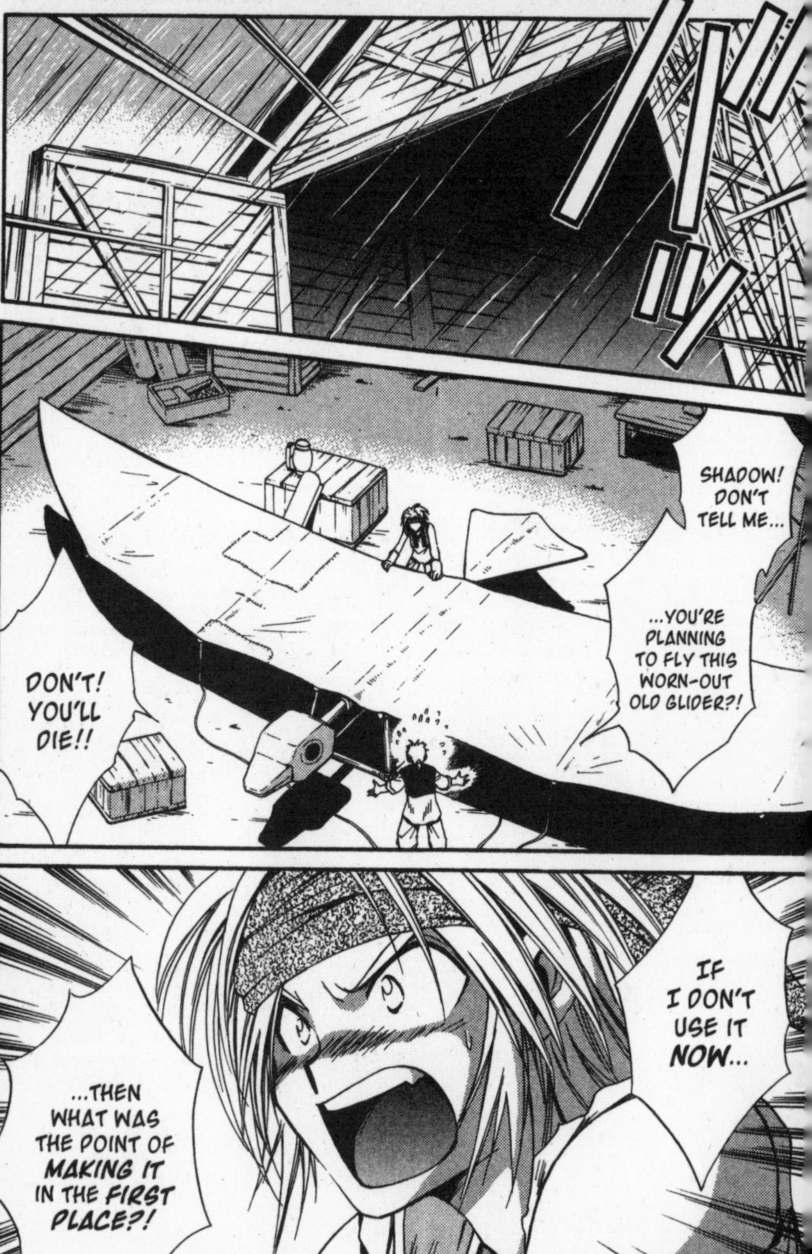
SHADOW! DON'T TELL ME...
...YOU'RE PLANNING TO FLY THIS WORN-OUT OLD GLIDER?!
DON'T! YOU'LL DIE!!
IF I DON'T USE IT NOW...
...THEN WHAT WAS THE POINT OF MAKING IT IN THE FIRST PLACE?!

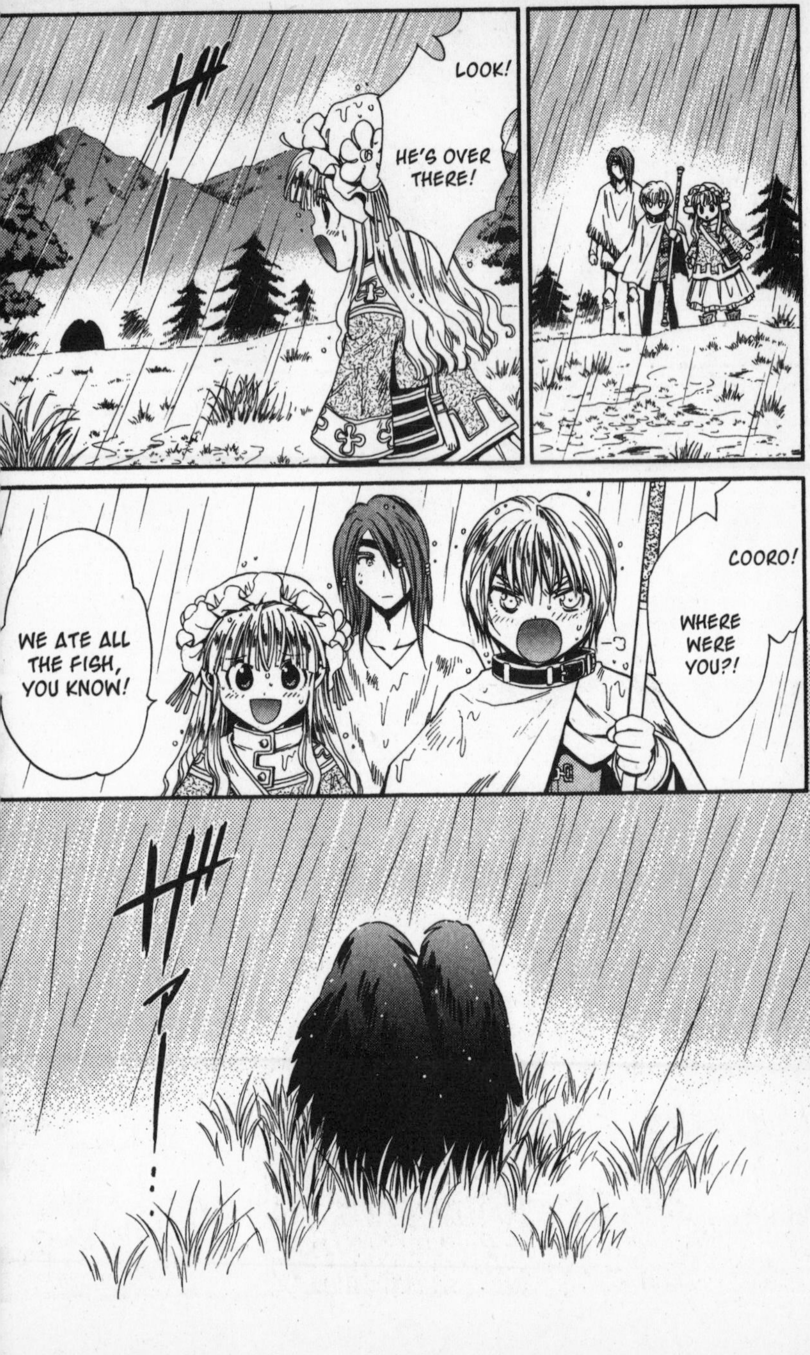
LOOK!
HE'S OVER THERE!
COORO!
WHERE WERE YOU?!
WE ATE ALL THE FISH, YOU KNOW!

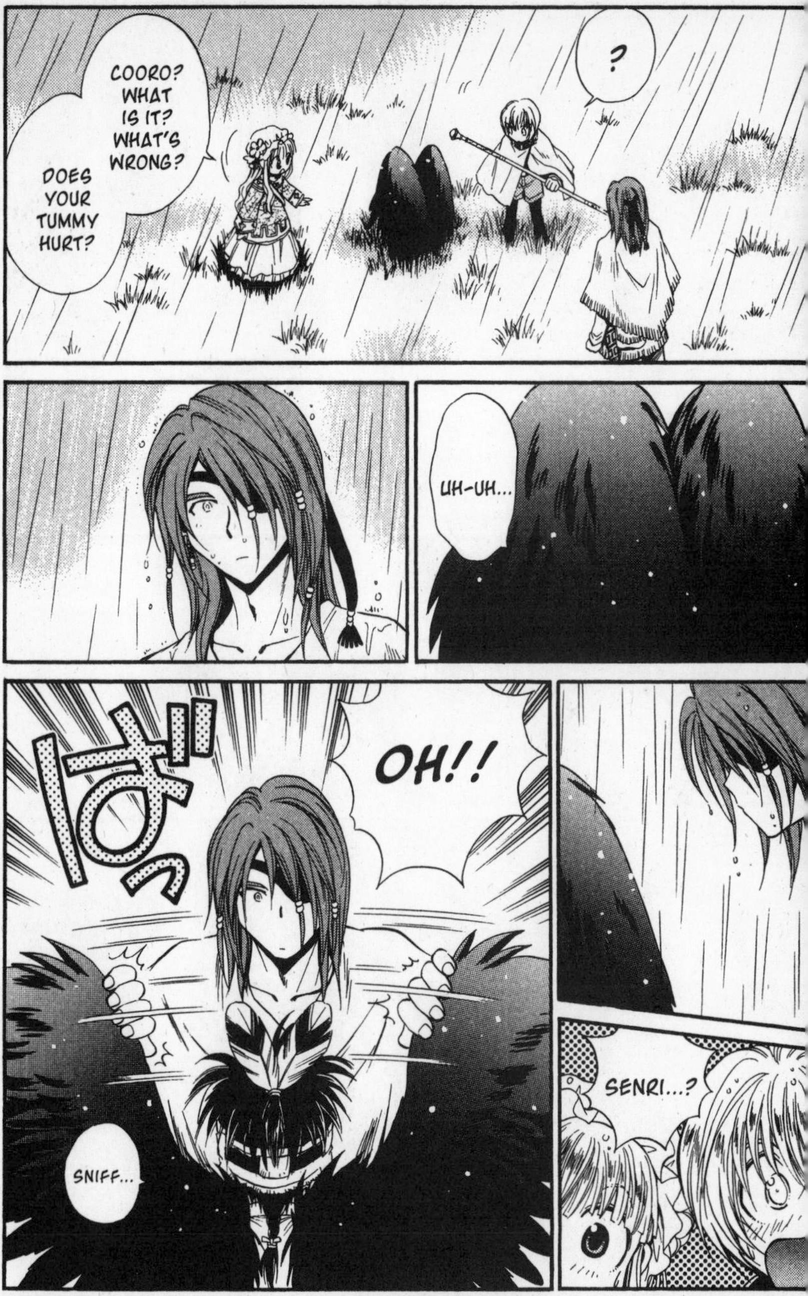
?
COORO? WHAT IS IT? WHAT'S WRONG?
DOES YOUR TUMMY HURT?
UH-UH...
SENRI...?
OH!!
ばっ
SNIFF...

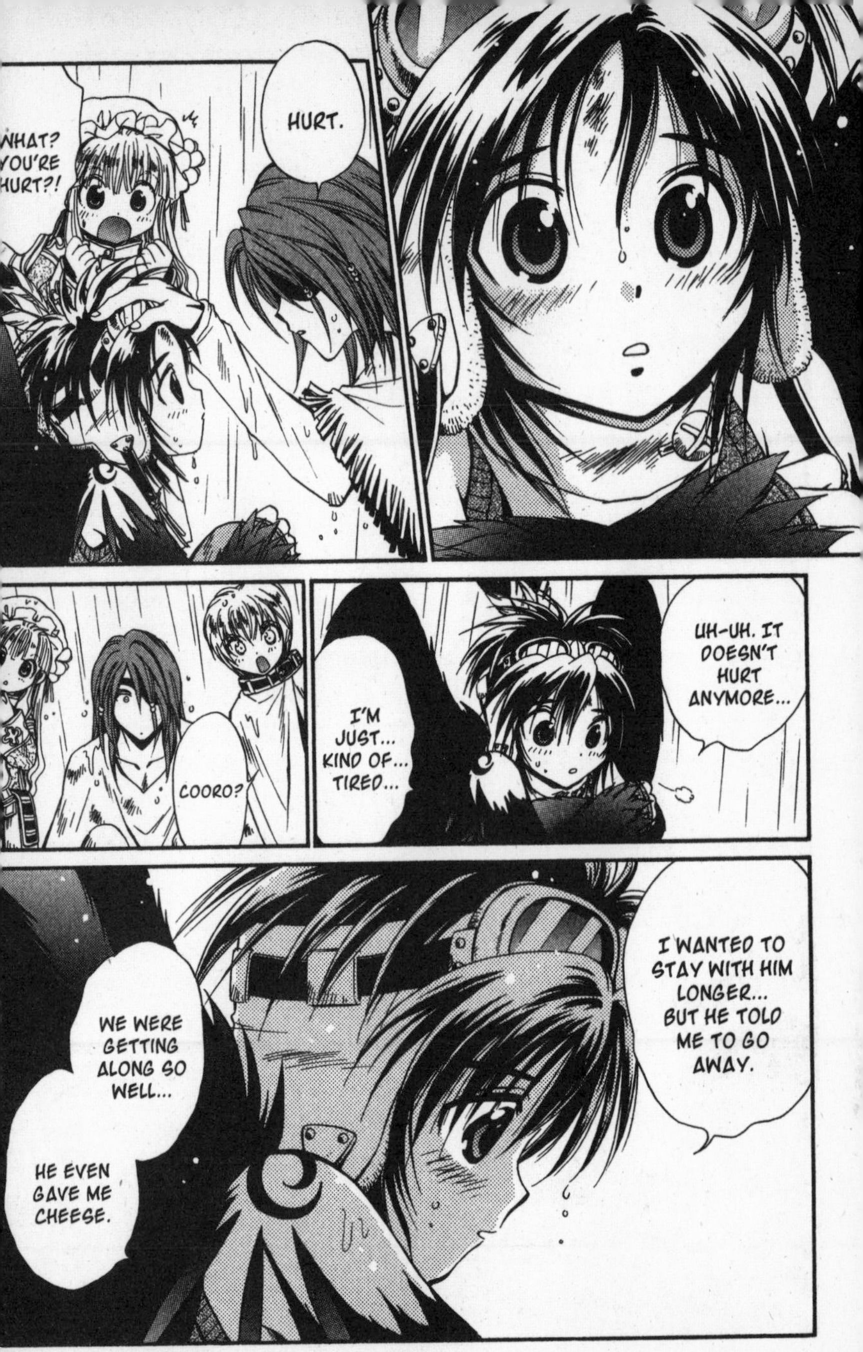
HURT.
WHAT? YOU'RE HURT?!
UH-UH. IT DOESN'T HURT ANYMORE...
I'M JUST... KIND OF... TIRED...
COORO?
I WANTED TO STAY WITH HIM LONGER... BUT HE TOLD ME TO GO AWAY.
WE WERE GETTING ALONG SO WELL...
HE EVEN GAVE ME CHEESE.

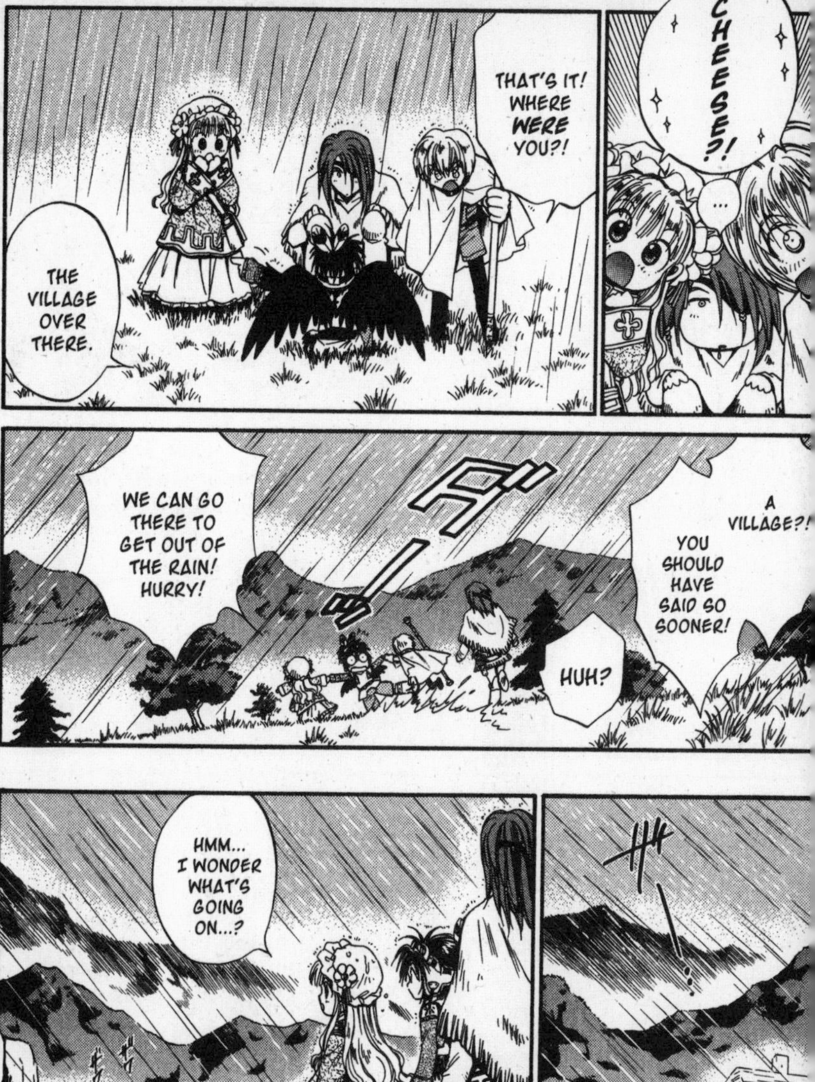
CHEESE?!
...
THAT'S IT! WHERE WERE YOU?!
THE VILLAGE OVER THERE.
A VILLAGE?!
YOU SHOULD HAVE SAID SO SOONER!
HUH?
WE CAN GO THERE TO GET OUT OF THE RAIN! HURRY!
HMM... I WONDER WHAT'S GOING ON...?

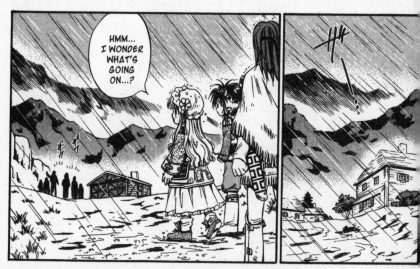

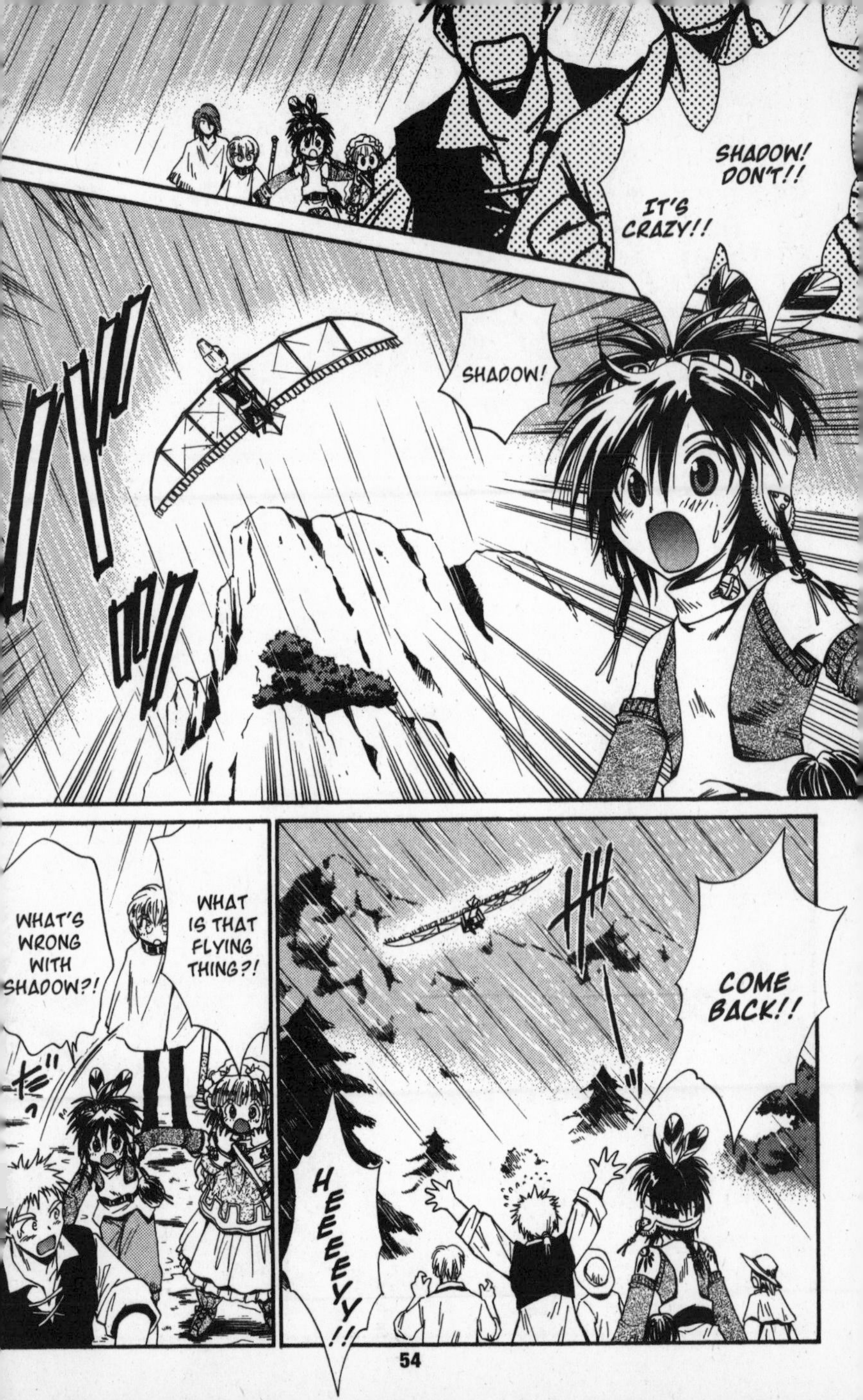
SHADOW! DON'T!!
IT'S CRAZY!!
SHADOW!
COME BACK!!
HEEEEYY!!
WHAT IS THAT FLYING THING?!
WHAT'S WRONG WITH SHADOW?!

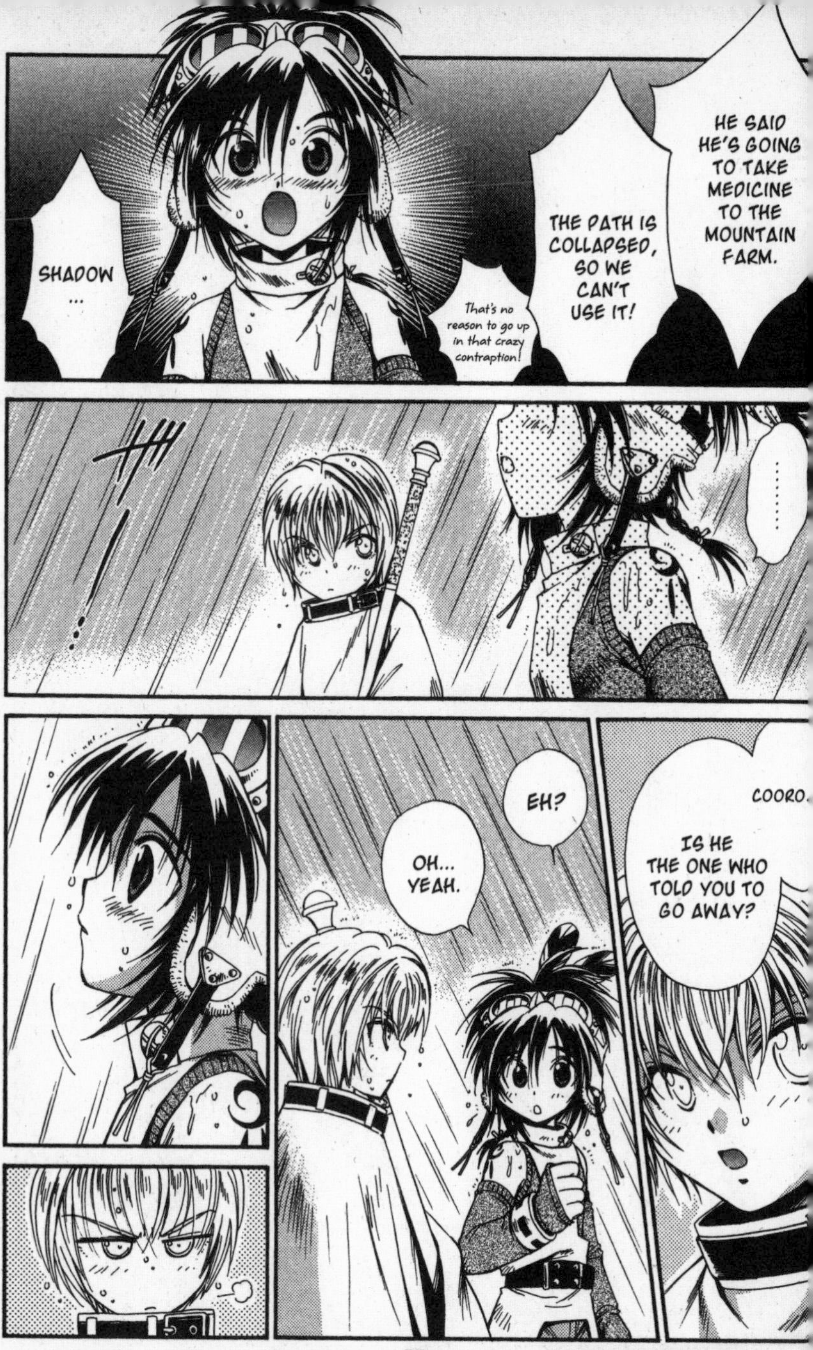
HE SAID HE'S GOING TO TAKE MEDICINE TO THE MOUNTAIN FARM.
THE PATH IS COLLAPSED, SO WE CAN'T USE IT!
That's no reason to go up in that crazy contraption!
SHADOW ...
......
COORO.
IS HE THE ONE WHO TOLD YOU TO GO AWAY?
EH?
OH... YEAH.

WHAT?!

AND *YOU'RE* THE BEST ONE TO HELP HIM, AREN'T YOU, HUSKY?

SIGH.

HE NEEDS SO MUCH HELP.

YEP.

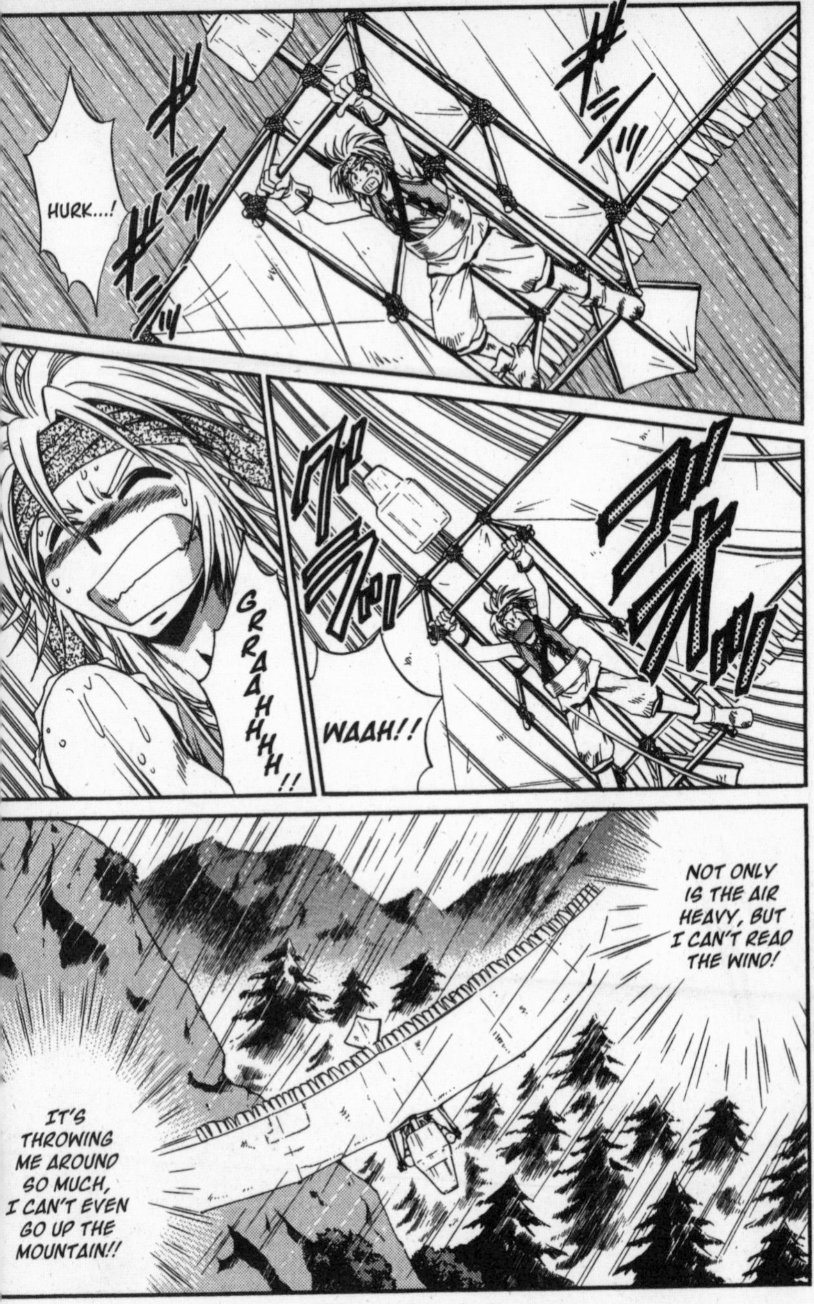
HURK...!
WAAH!!
GRRAAHHHH!!
NOT ONLY IS THE AIR HEAVY, BUT I CAN'T READ THE WIND!
IT'S THROWING ME AROUND SO MUCH, I CAN'T EVEN GO UP THE MOUNTAIN!!

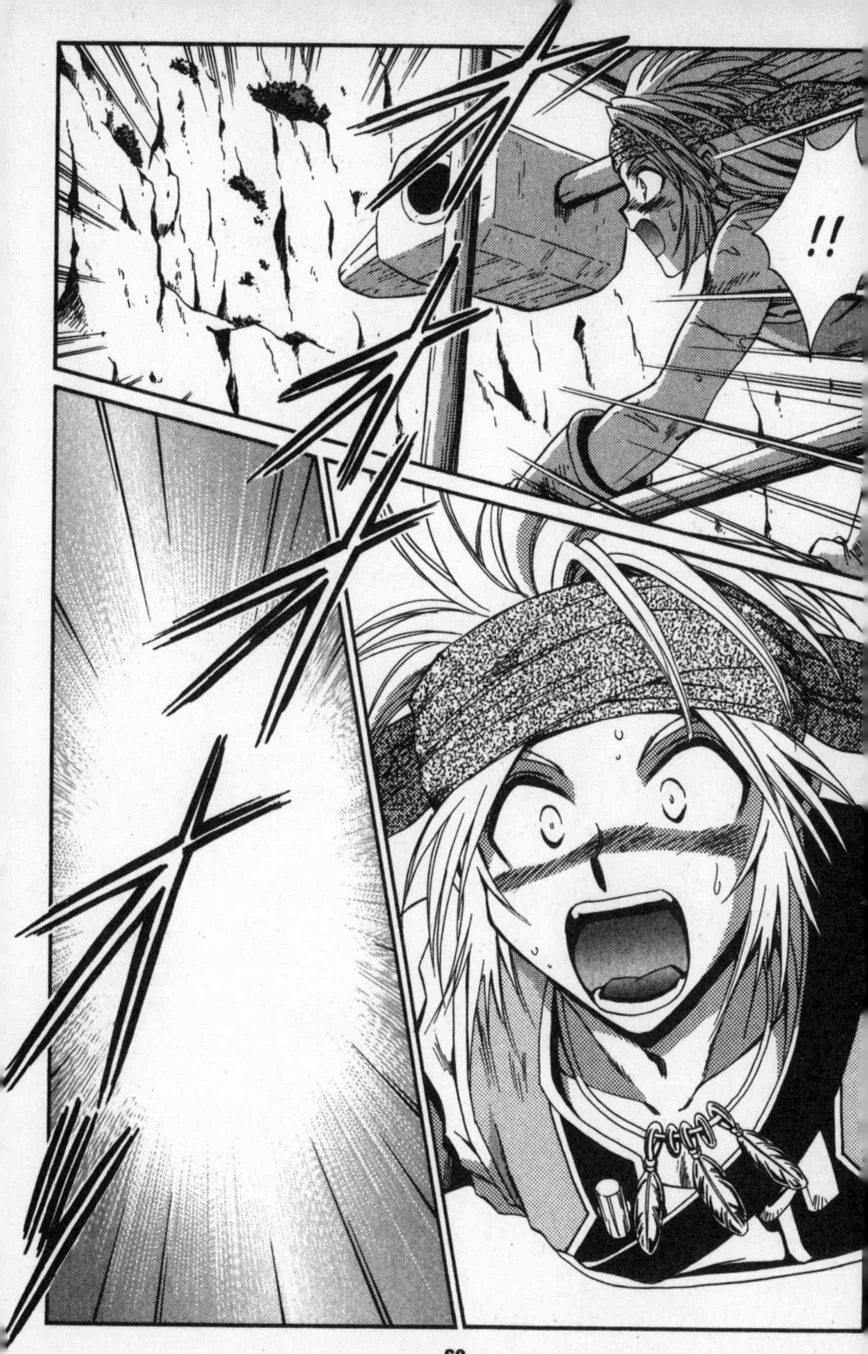
!!

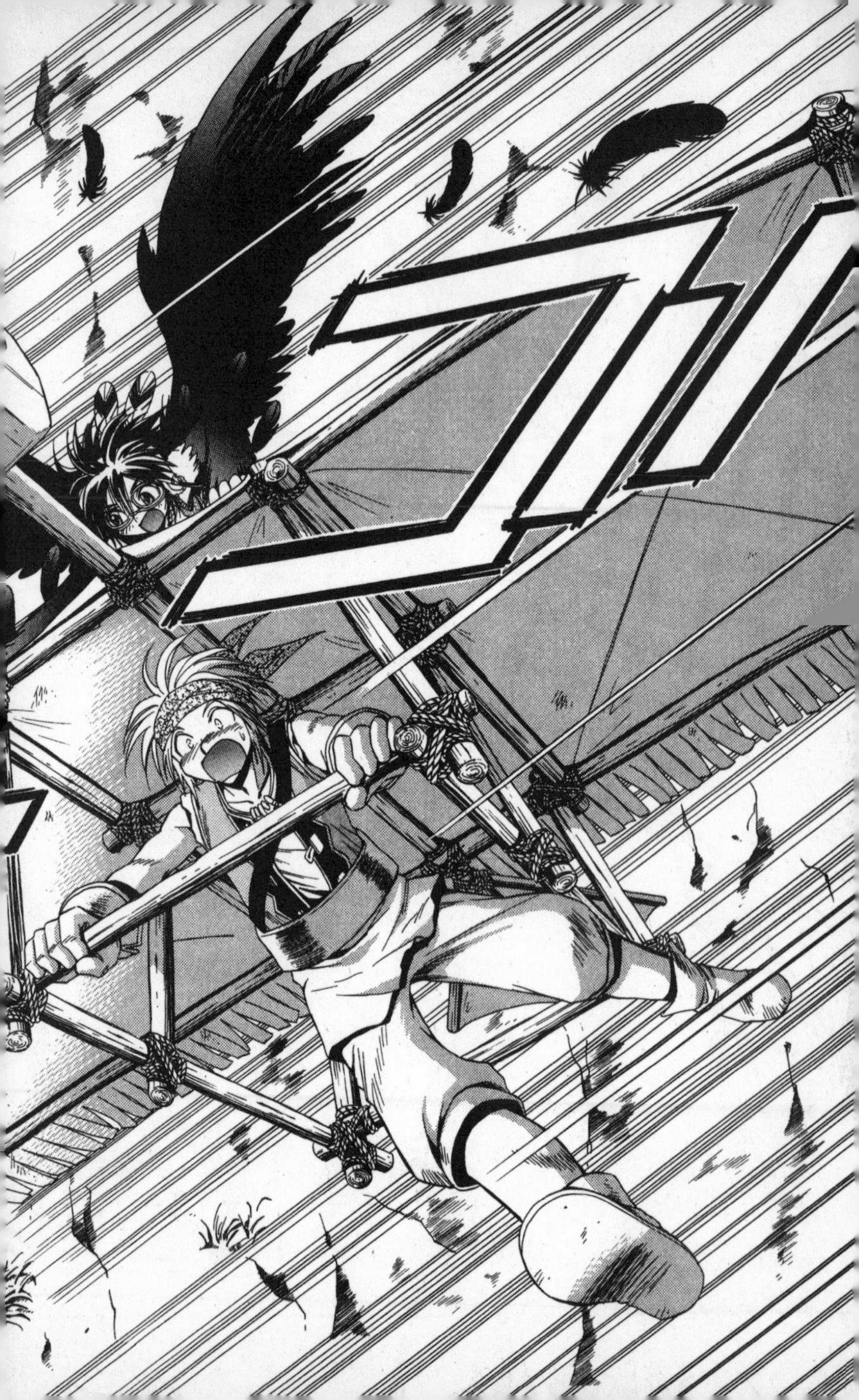

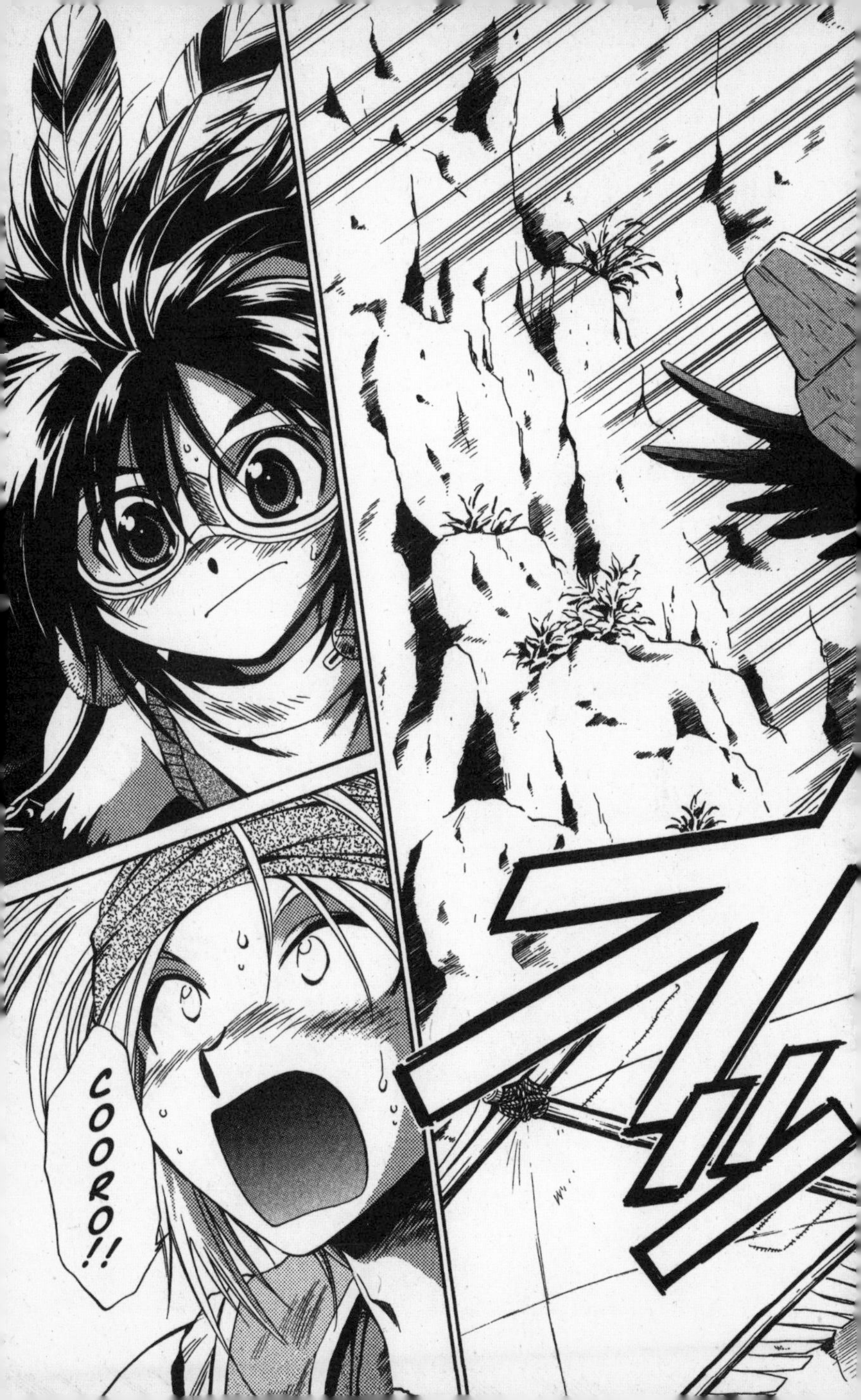
COOORO!!

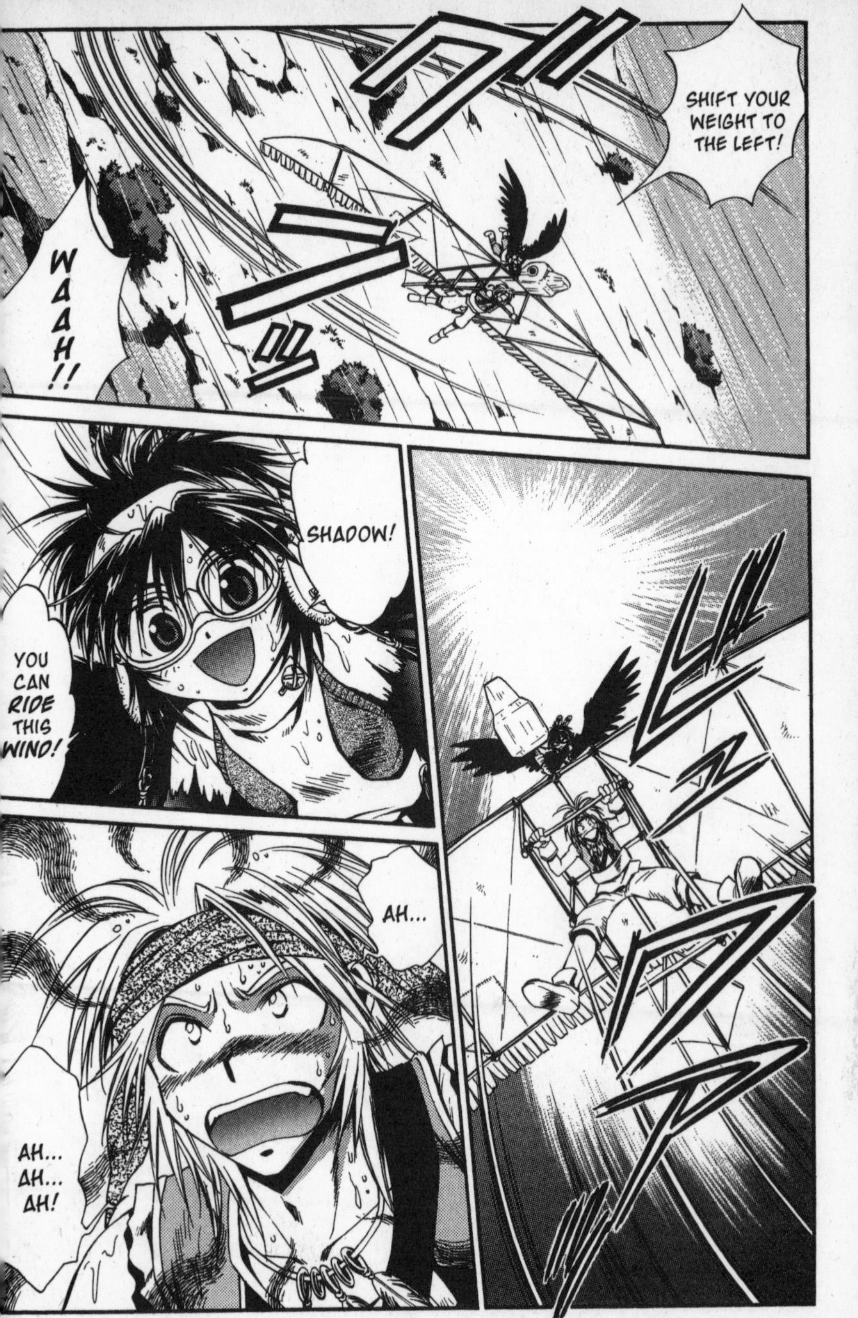
SHIFT YOUR WEIGHT TO THE LEFT!
WAAAH!!
SHADOW!
YOU CAN RIDE THIS WIND!
AH...
AH... AH... AH!

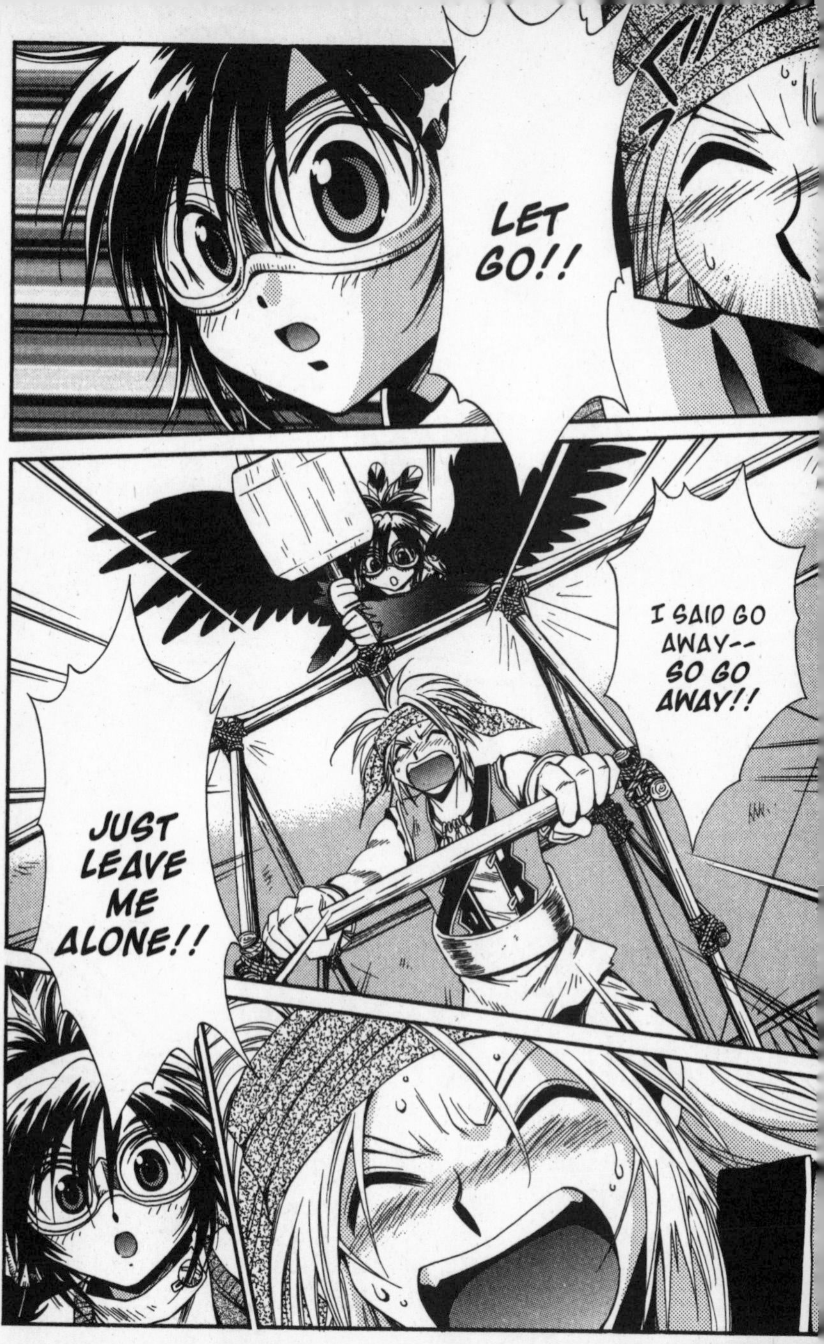
LET GO!!
I SAID GO AWAY-- SO GO AWAY!!
JUST LEAVE ME ALONE!!

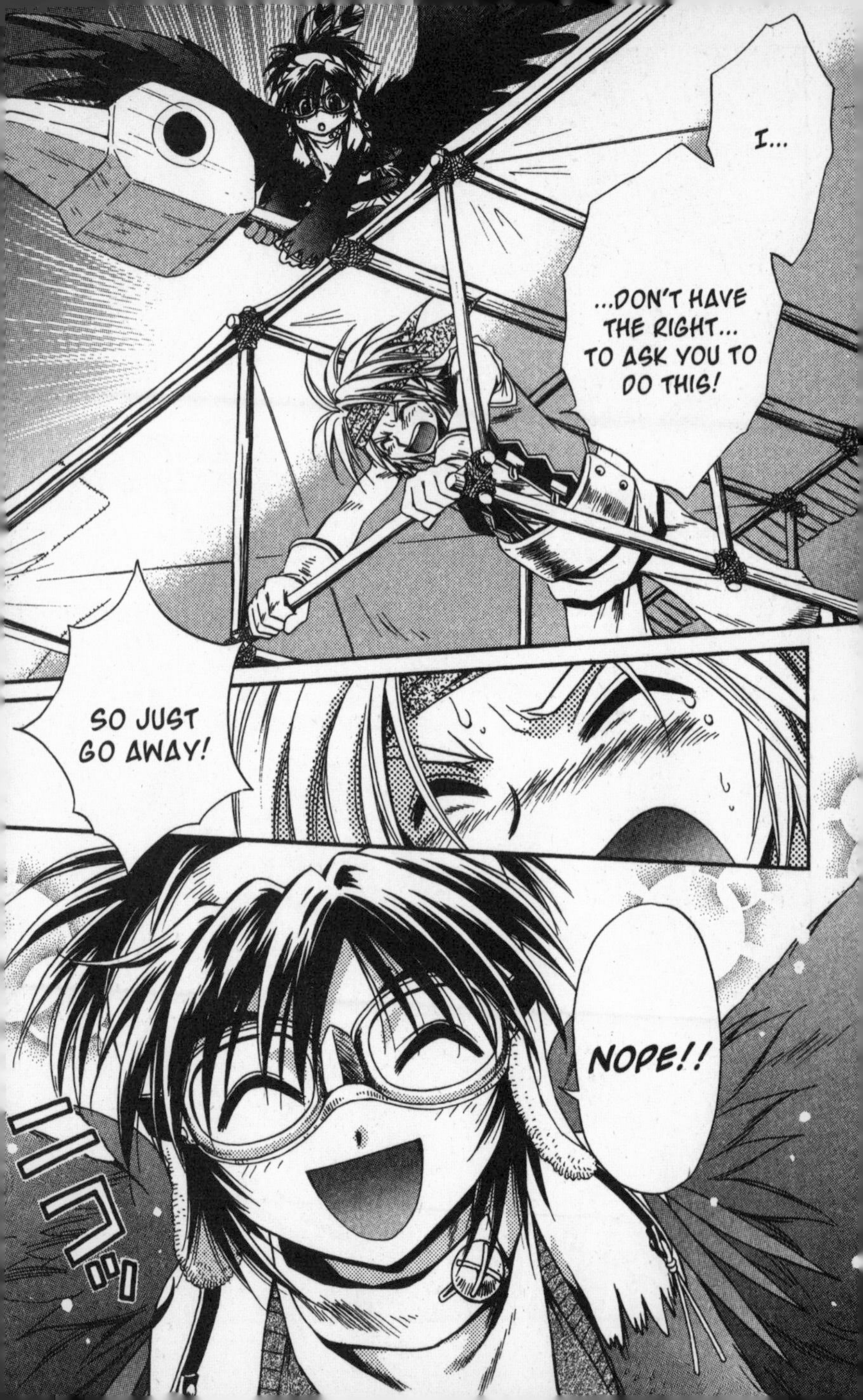
I...
...DON'T HAVE THE RIGHT... TO ASK YOU TO DO THIS!
SO JUST GO AWAY!
NOPE!!

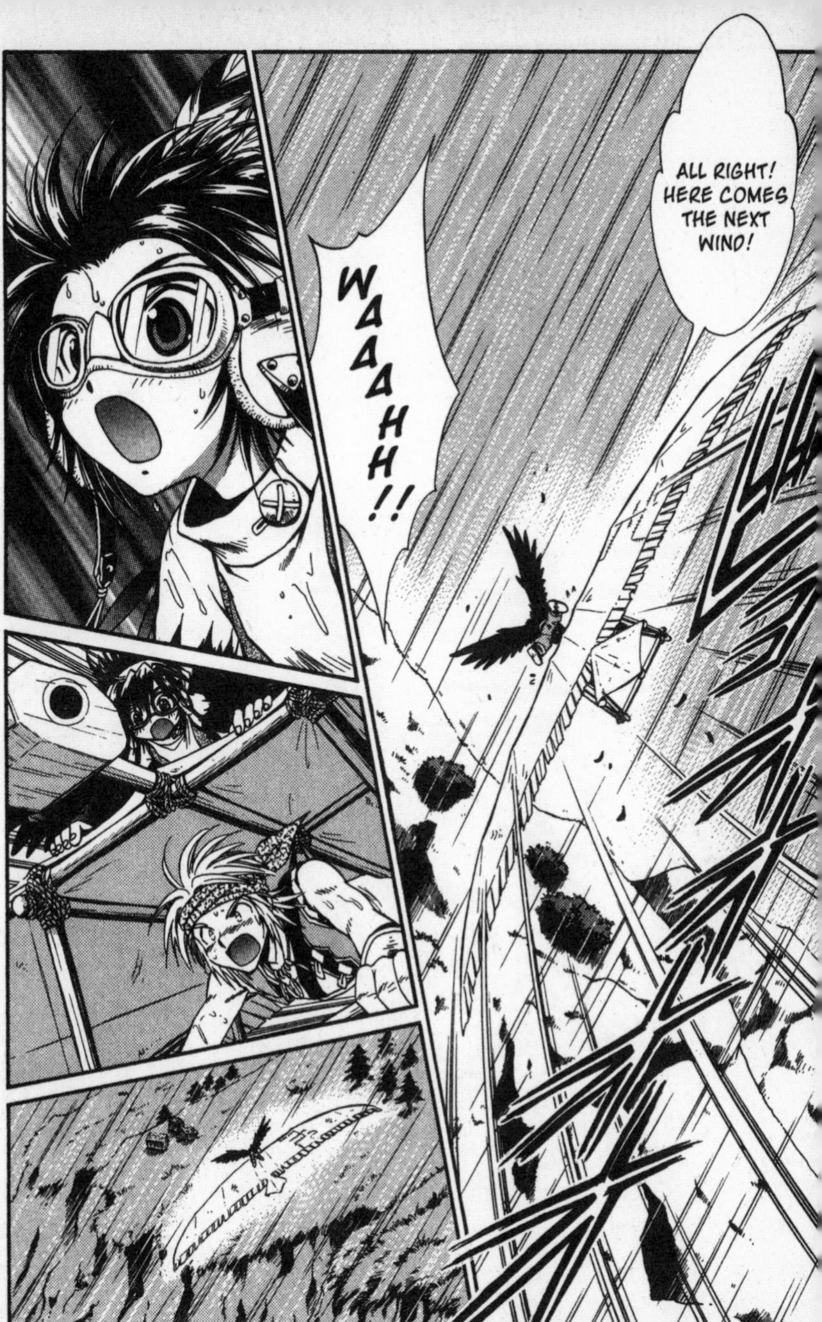
ALL RIGHT! HERE COMES THE NEXT WIND!
WAAAAHH!!

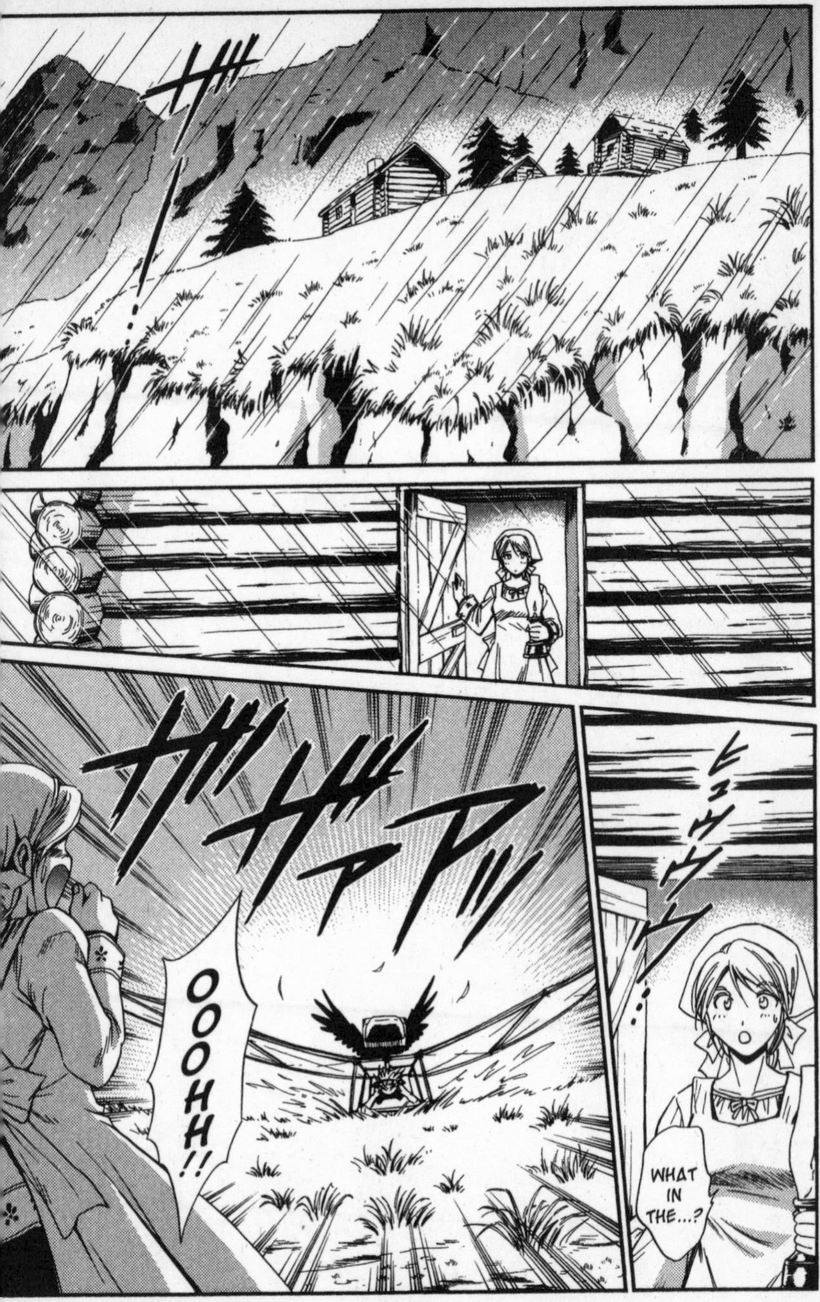
WHAT IN THE...?
OOOOHH!!

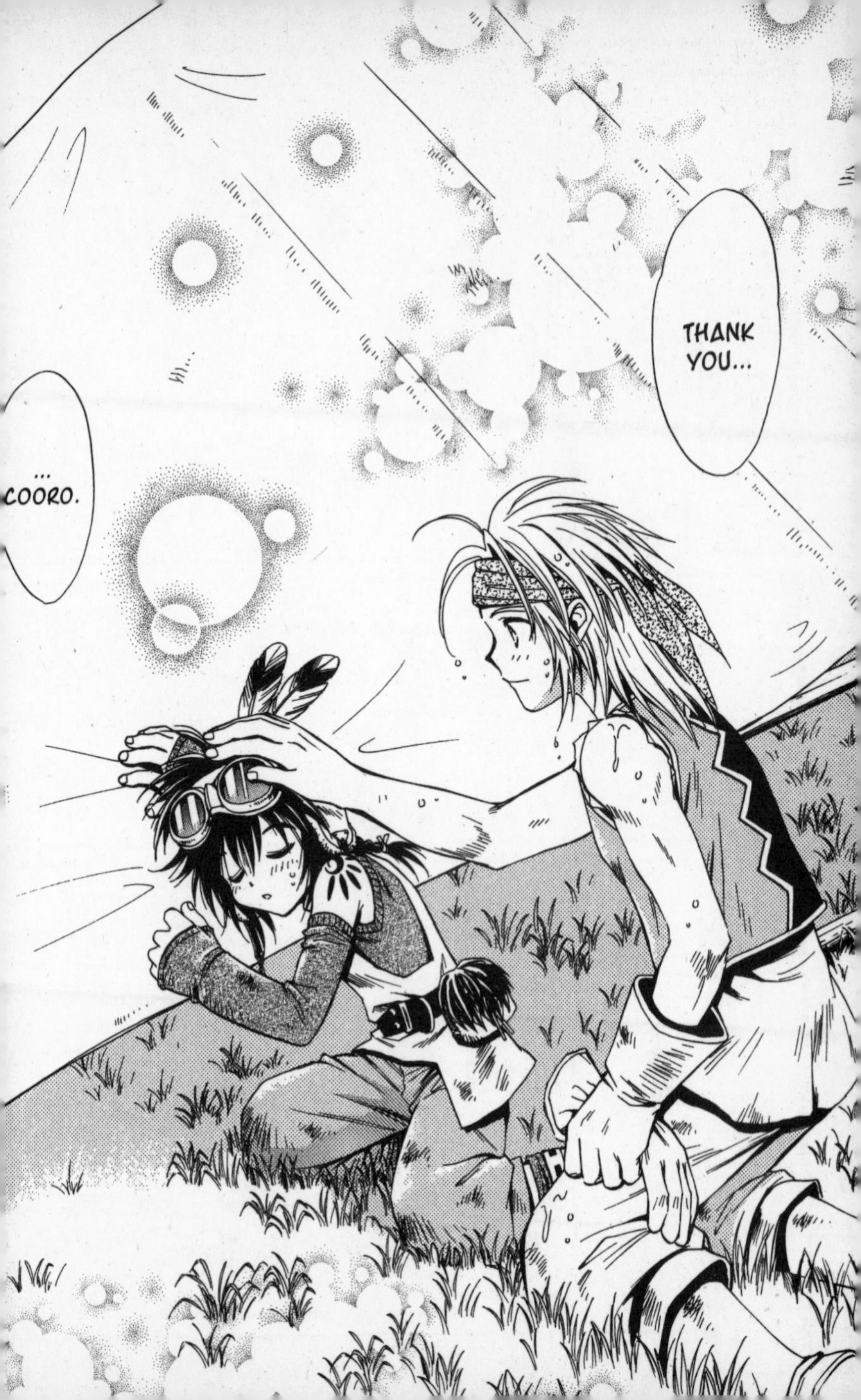
THANK YOU...
... COORO.

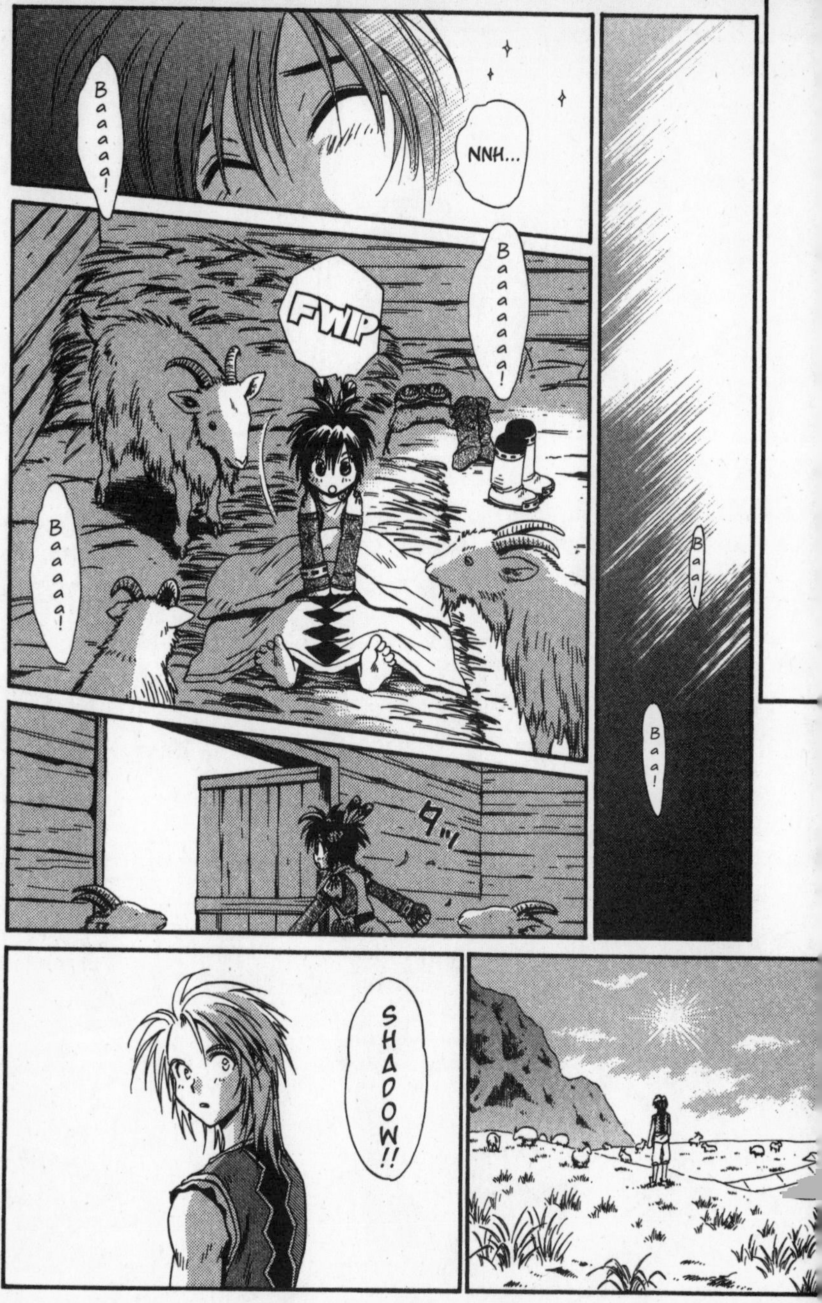
Baa!
Baa!
NNH...
Baaaaa!
Baaaaaaaa!
FWIP
Baaaaa!
タッ
SHADOW!!

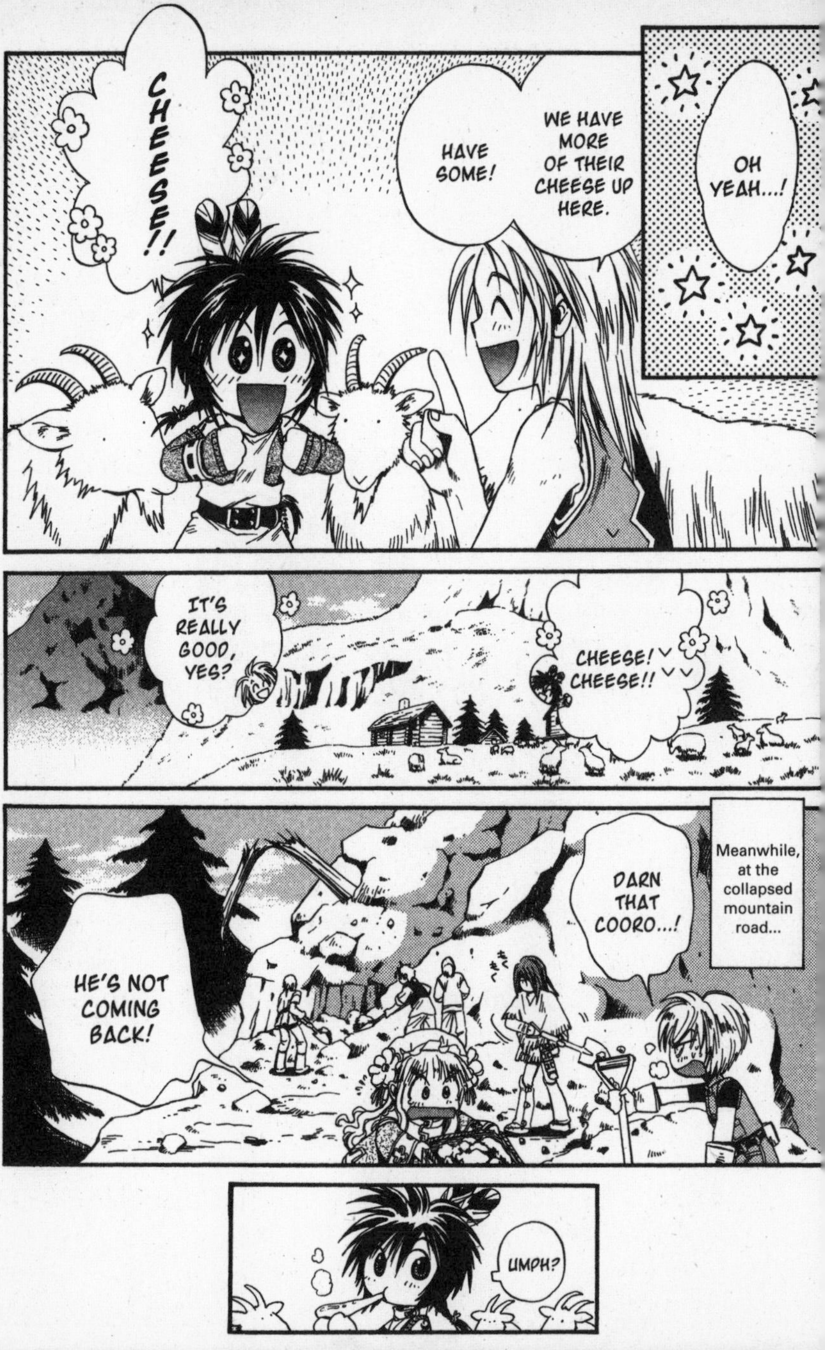
OH YEAH...!
WE HAVE MORE OF THEIR CHEESE UP HERE.
HAVE SOME!
CHEESE!!
CHEESE! CHEESE!!
IT'S REALLY GOOD, YES?
Meanwhile, at the collapsed mountain road...
DARN THAT COORO...!
HE'S NOT COMING BACK!
UMPH?

Antimonopoly !

Chapter 11: Guardian Heart—Part 1

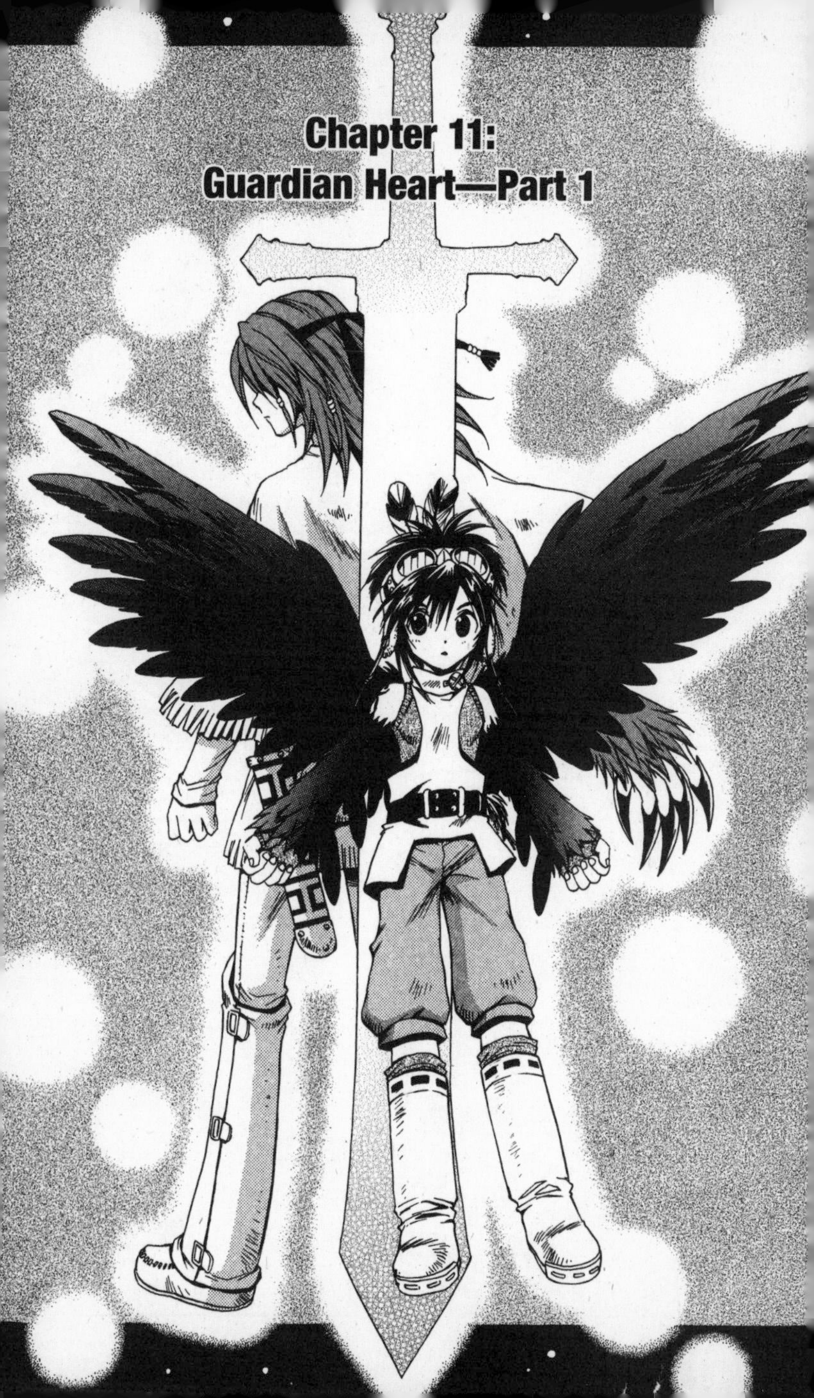

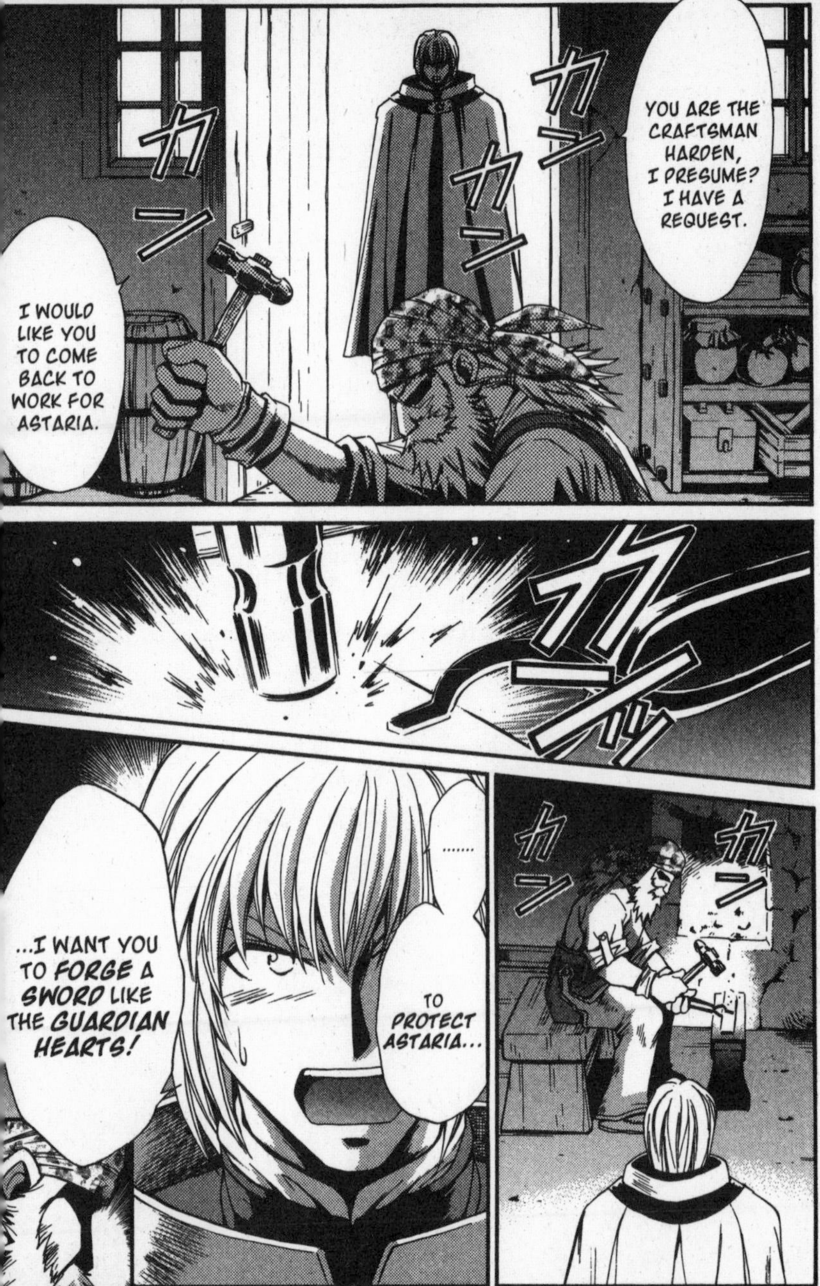
YOU ARE THE CRAFTSMAN HARDEN, I PRESUME? I HAVE A REQUEST.
I WOULD LIKE YOU TO COME BACK TO WORK FOR ASTARIA.
……
TO PROTECT ASTARIA…
…I WANT YOU TO FORGE A SWORD LIKE THE GUARDIAN HEARTS!

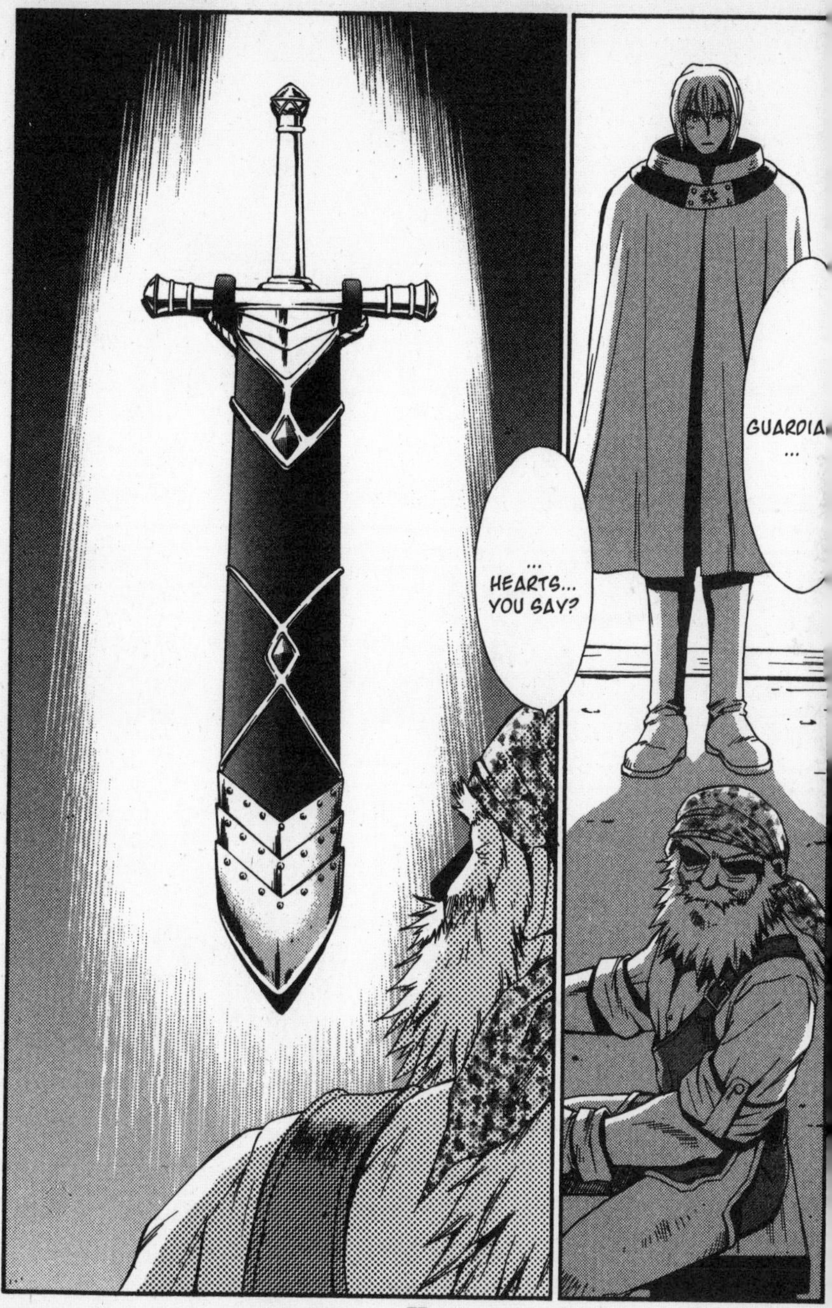
GUARDIA ...
... HEARTS... YOU SAY?

...MAINLY BECAUSE THE ASTARIAN GOVERNMENT CONTROLS THE IRON.

BESIDES, IRON-EDGED TOOLS ARE REALLY EXPENSIVE...

YOU'RE TOO YOUNG FOR SOMETHING LIKE THAT, COORO.

I WANT AN IRON HATCHET OR AXE LIKE SENRI'S!

I CAN'T CUT WOOD WITH MY DULL OLD STONE KNIFE.

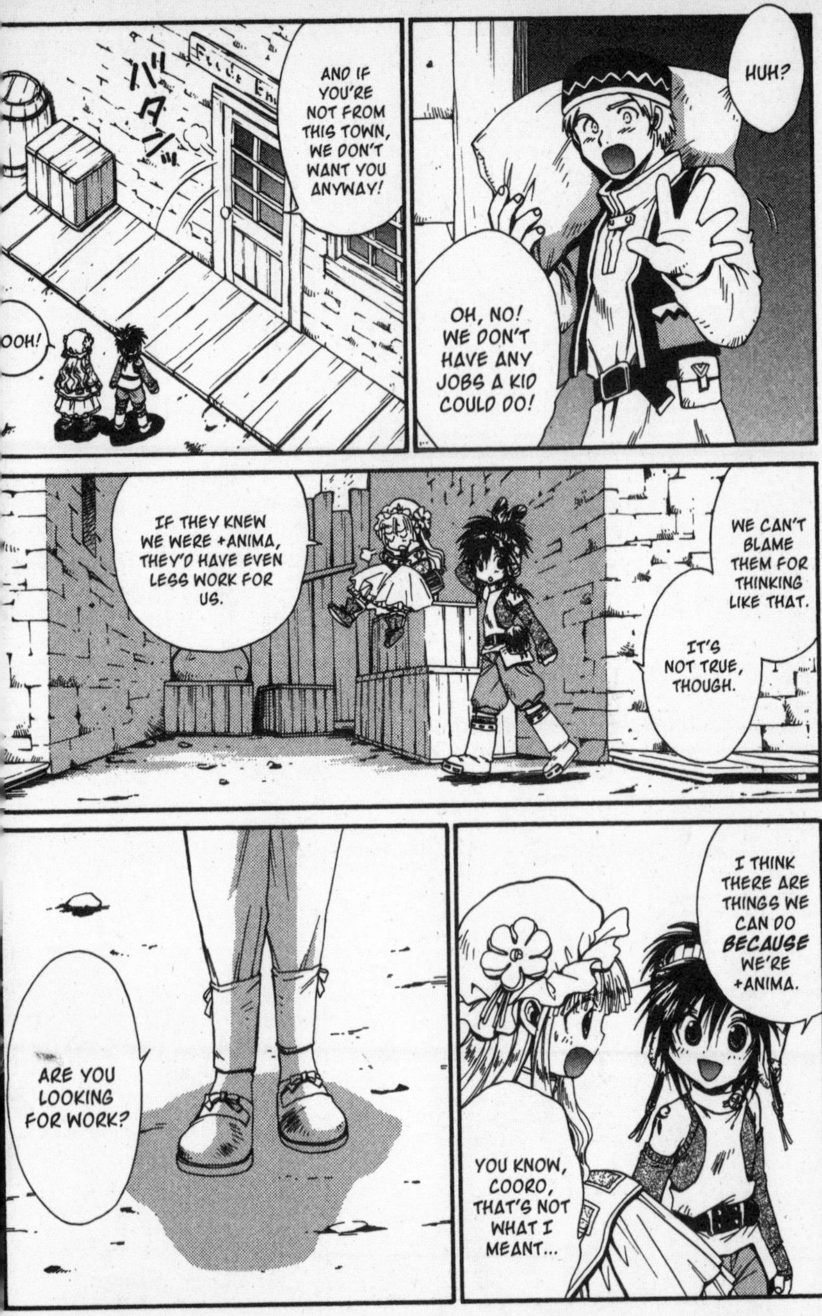
HUH?
OH, NO! WE DON'T HAVE ANY JOBS A KID COULD DO!
バタン
AND IF YOU'RE NOT FROM THIS TOWN, WE DON'T WANT YOU ANYWAY!
OOH!
WE CAN'T BLAME THEM FOR THINKING LIKE THAT.
IT'S NOT TRUE, THOUGH.
IF THEY KNEW WE WERE +ANIMA, THEY'D HAVE EVEN LESS WORK FOR US.
I THINK THERE ARE THINGS WE CAN DO **BECAUSE** WE'RE +ANIMA.
YOU KNOW, COORO, THAT'S NOT WHAT I MEANT...
ARE YOU LOOKING FOR WORK?

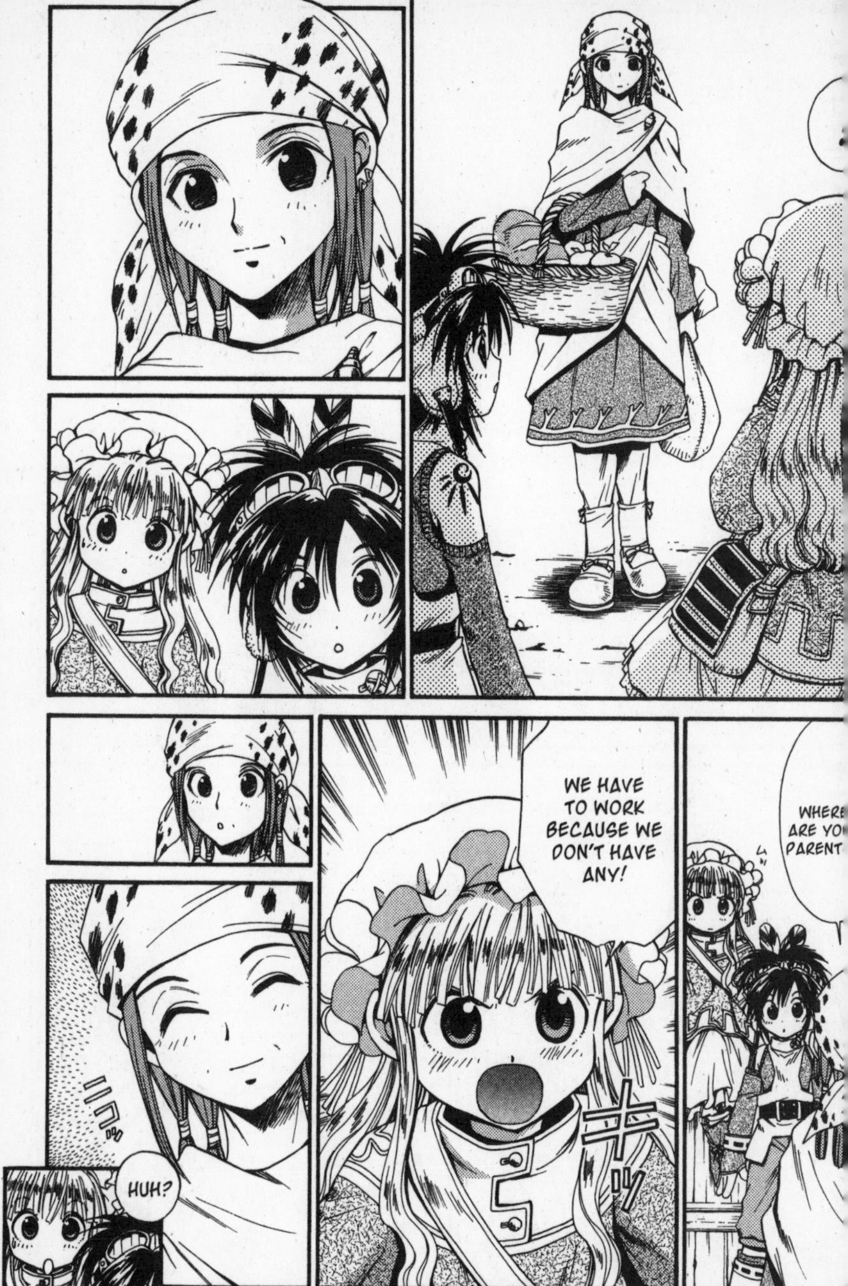
WHERE ARE YO PARENT
WE HAVE TO WORK BECAUSE WE DON'T HAVE ANY!
HUH?

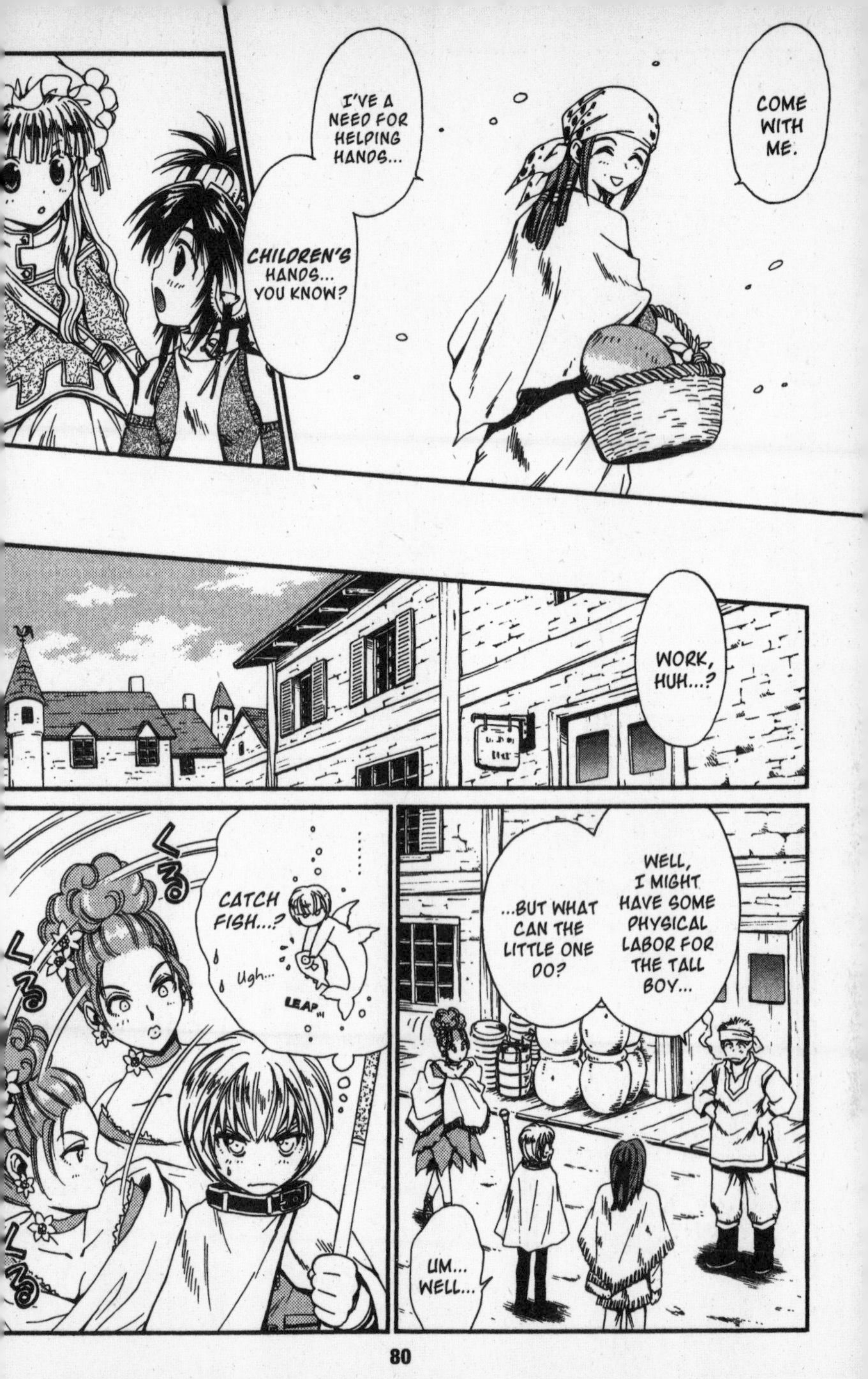
COME WITH ME.
I'VE A NEED FOR HELPING HANDS...
CHILDREN'S HANDS... YOU KNOW?
WORK, HUH...?
WELL, I MIGHT HAVE SOME PHYSICAL LABOR FOR THE TALL BOY...
...BUT WHAT CAN THE LITTLE ONE DO?
UM... WELL...
CATCH FISH...?
Ugh...
LEAP

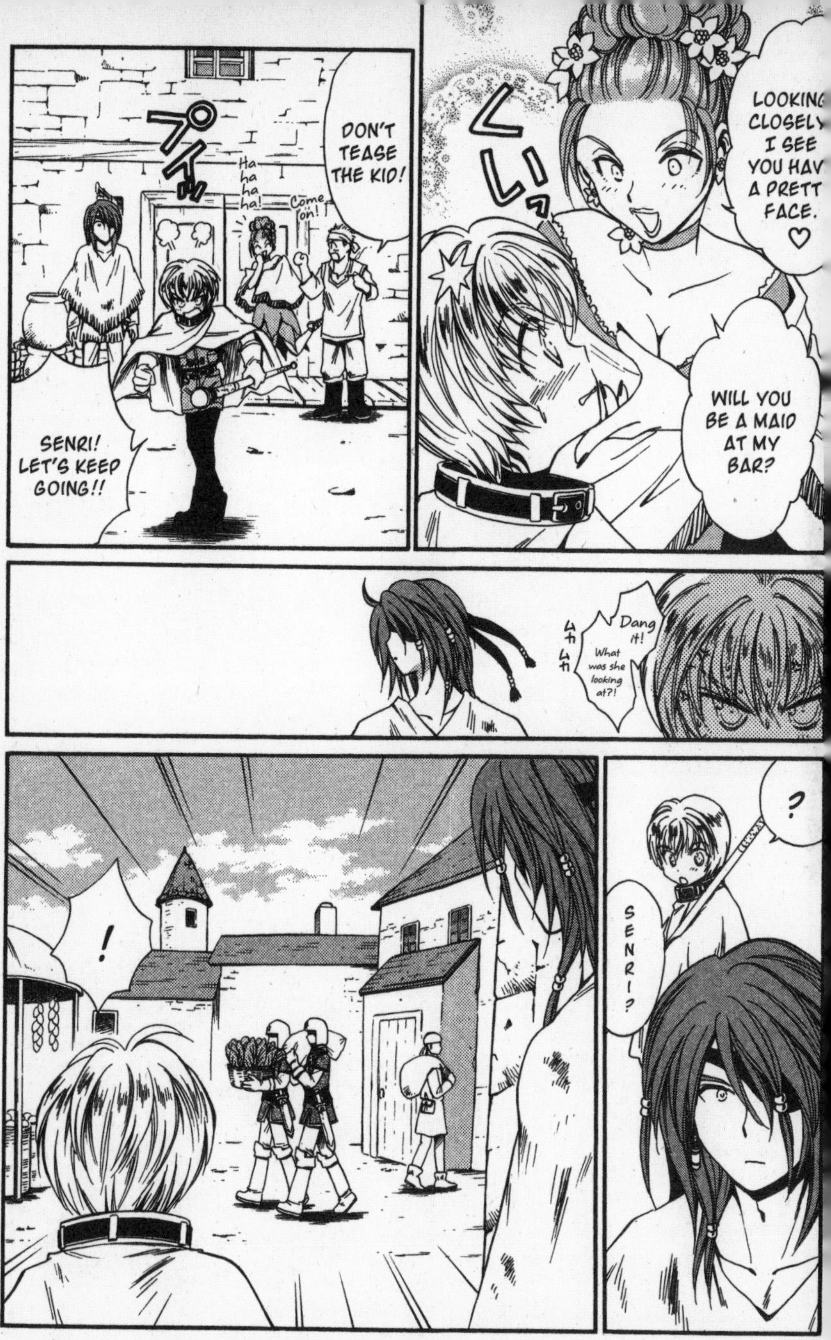
くいっ
LOOKING CLOSELY I SEE YOU HAV A PRETT FACE. ♡
WILL YOU BE A MAID AT MY BAR?
DON'T TEASE THE KID!
プイッ
Ha ha ha ha!
Come on!
SENRI! LET'S KEEP GOING!!
Dang it!
What was she looking at?!
ムカムカ
?
SENRI?
!

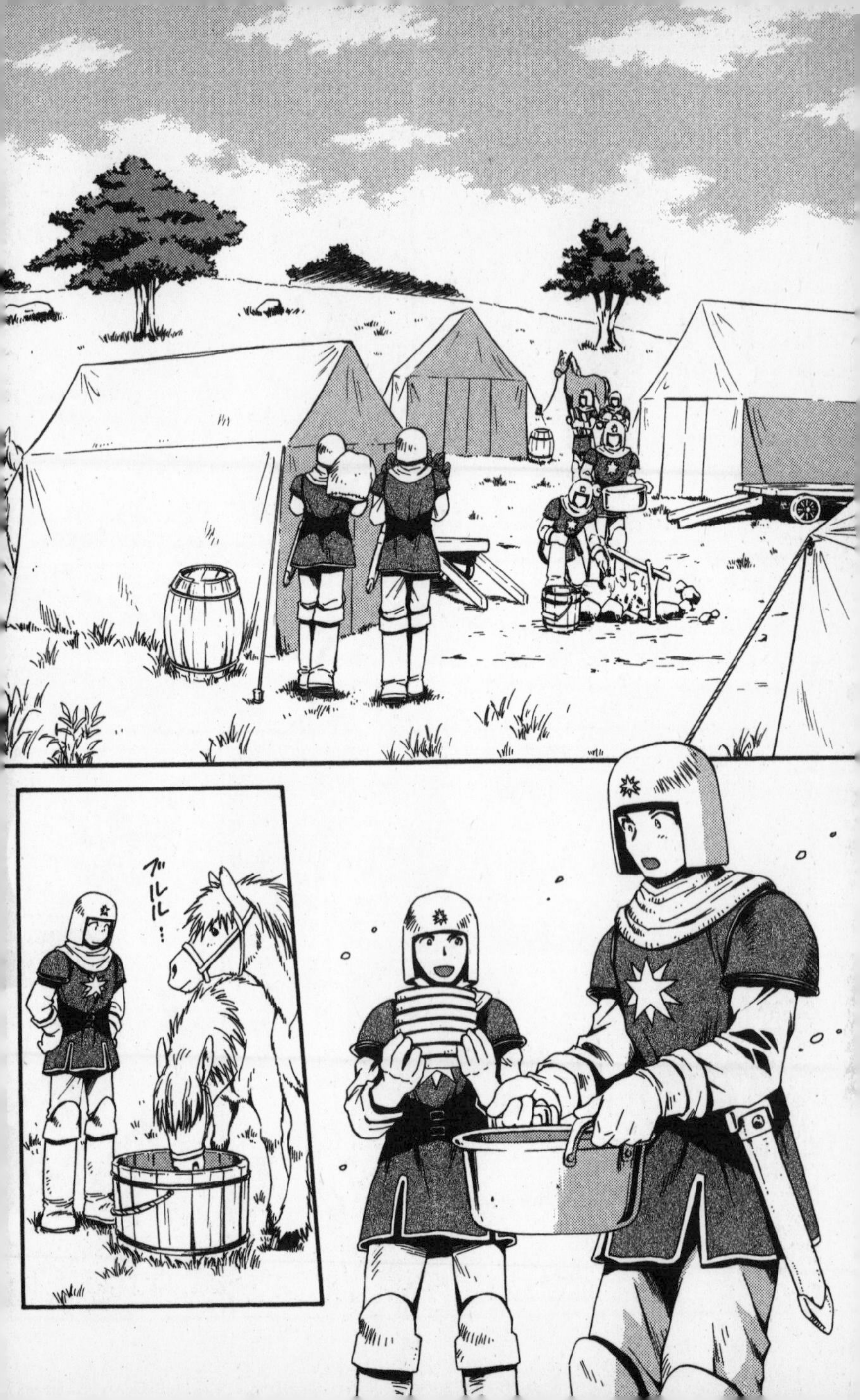
ブルル…

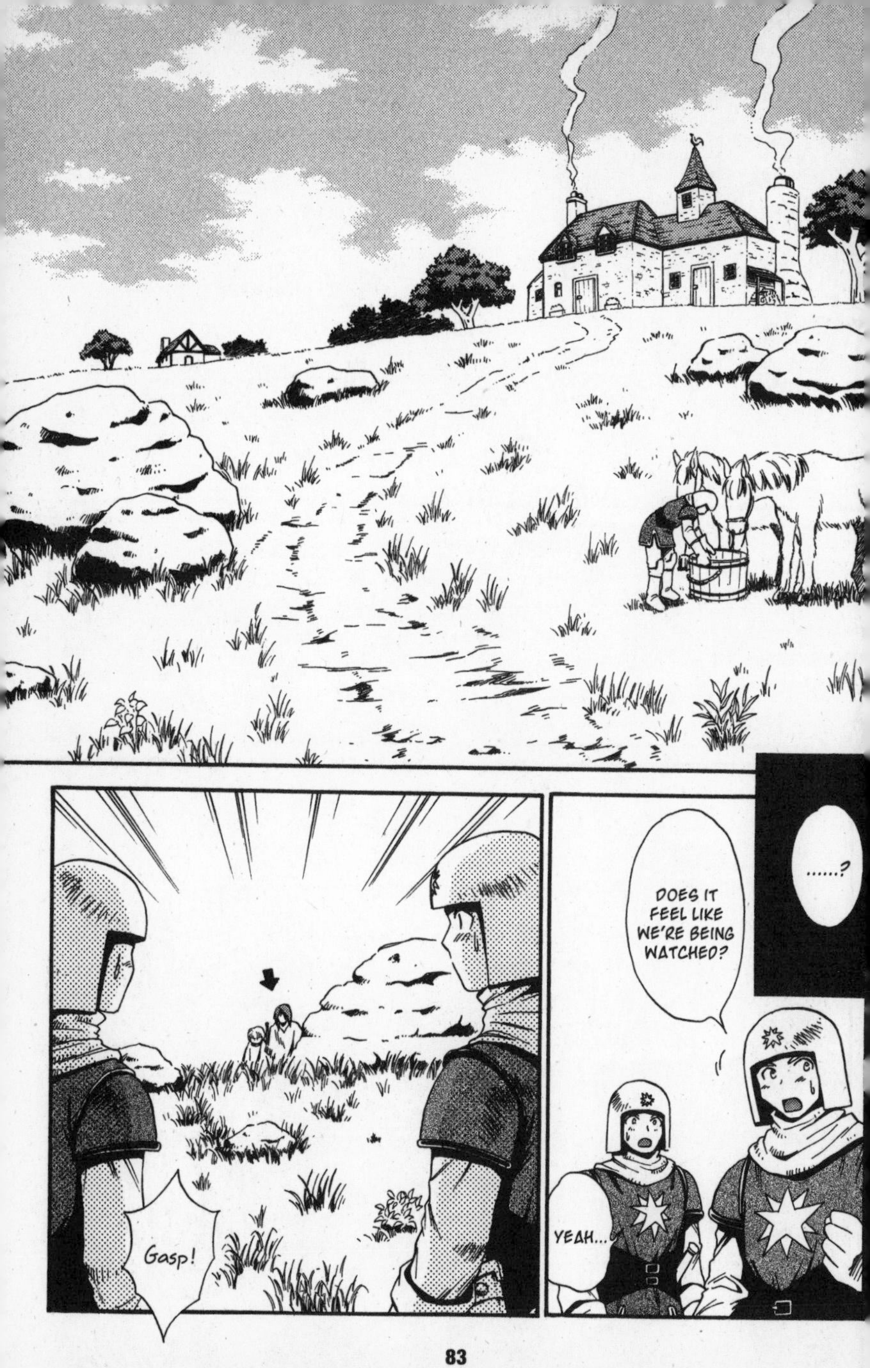
......?
DOES IT FEEL LIKE WE'RE BEING WATCHED?
YEAH...
Gasp!

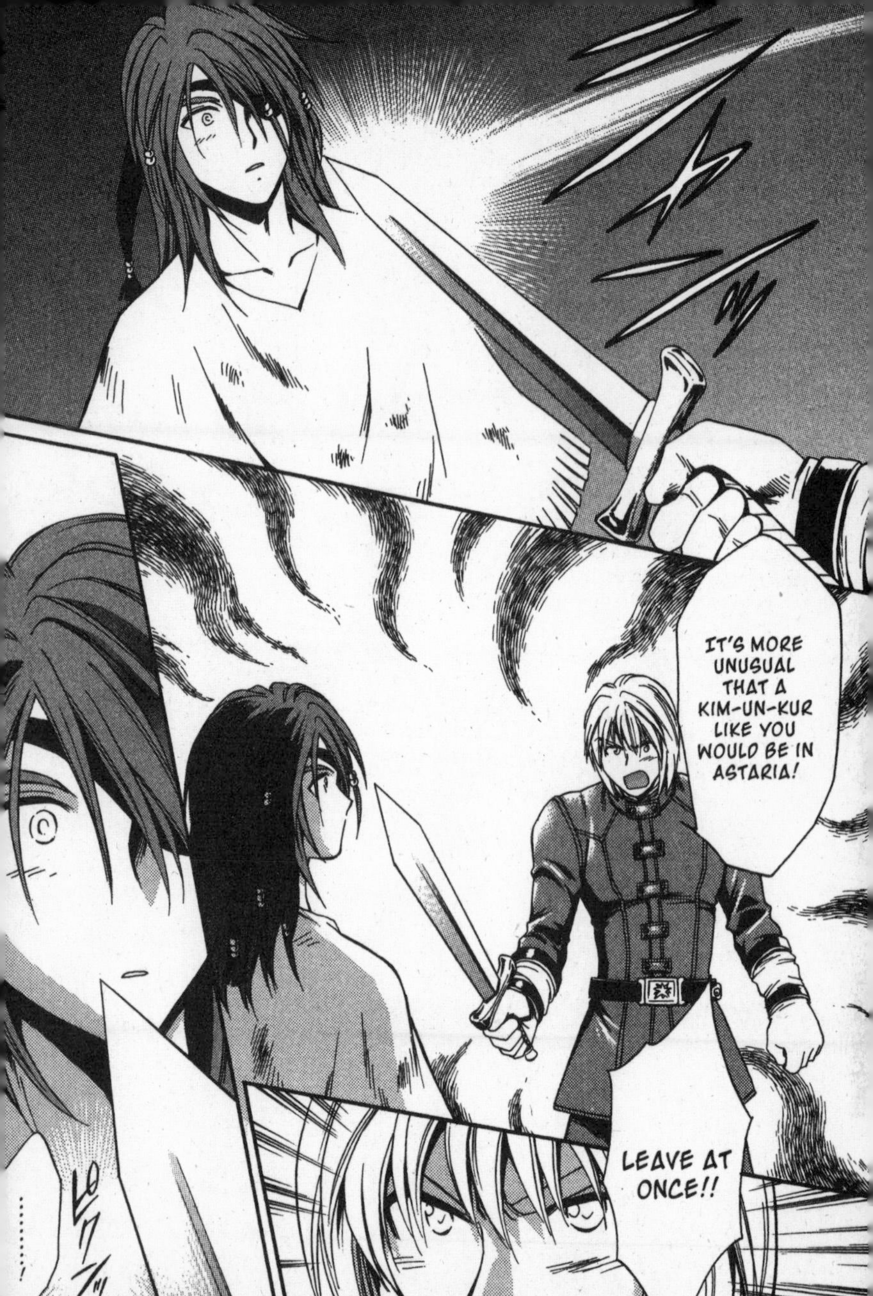
IT'S MORE UNUSUAL THAT A KIM-UN-KUR LIKE YOU WOULD BE IN ASTARIA!
LEAVE AT ONCE!!
......!

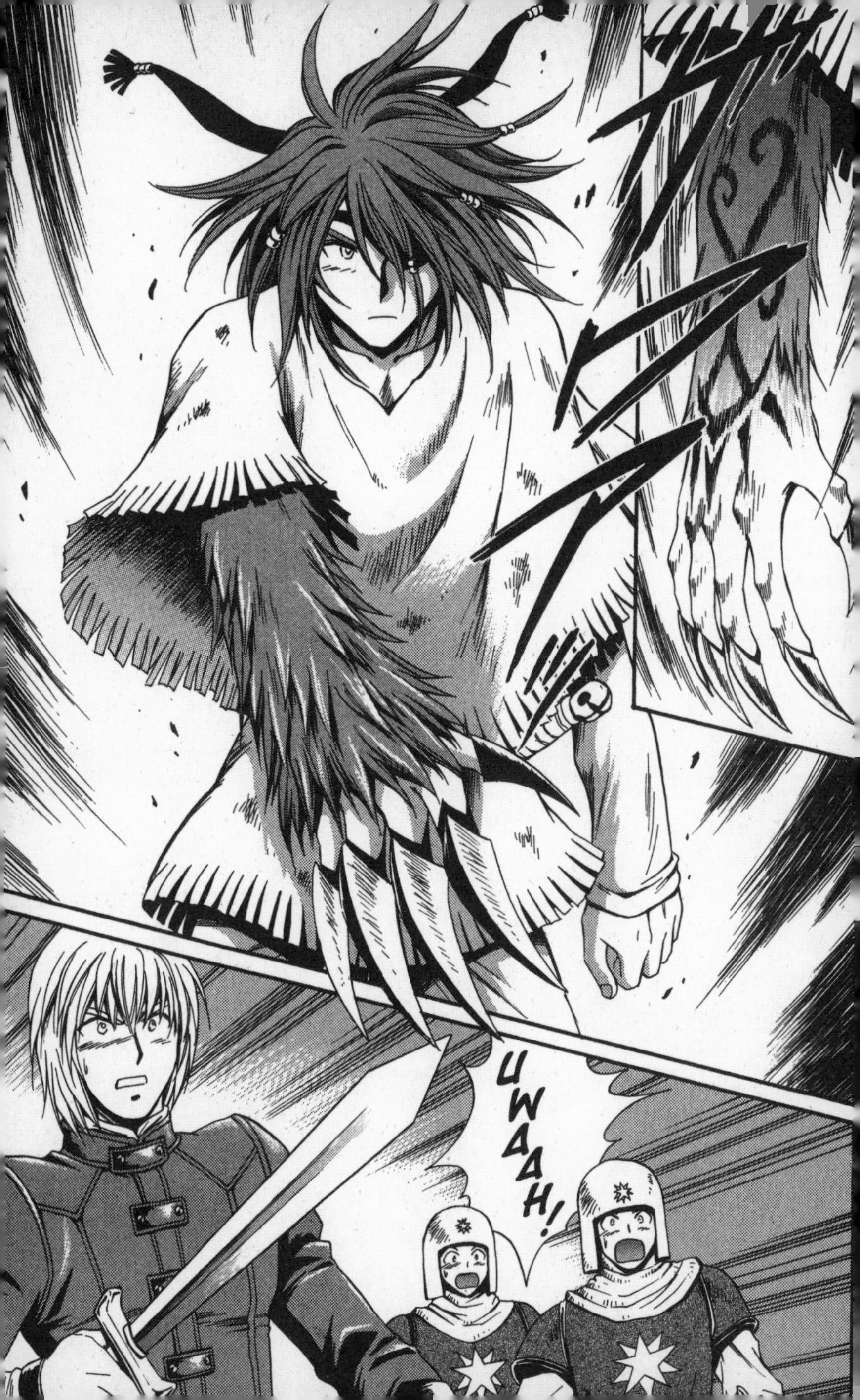
UWAAH!

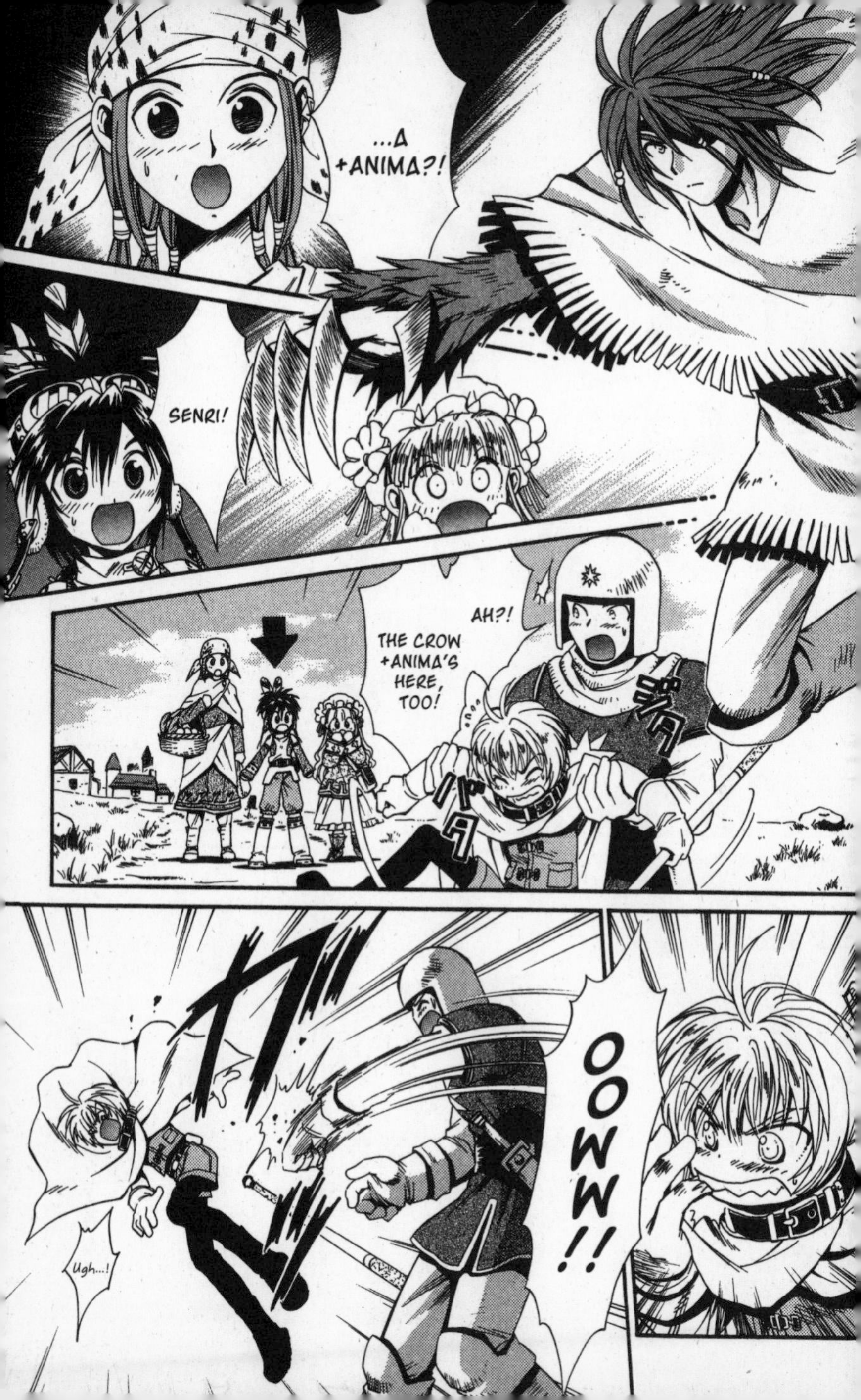
...A +ANIMA?!
SENRI!
AH?!
THE CROW +ANIMA'S HERE, TOO!
OOWW!!
Ugh...!

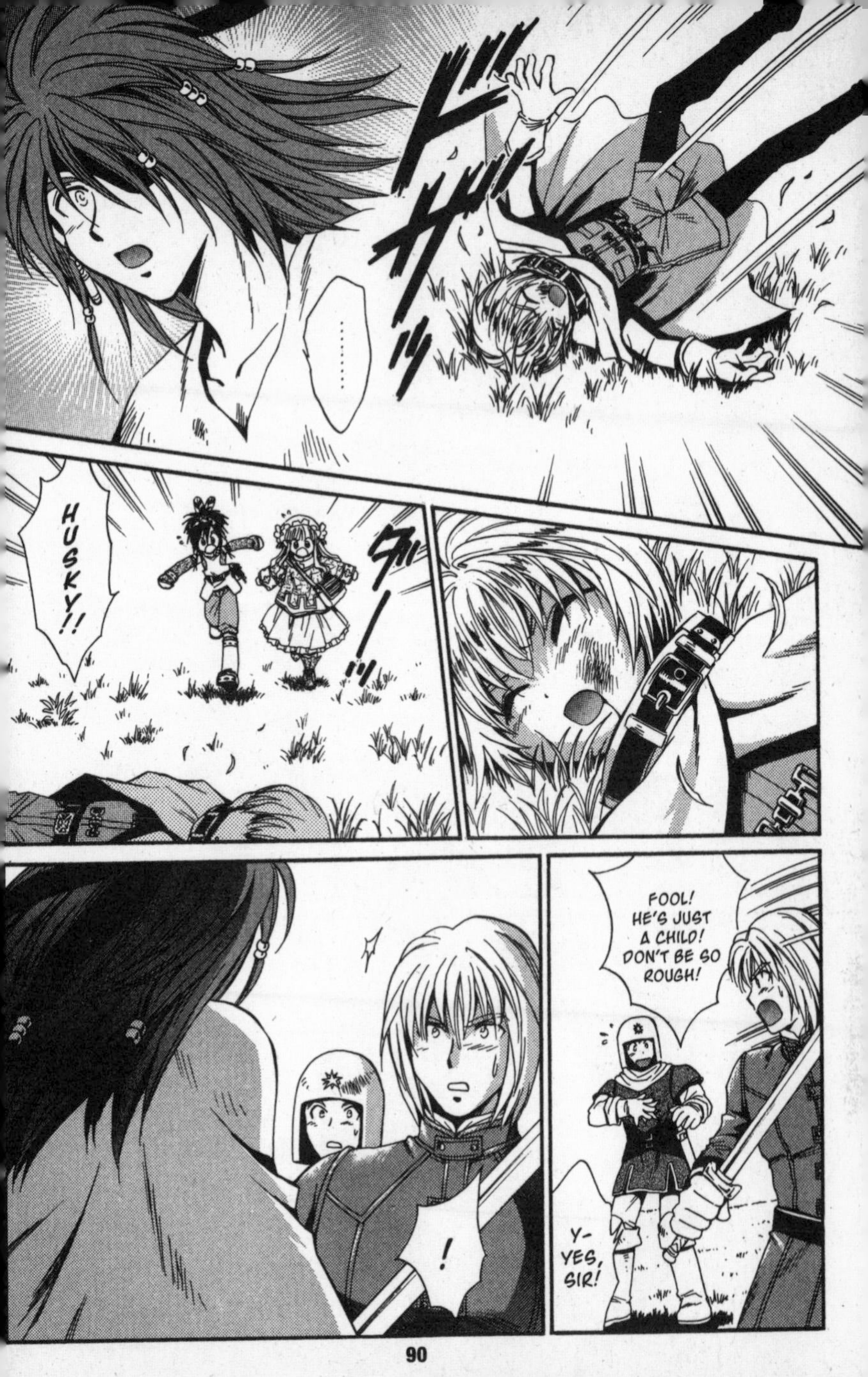
......
HUSKY!!
FOOL! HE'S JUST A CHILD! DON'T BE SO ROUGH!
Y-YES, SIR!
!

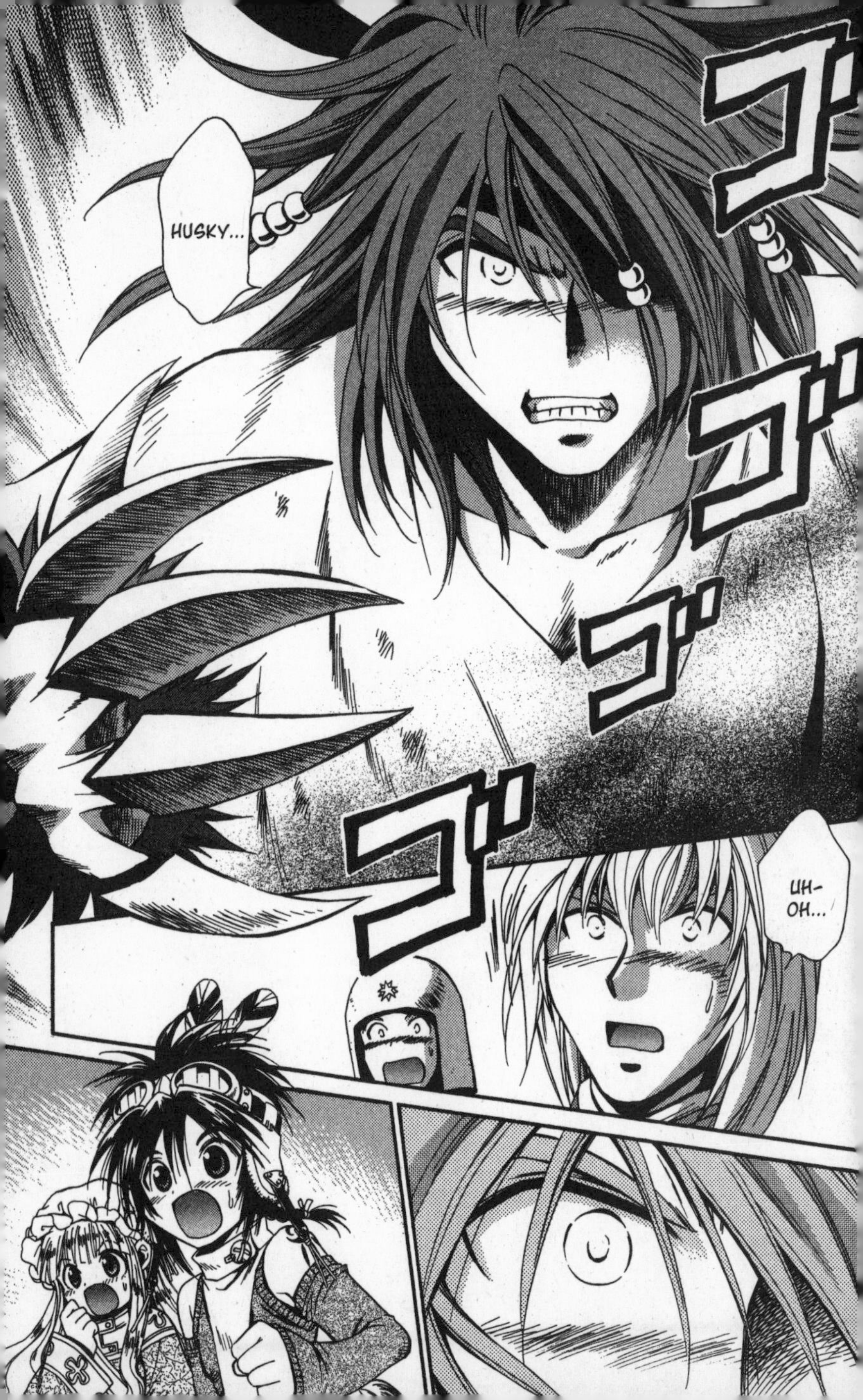
HUSKY...
ゴゴゴゴ
UH-OH...

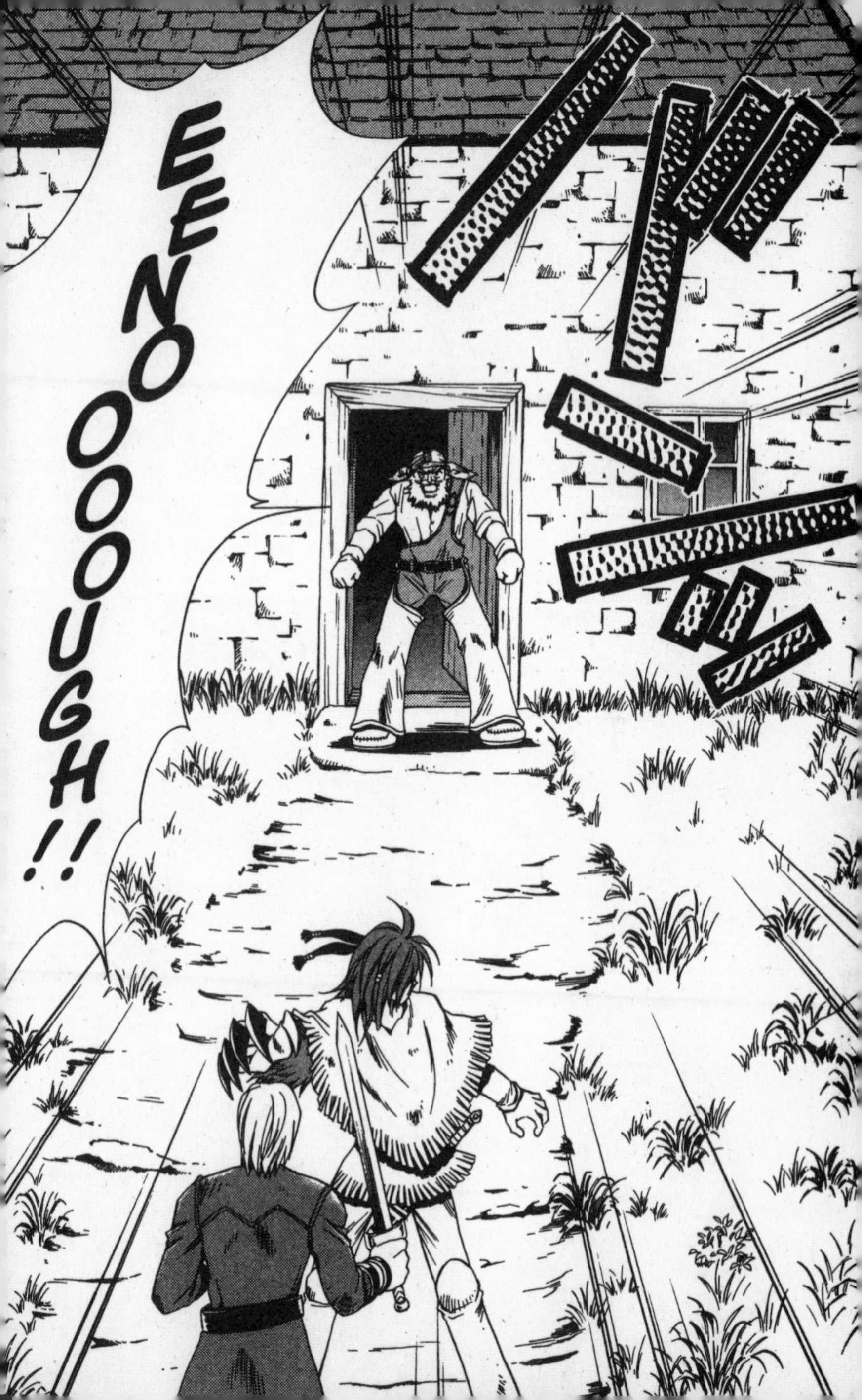
EEENOOOOOOUGH!!

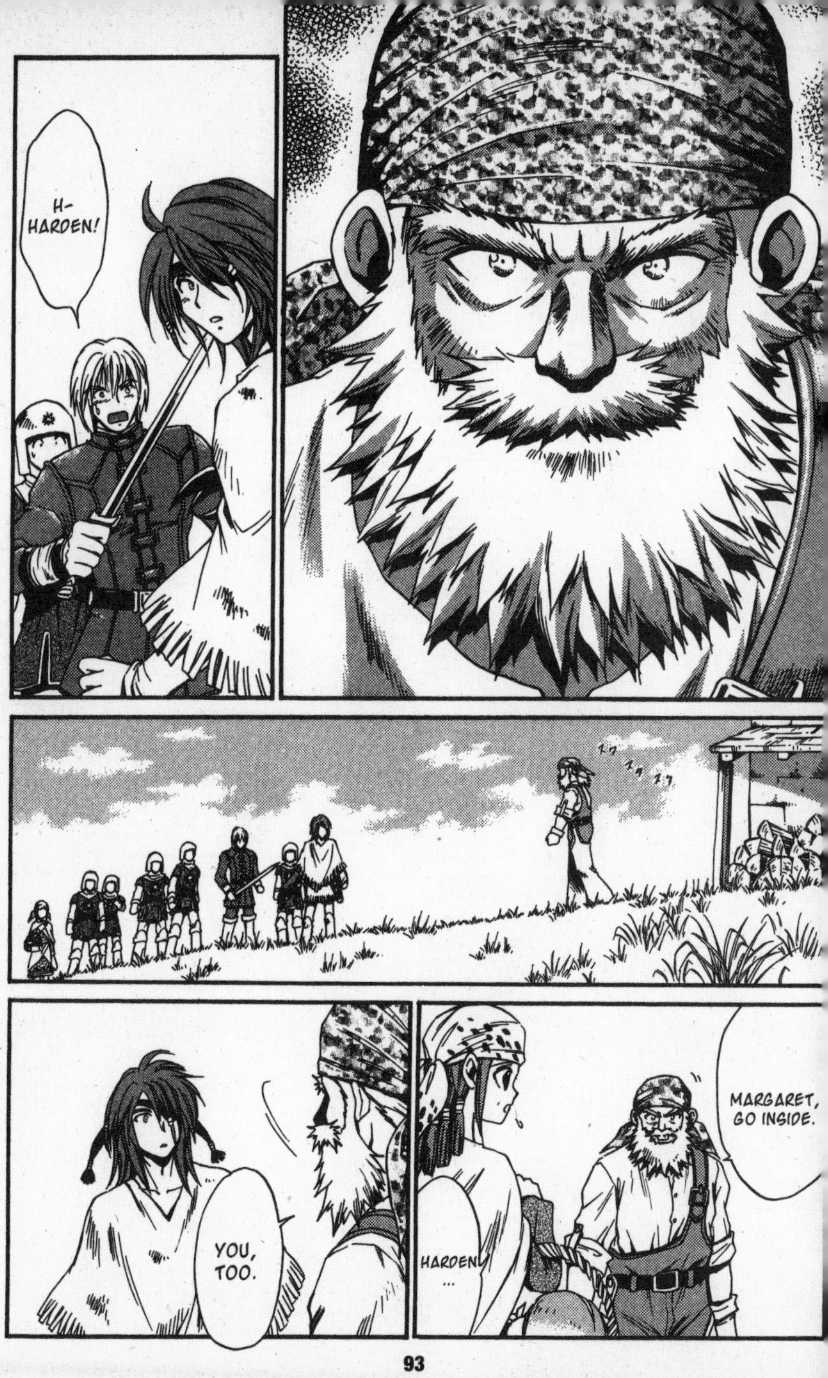
H- HARDEN!
MARGARET, GO INSIDE.
HARDEN ...
YOU, TOO.

AH!

SENRI! THIS WAY...!

HARDEN...

SO YOU TAKE THE SIDE OF +ANIMA...

ギィ...
バタン

......

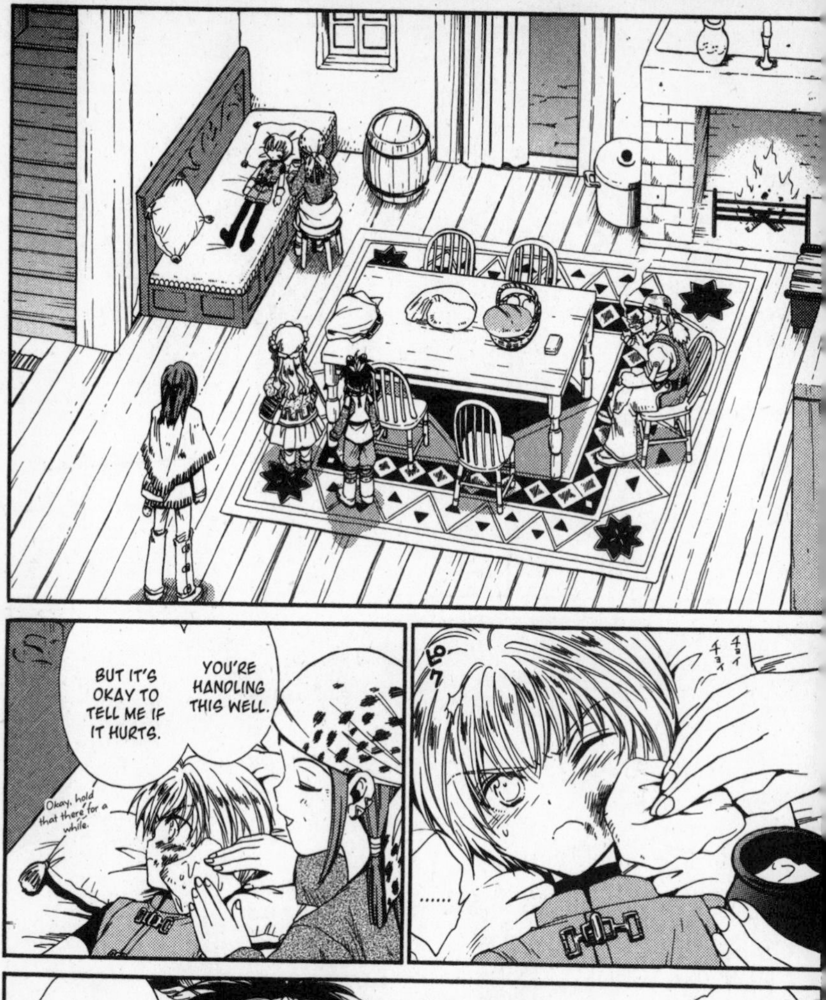
......
YOU'RE HANDLING THIS WELL.
BUT IT'S OKAY TO TELL ME IF IT HURTS.
Okay, hold that there for a while.
OOOH, REALLY! WHAT WAS WITH THEM?!
THEY WERE THE ONES WE MET WHEN WE WERE CROSSING THE MOUNTAINS WITH ROSE AND MARGOT, RIGHT?

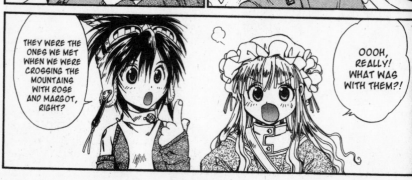

...I WON'T FORGE SWORDS FOR BATTLE AGAIN!

EVEN THOUGH I'M...NOT A SWORD-SMITH ANY-MORE...

THEY EVEN BROUGHT A MOUNTAIN OF IRON SWORDS FOR ME TO WORK WITH.

THEY CAME HERE SAYING THEY WANTED ME TO REFORGE THEIR SWORDS.

WHOA!!

THAT'S A BIG SWORD!!

WHAT IS IT...?

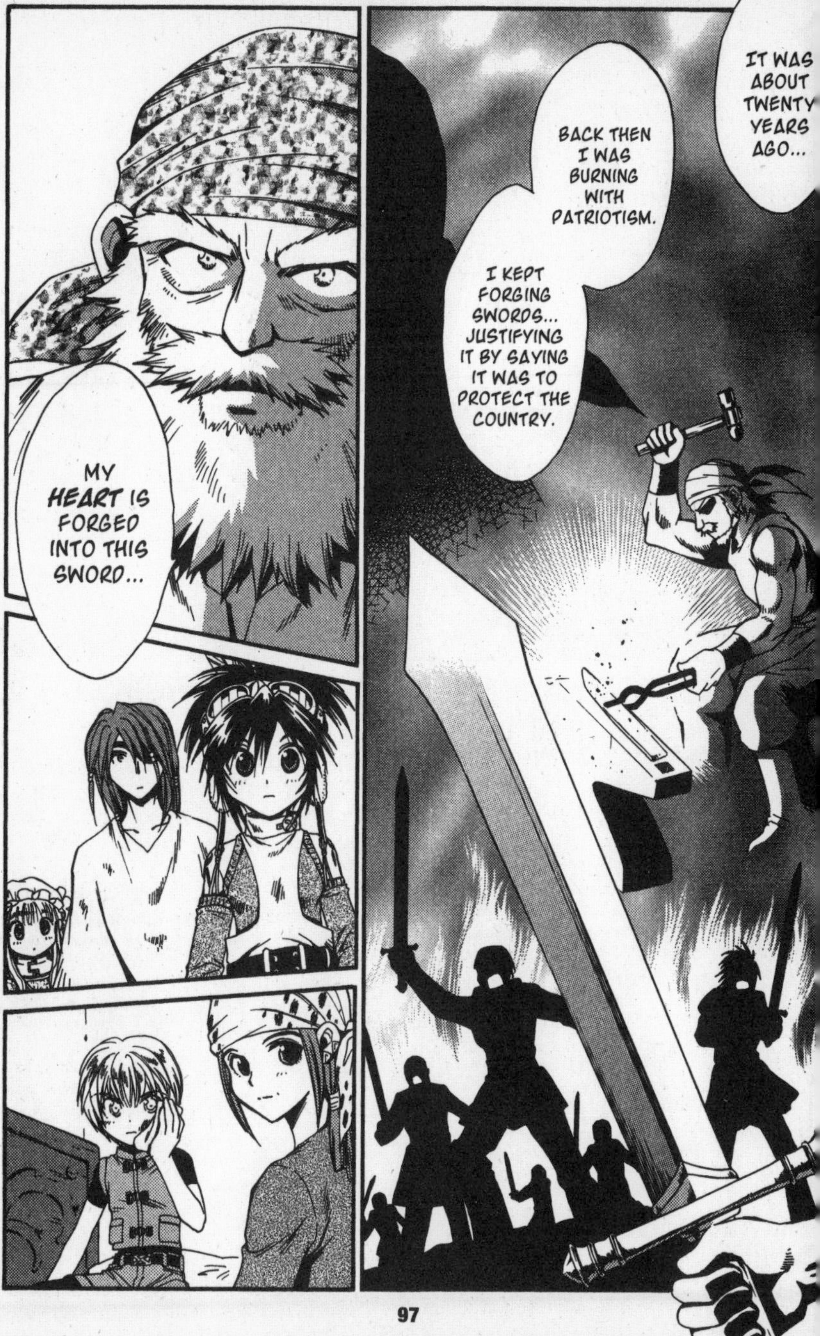
IT WAS ABOUT TWENTY YEARS AGO...
BACK THEN I WAS BURNING WITH PATRIOTISM.
I KEPT FORGING SWORDS... JUSTIFYING IT BY SAYING IT WAS TO PROTECT THE COUNTRY.
MY HEART IS FORGED INTO THIS SWORD...

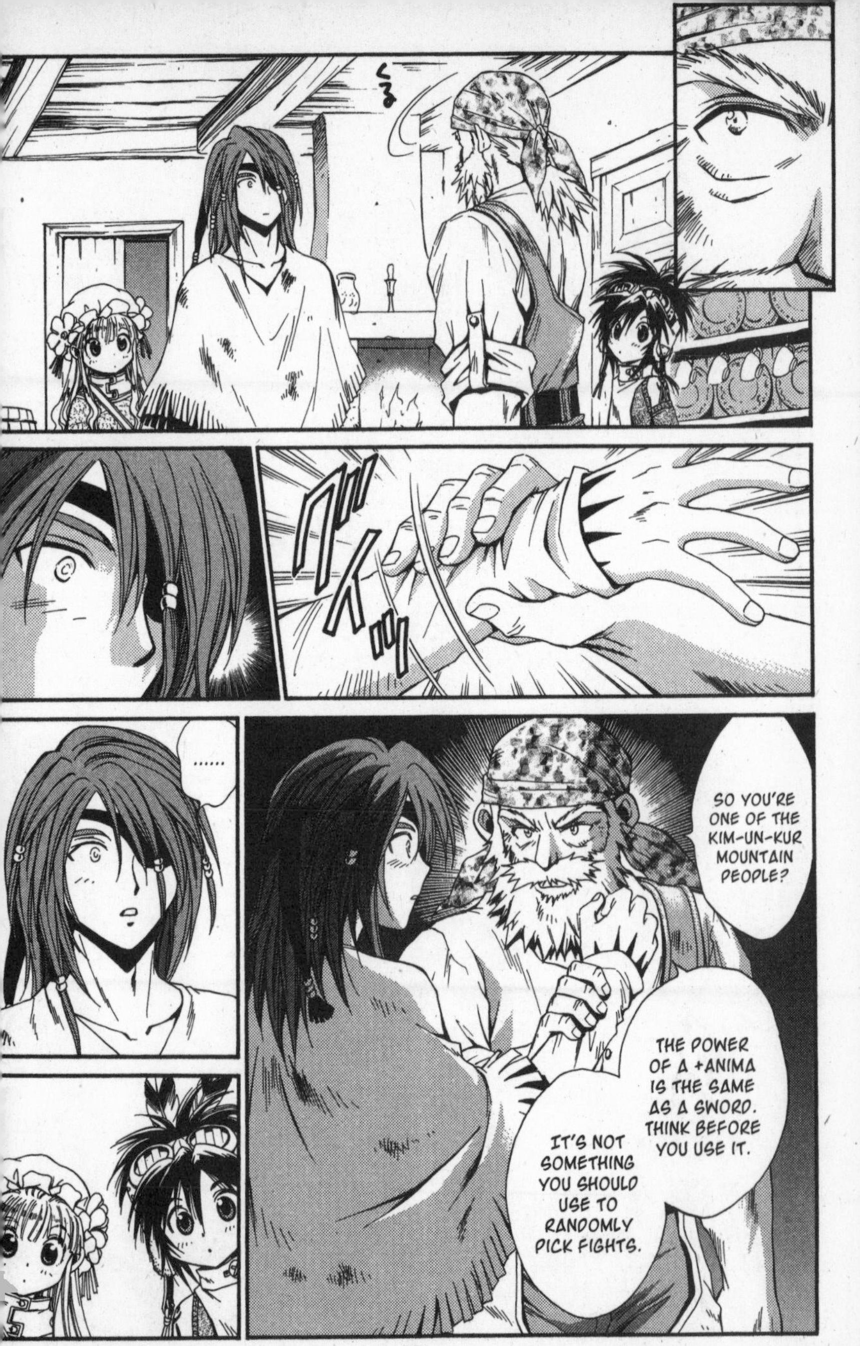
くる
グイッ
SO YOU'RE ONE OF THE KIM-UN-KUR MOUNTAIN PEOPLE?
THE POWER OF A +ANIMA IS THE SAME AS A SWORD. THINK BEFORE YOU USE IT.
IT'S NOT SOMETHING YOU SHOULD USE TO RANDOMLY PICK FIGHTS.
......

YUMMM!! ♡♡

THAT'S ENOUGH TALK! LET'S HAVE DINNER!

AL RIGI

♪ THANK YOU... ♪

I WONDER IF YOU CAN HANDLE COLD SOUP?

YOU CAN'T EAT SOLID FOODS, CAN YOU?

WORK...?

YES!

YUMMY BREEEAD! ♡

UUMMM!! ♡♡

EAT YOUR FILL SO YOU CAN HAVE ENERGY TO WORK!

I'M GOING TO MAKE THEM MY ASSIS- TANTS!

REALLY?

CHILDREN'S SMALL FINGERS ARE VERY USEFUL FOR THIS.

WE'RE GOING TO TAKE APART THESE OLD CLOTHES AND MAKE NEW ONES.

YAY! ♡

Take apart...

THEY'RE BOTH NICE, AREN'T THEY?

...

We take this apart, right?

I'LL LEAVE YOU AT IT, THEN. GOOD LUCK--I'M COUNTING ON YOU!

IT LOOKED LIKE THAT MAN UNDER-STANDS A LOT ABOUT +ANIMA.

MAYBE...

MAYBE THEY GET BETTER AT HIDING IT WHEN THEY'RE OLDER.

But I wouldn't know, anyway.

?

EH?

I DIDN'T SENSE A +ANIMA...

THEY'LL THINK MORE AND MORE THAT WE'RE THEIR ENEMIES!

TO THINK WE'D END UP STAYING AT THE HOUSE OF AN OLD MAN WHO'S GOING AGAINST THE MILITARY!

SO WHAT IF HE IS?

HE TALKS ALL HIGH AND MIGHTY!

THAT'S WHY IT'S EVEN MORE ANNOYING!

THAT'S NOT BAD.

HE JUST DOESN'T WANT TO MAKE A SWORD.

YOU THINK THAT'S A GOOD ENOUGH EXCUSE FOR THE MILITARY?!

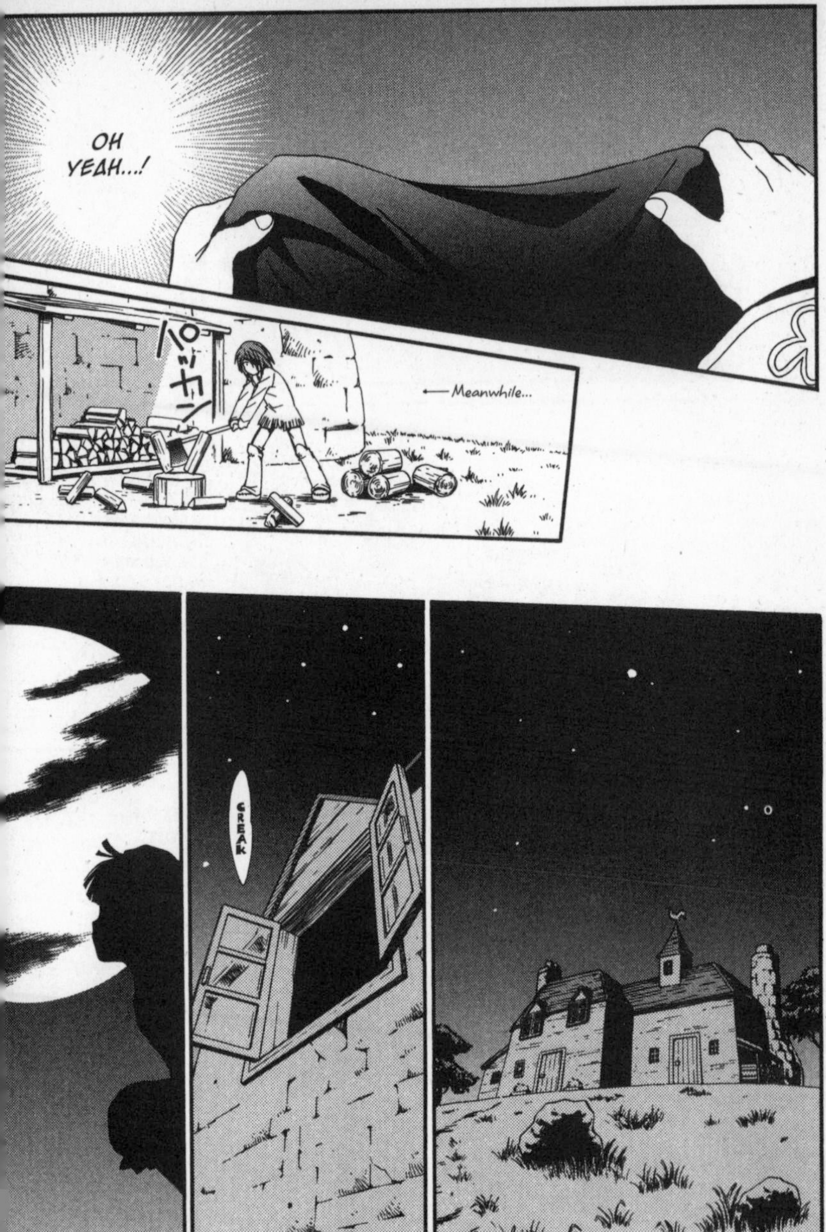
OH YEAH...!
パッカーン
Meanwhile...
CREAK

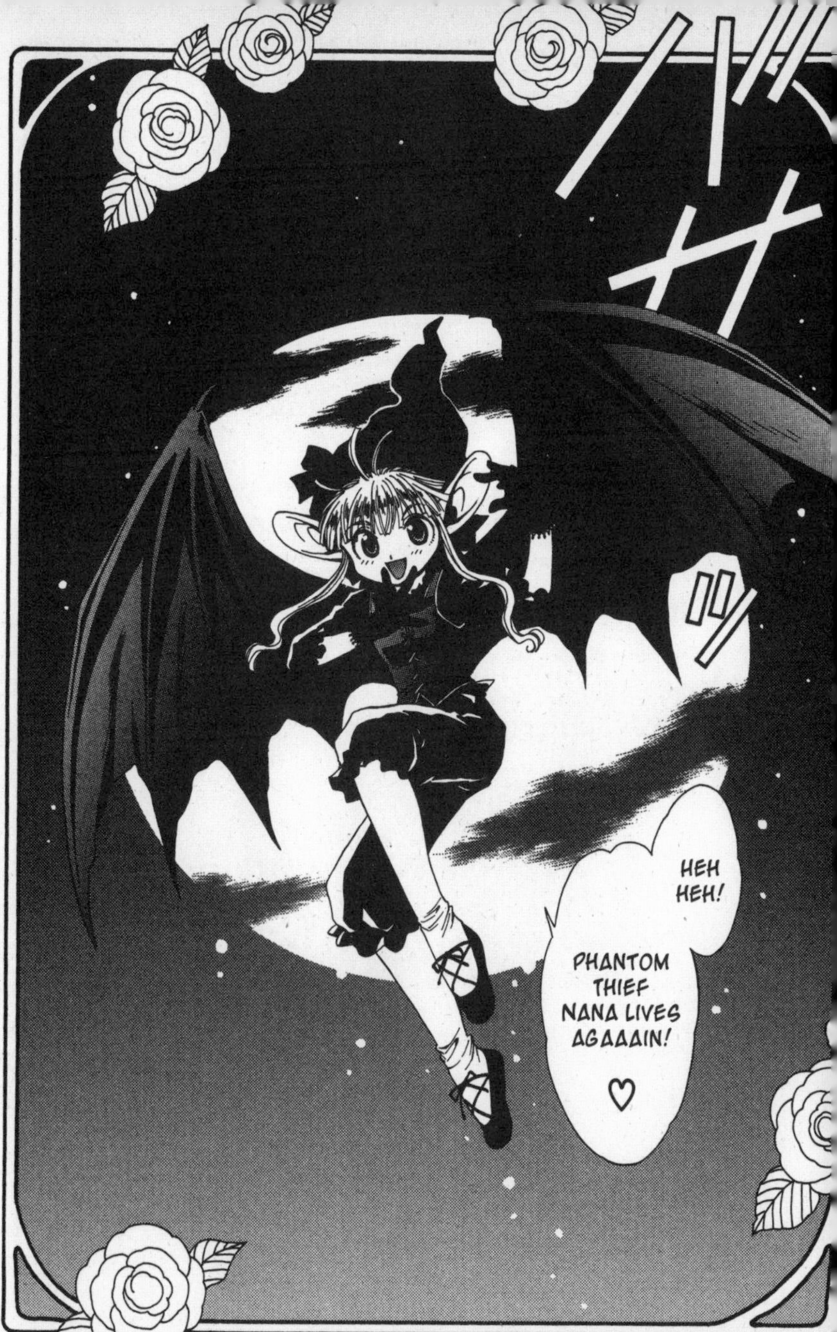
HEH HEH!
PHANTOM THIEF NANA LIVES AGAAAIN! ♡

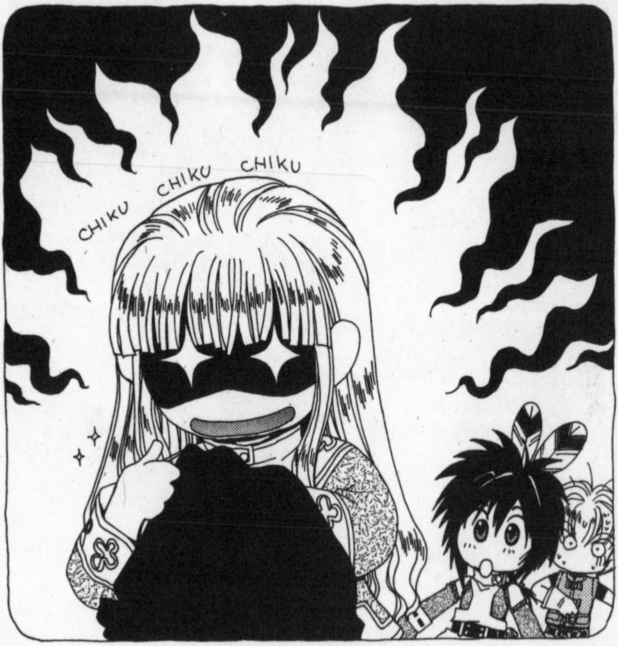
CHIKU CHIKU CHIKU

Prank Girl !

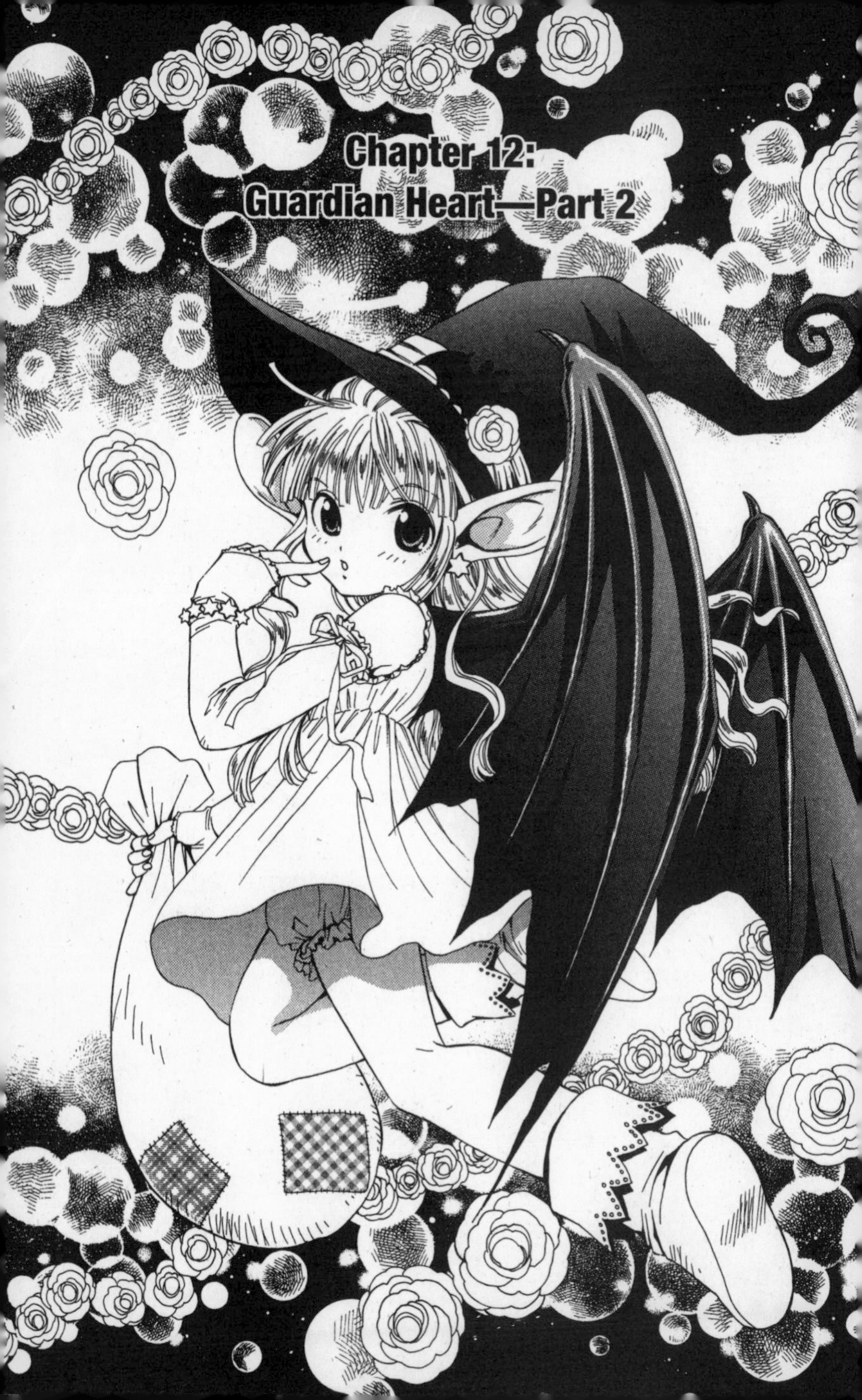
Chapter 12:
Guardian Heart—Part 2

OW!!

UUWAH...

HM?

Zzzz...

Snort!

COORO, YOU LITTLE--

108

A BLADE UNWILLINGLY FORGED IS DOOMED TO TURN *AGAINST YOU* IN YOUR *HOUR* OF *NEED!!*

WHAT IS THIS VOICE...

IF YOU FORCE HARDEN TO FORGE A SWORD FOR YOU, DO SO AT YOUR OWN PERIL...

...ECHOING IN MY HEAD ...?!

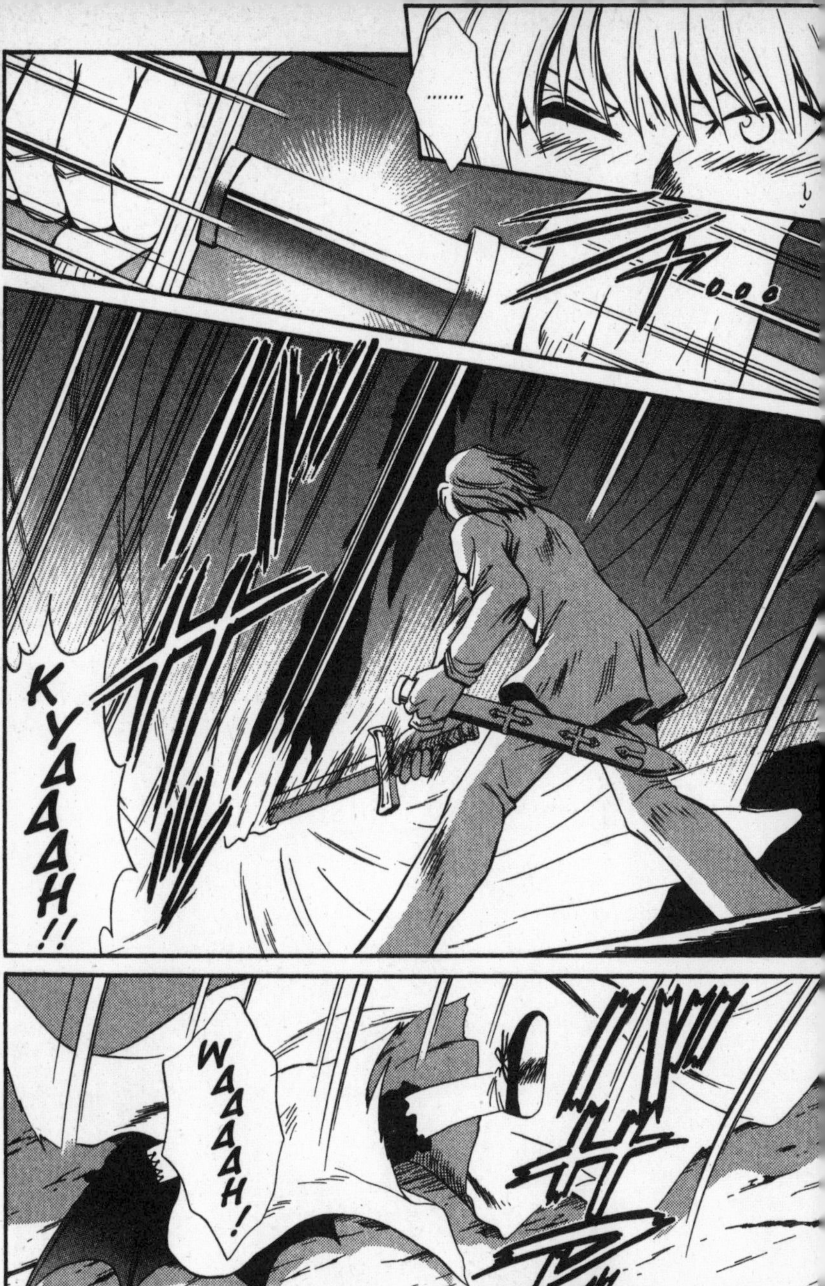
......
KYAAAAH!!
WAAAAH!

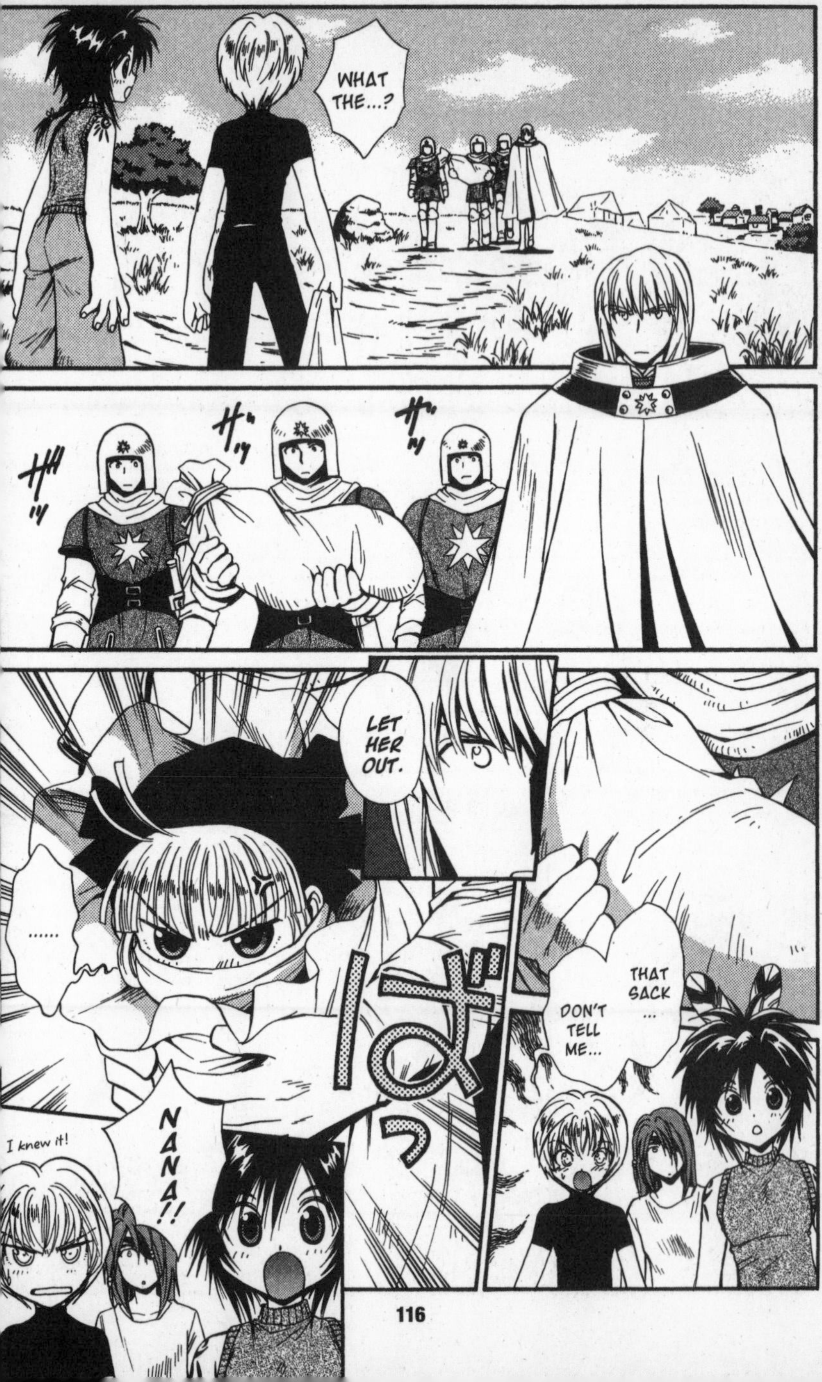
WHAT THE...?
LET HER OUT.
THAT SACK...
DON'T TELL ME...
......
ばっ
NANA!!
I knew it!

117

YES. IT WAS A BATTLE WITH THE KIM-UN-KUR.

HARDEN...

DO YOU REMEMBER THE BATTLE OF MOSS MOUNTAIN?

MURDERED BY A *BEAR* +ANIMA, AS A MATTER OF FACT!

MY GRANDFATHER WAS KILLED BY A +ANIMA DURING THAT BATTLE.

I WILL PARDON THE GIRL...

...AND IN EXCHANGE, I WOULD HAVE YOU FORGE ME A SWORD.

NOW, ASTARIA NEEDS YOUR STRENGTH AGAIN.

119

......

THANKS!

HEY, HEY, MISTER COMMANDER...?

WILL YOU LET ME HOLD THAT AXE?

EH?

と た た た

MMPH MM-MM-MMMM!

It's too heavy.

IT'S IMPOSSIBLE FOR YOU, TOO, NANA.

HERE YOU GO...

BOY...IT SURE IS HEAVY!

I CAN'T EVEN FLY WHILE HOLDING THIS.

Nana, we're going.

N y a a a h...

......

NEXT TIME YOU WON'T FIND MERCY, GIRL.

120

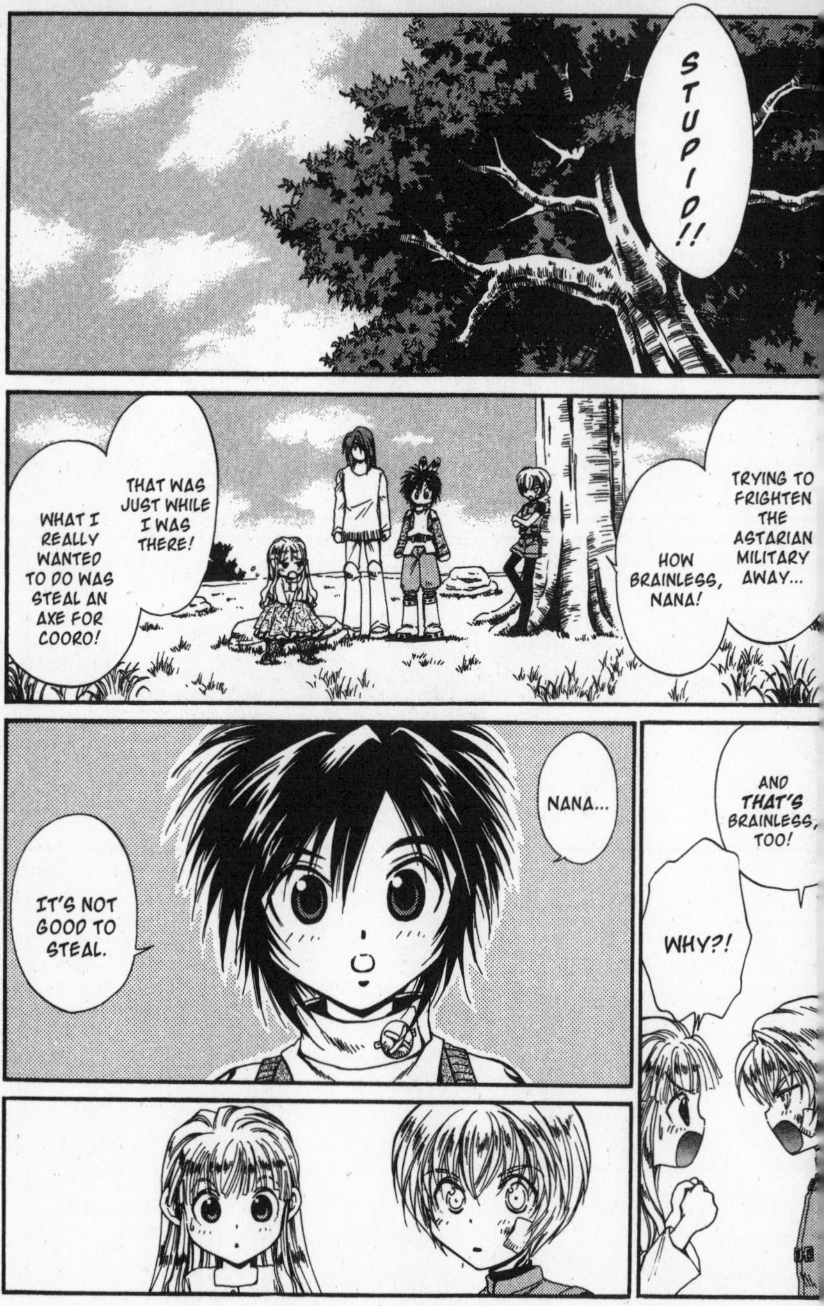
STUPID!!
TRYING TO FRIGHTEN THE ASTARIAN MILITARY AWAY...
HOW BRAINLESS, NANA!
THAT WAS JUST WHILE I WAS THERE!
WHAT I REALLY WANTED TO DO WAS STEAL AN AXE FOR COORO!
AND *THAT'S* BRAINLESS, TOO!
WHY?!
NANA...
IT'S NOT GOOD TO STEAL.

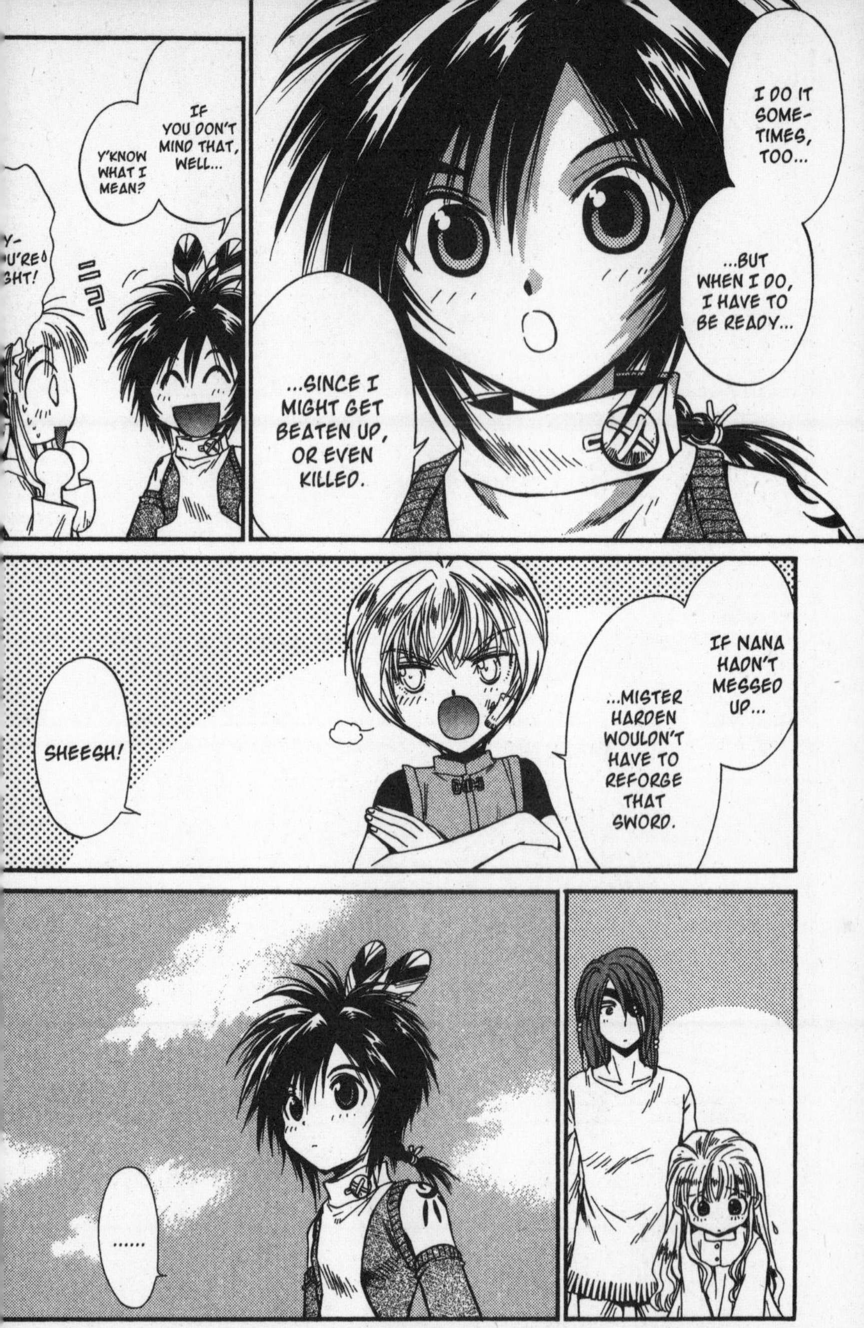
I DO IT SOMETIMES, TOO...
...BUT WHEN I DO, I HAVE TO BE READY...
...SINCE I MIGHT GET BEATEN UP, OR EVEN KILLED.
IF YOU DON'T MIND THAT, WELL...
Y'KNOW WHAT I MEAN?
ニコー
IF NANA HADN'T MESSED UP...
...MISTER HARDEN WOULDN'T HAVE TO REFORGE THAT SWORD.
SHEESH!
......

...THOUGH NO GOOD WILL COME OF IT.

YES, I AM...

ARE YOU GOING TO REFORGE ALL OF THEM?

WHOA! THERE'RE SO MANY!

WHEN I MET MARGARET, I CHANGED...

THESE DAYS, I'M A SMITH WHO MAKES TOOLS FOR DAILY LIFE.

MISS MAR-GARET?

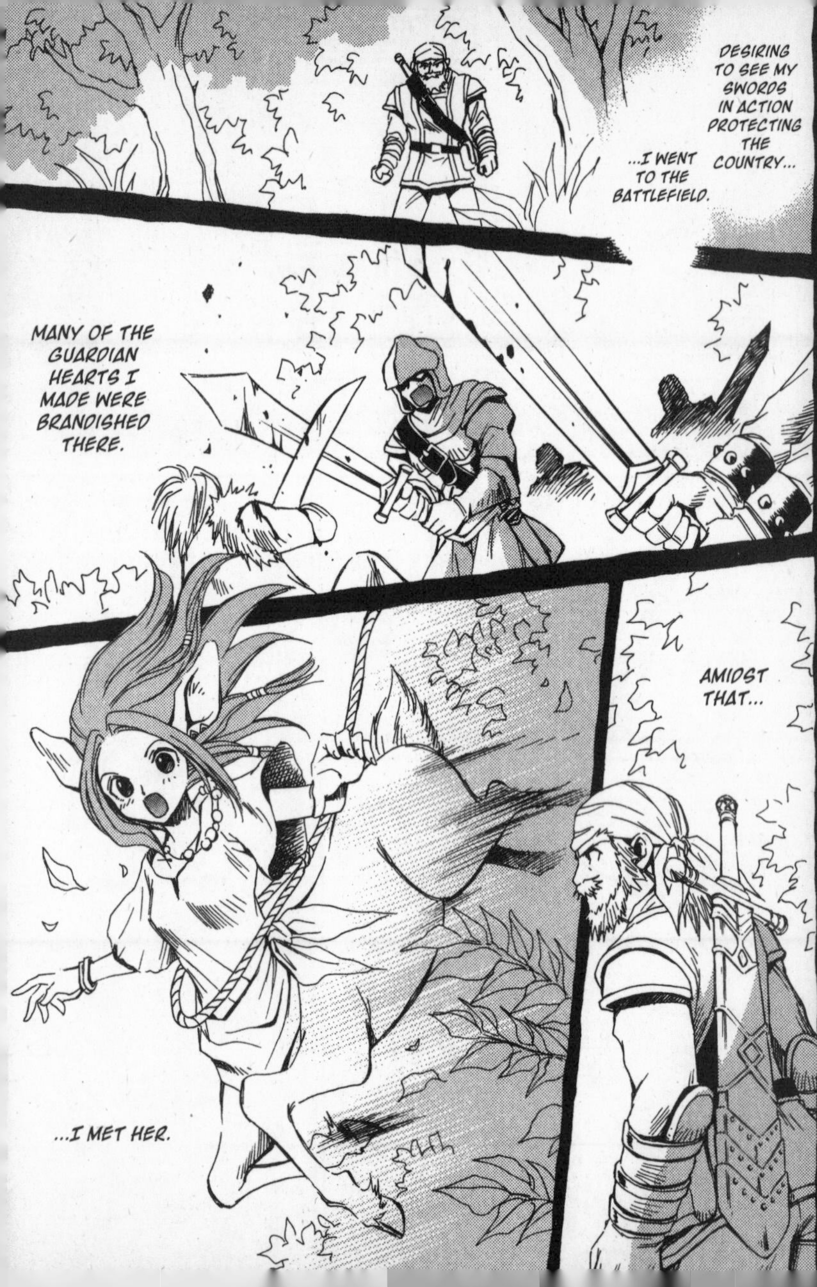
DESIRING TO SEE MY SWORDS IN ACTION PROTECTING THE COUNTRY...
...I WENT TO THE BATTLEFIELD.
MANY OF THE GUARDIAN HEARTS I MADE WERE BRANDISHED THERE.
AMIDST THAT...
...I MET HER.

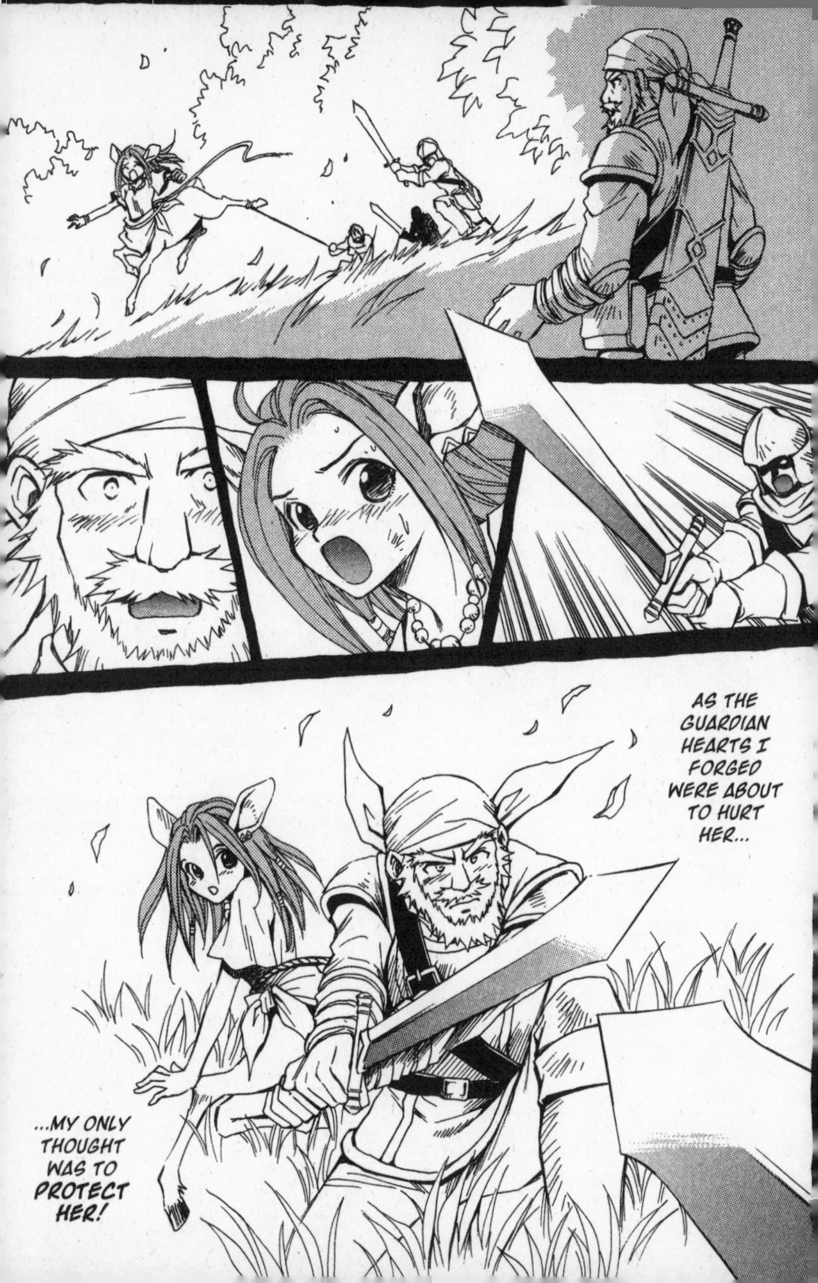
AS THE GUARDIAN HEARTS I FORGED WERE ABOUT TO HURT HER...
...MY ONLY THOUGHT WAS TO PROTECT HER!

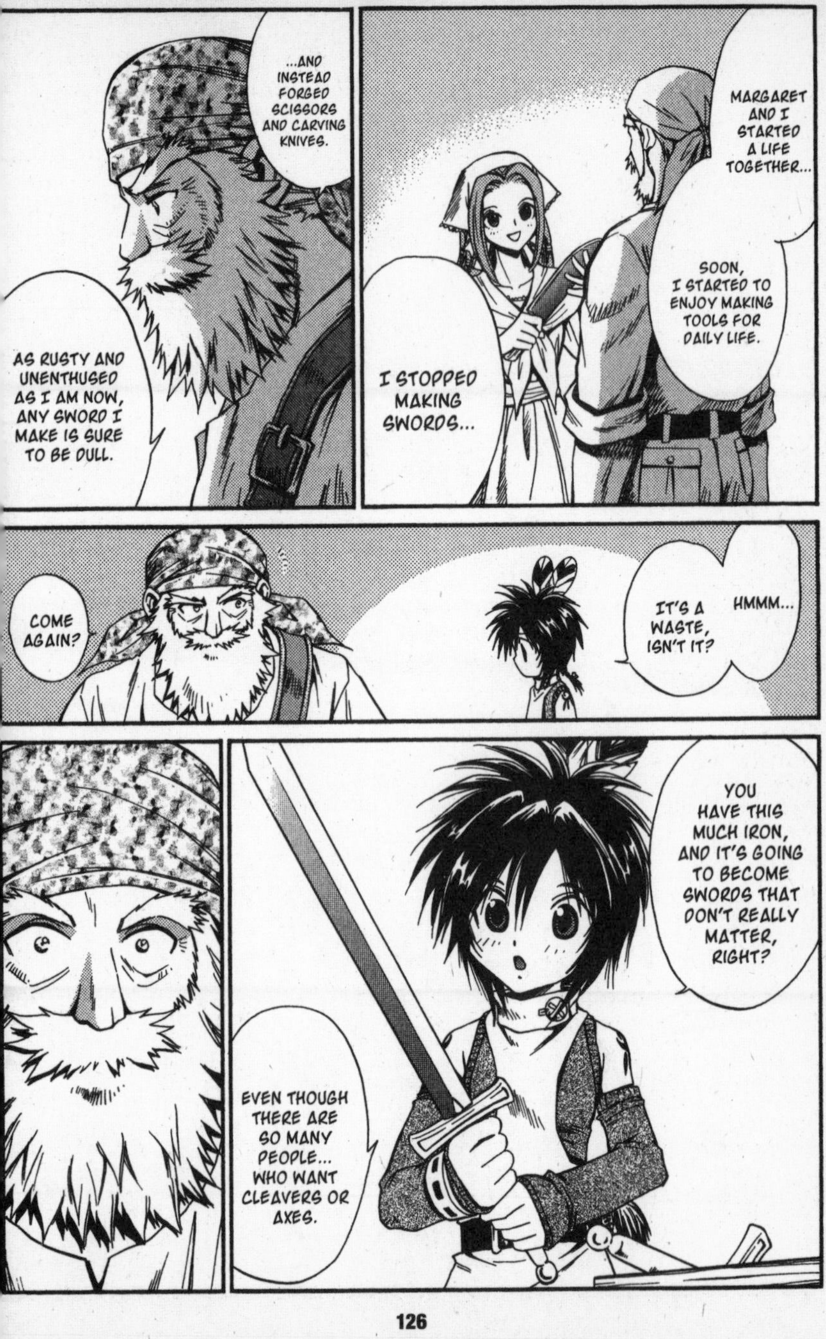
MARGARET AND I STARTED A LIFE TOGETHER...
SOON, I STARTED TO ENJOY MAKING TOOLS FOR DAILY LIFE.
I STOPPED MAKING SWORDS...
...AND INSTEAD FORGED SCISSORS AND CARVING KNIVES.
AS RUSTY AND UNENTHUSED AS I AM NOW, ANY SWORD I MAKE IS SURE TO BE DULL.
HMMM...
IT'S A WASTE, ISN'T IT?
COME AGAIN?
YOU HAVE THIS MUCH IRON, AND IT'S GOING TO BECOME SWORDS THAT DON'T REALLY MATTER, RIGHT?
EVEN THOUGH THERE ARE SO MANY PEOPLE... WHO WANT CLEAVERS OR AXES.

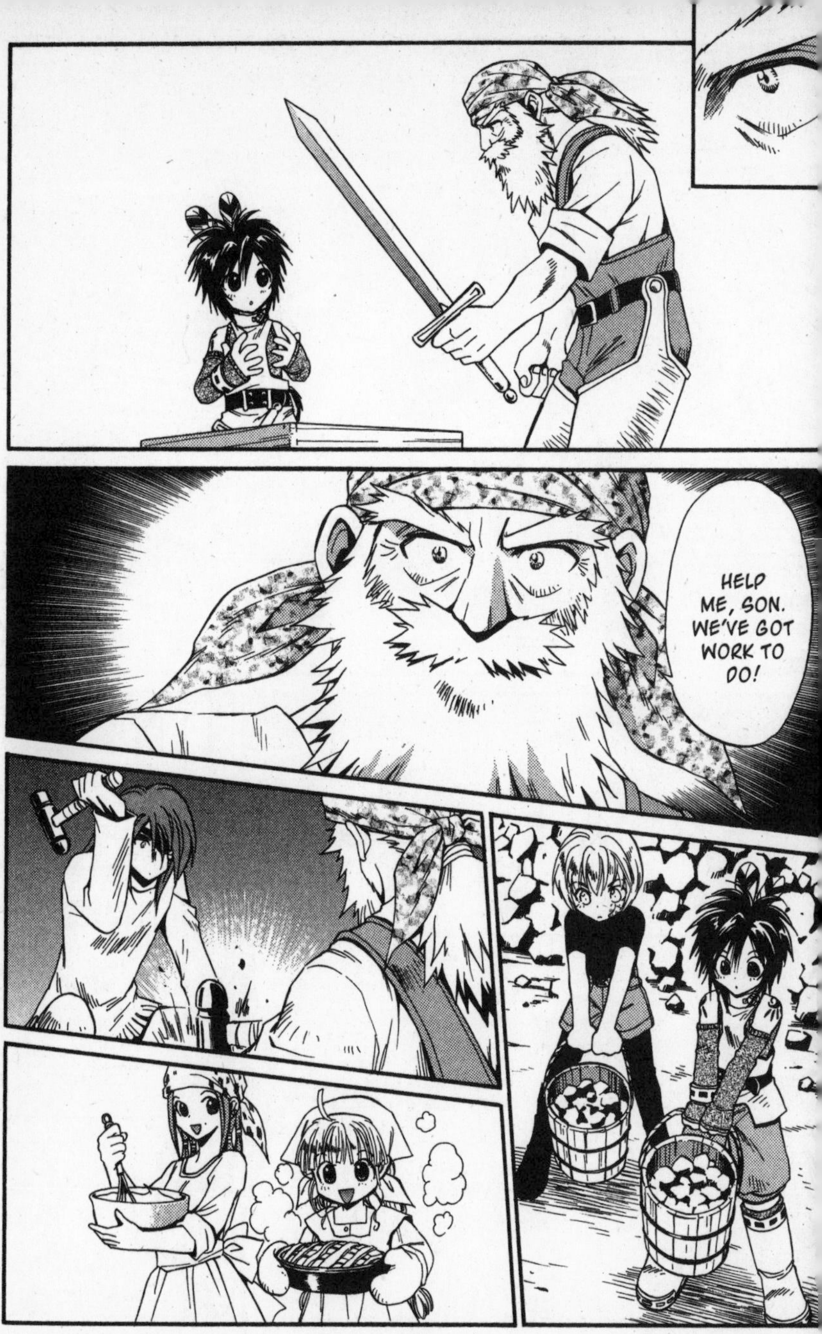
HELP ME, SON. WE'VE GOT WORK TO DO!

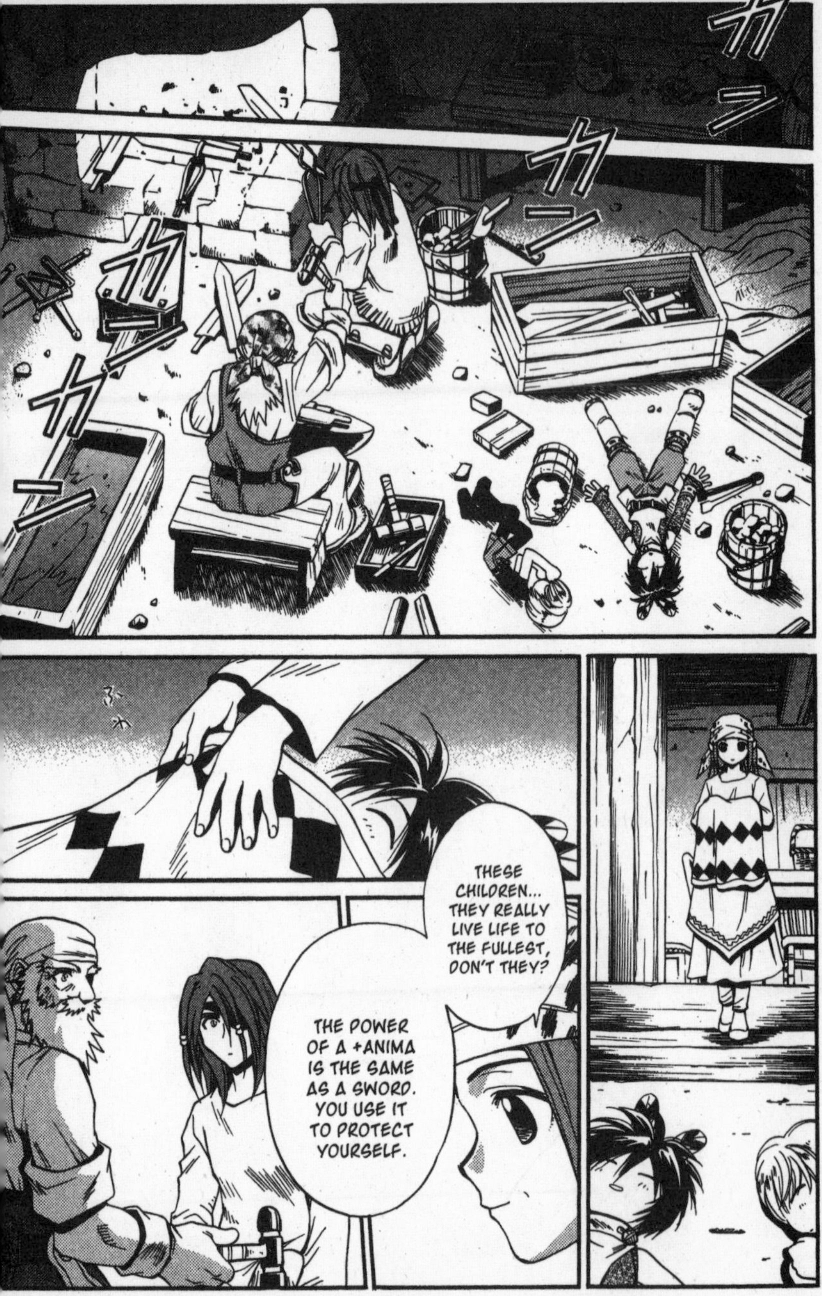
THESE CHILDREN... THEY REALLY LIVE LIFE TO THE FULLEST, DON'T THEY?
THE POWER OF A +ANIMA IS THE SAME AS A SWORD. YOU USE IT TO PROTECT YOURSELF.

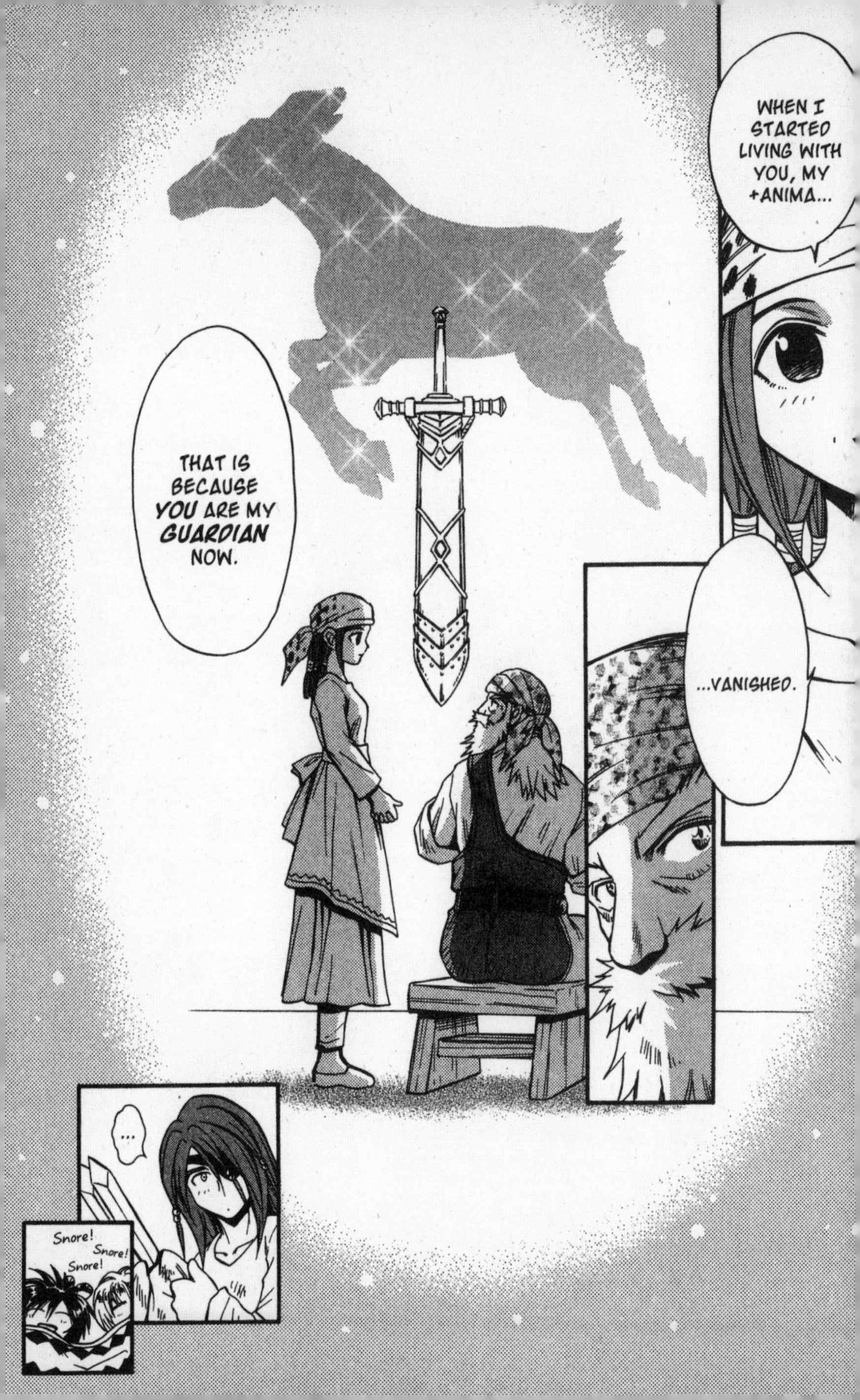
WHEN I STARTED LIVING WITH YOU, MY +ANIMA...
...VANISHED.
THAT IS BECAUSE *YOU* ARE MY ***GUARDIAN*** NOW.
...
Snore! Snore! Snore!

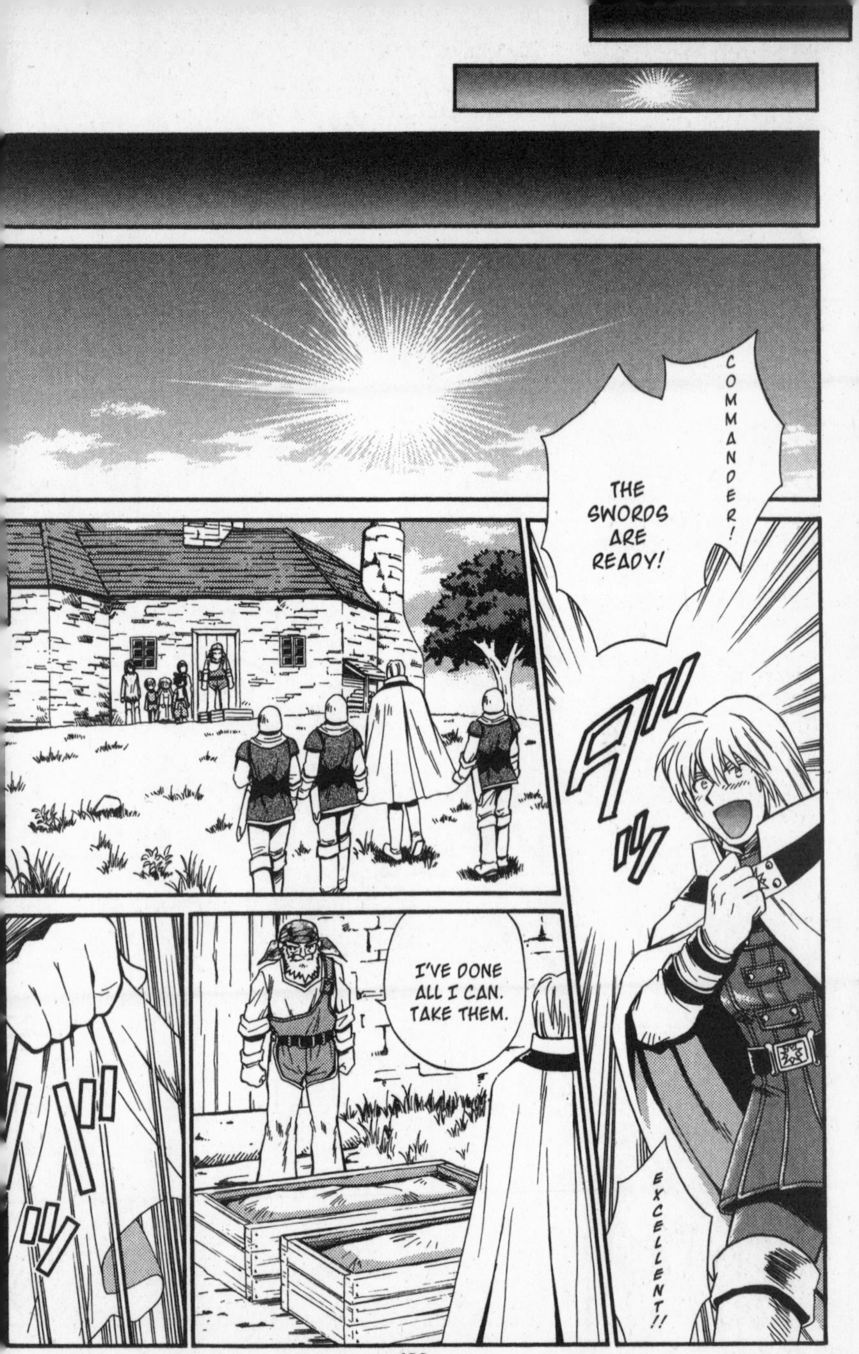
COMMANDER!
THE SWORDS ARE READY!
EXCELLENT!!
I'VE DONE ALL I CAN. TAKE THEM.

131

WHEN I PUT MY HEART INTO THEM, THIS IS WHAT THEY BECAME.

HARDEN!! JUST WHAT IS THE MEANING OF THIS?!

MY HANDS NATURALLY FORGED THEM.

...

......

I'D LOVE TO LET MY WIFE USE THIS...

ほ————っ

...THESE ARE VERY WELL MADE...

Y'KNOW...

WOULDN'T YOU?

132

133

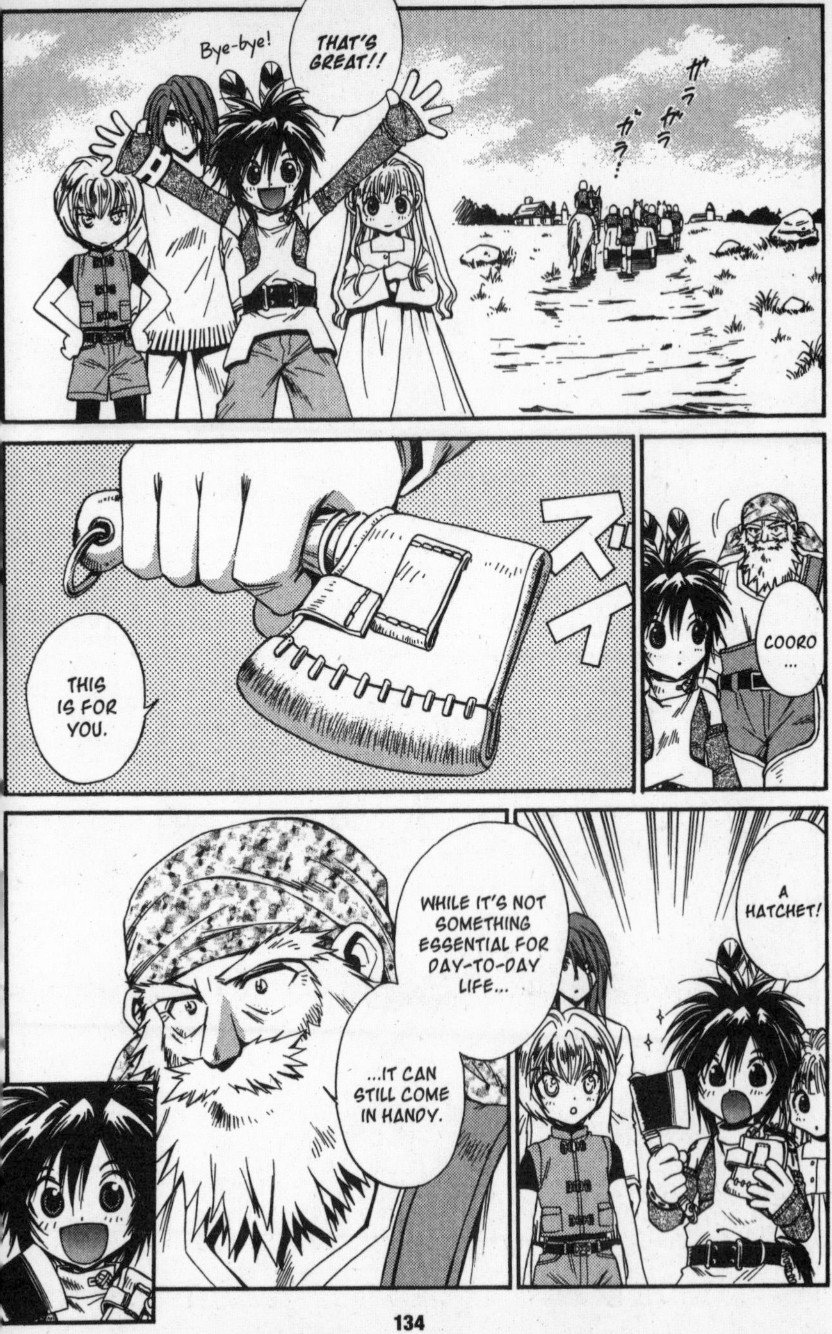
ガラ ガラ ガラ…
THAT'S GREAT!!
Bye-bye!
COORO ...
ズイ
THIS IS FOR YOU.
A HATCHET!
WHILE IT'S NOT SOMETHING ESSENTIAL FOR DAY-TO-DAY LIFE...
...IT CAN STILL COME IN HANDY.

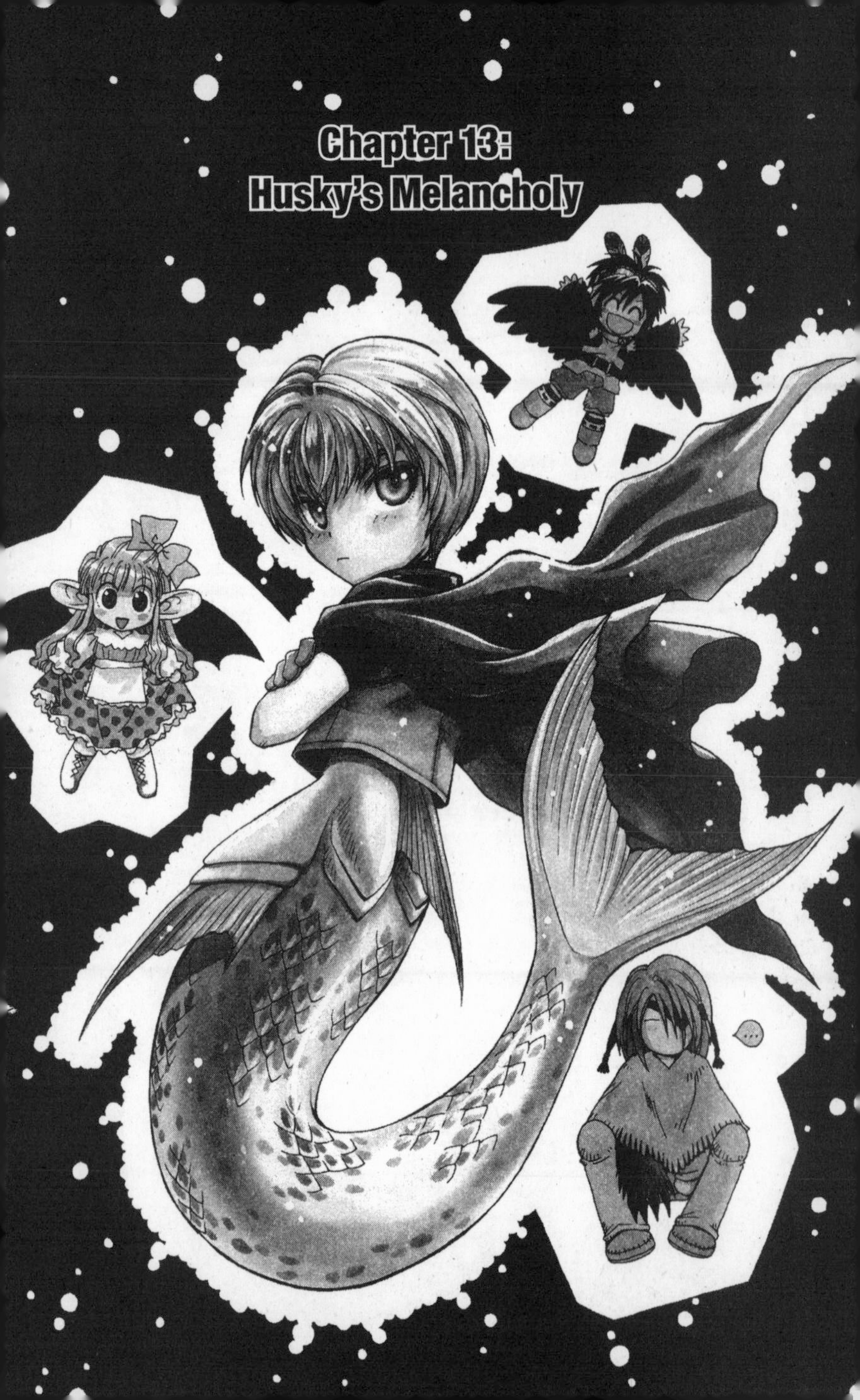
Chapter 13:
Husky's Melancholy
...

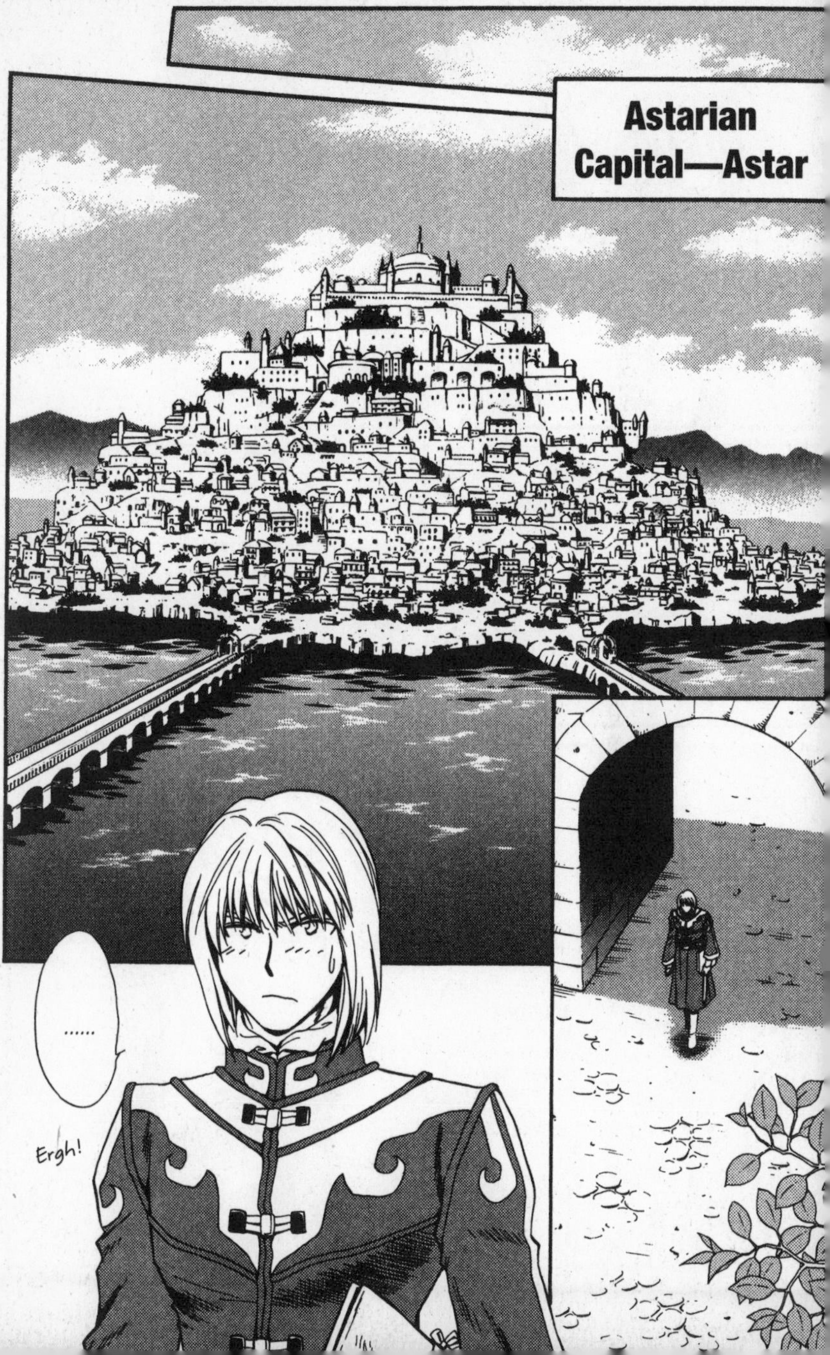
Astarian Capital—Astar
......
Ergh!

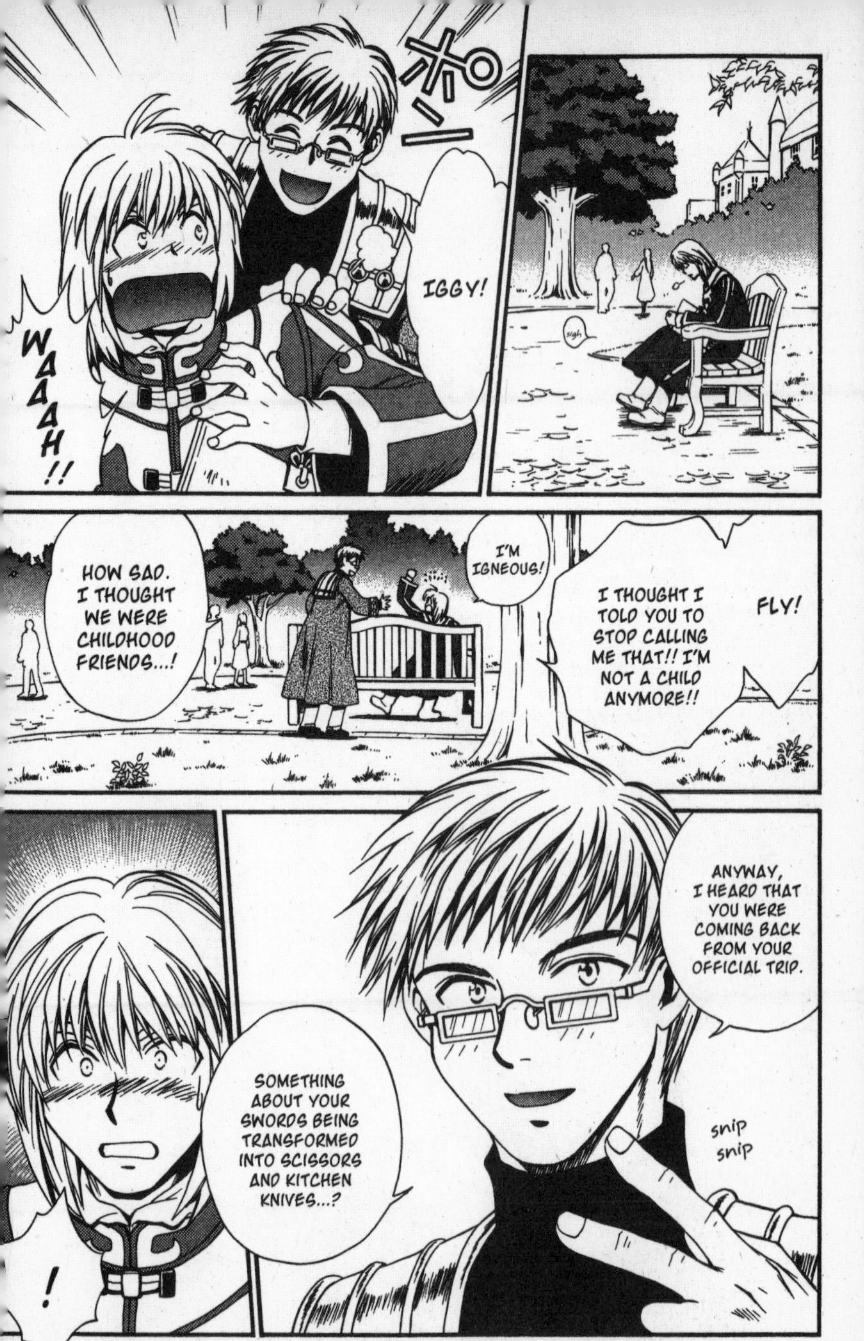
sigh
IGGY!
WAAAH!!
I THOUGHT I TOLD YOU TO STOP CALLING ME THAT!! I'M NOT A CHILD ANYMORE!!
FLY!
I'M IGNEOUS!
HOW SAD. I THOUGHT WE WERE CHILDHOOD FRIENDS...!
ANYWAY, I HEARD THAT YOU WERE COMING BACK FROM YOUR OFFICIAL TRIP.
snip snip
SOMETHING ABOUT YOUR SWORDS BEING TRANSFORMED INTO SCISSORS AND KITCHEN KNIVES...?
!

HOW DO YOU KNOW ABOUT THAT?!

IT'S SUPPOSED TO BE A MILITARY SECRET!

HAS IT LEAKED AS FAR AS THE RESEARCH-ERS?!

Oh!

......

OH YEAH... I KEEP FORGETTING.

WELL, YOU SEE... I'M SPECIAL. HEH HEH...

EVER SINCE I MET THOSE +ANIMA, THINGS KEEP GOING WRONG!

I JUST FILED A REPORT!

+ANIMA?

WELL, THERE GOES MY REPUTATION ...!

139

......

THAT'S NOT NECESSARILY TRUE...

WHAT?

MIGHT IT BE THAT A TIME HAS COME WHEN PEOPLE SHOULD ACCEPT +ANIMA POWERS?

YOU'RE SUCH AN OPTIMIST, FLY...

THAT'S RIGHT. SO YOU DO UNDERSTAND, IGGY!

I SAID STOP THAT!

THAT'S WHAT I THINK.

THEY'RE MILITARY PROPERTY, BUB!

I JUST WISH I COULD HAVE ONE OF THOSE SWORDS THAT BECAME A KNIFE...

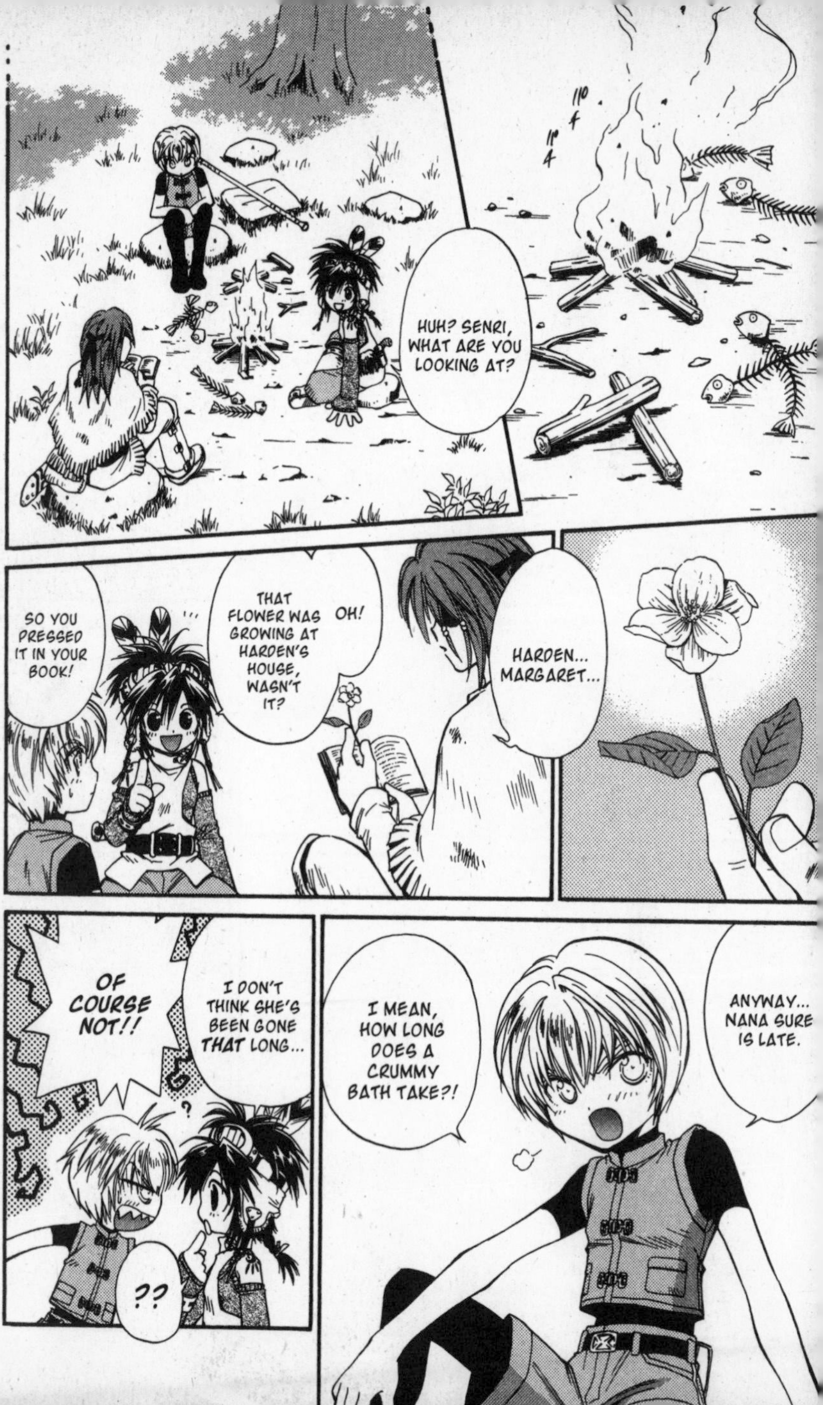
HUH? SENRI, WHAT ARE YOU LOOKING AT?
HARDEN... MARGARET...
OH!
THAT FLOWER WAS GROWING AT HARDEN'S HOUSE, WASN'T IT?
SO YOU PRESSED IT IN YOUR BOOK!
ANYWAY... NANA SURE IS LATE.
I MEAN, HOW LONG DOES A CRUMMY BATH TAKE?!
I DON'T THINK SHE'S BEEN GONE **THAT** LONG...
OF COURSE NOT!!
??

SORRY I TOOK SO LONG!

TADAH!!

WHAT DO YOU THINK?

I HAD MARGARET MAKE THEM. AREN'T THEY NICE?

NANA, HOW DID YOU GET THEM?

AH! YOUR CLOTHES!

SIGH... SEE? THIS IS WHY I HATE GIRLS!

THEY FUSS OVER THINGS LIKE THAT, AND MAKE PEOPLE WAIT FOREVER WHILE THEY TAKE A BATH!

......

......

WHAT DO YOU MEAN?

LEAVES...?

YOU THINK I CAN STAND WEARING LEAVES?!

HUSKY, YOU WERE FUSSING OVER CLOTHES, TOO!

LET'S GO, SENRI!

NO PROBLEM!

C-COORO, SENRI!

GO TAKE A BATH!

NOPE.

YOU'RE NOT GOING, HUSKY?

Taking a bath... Taking a bath...

146

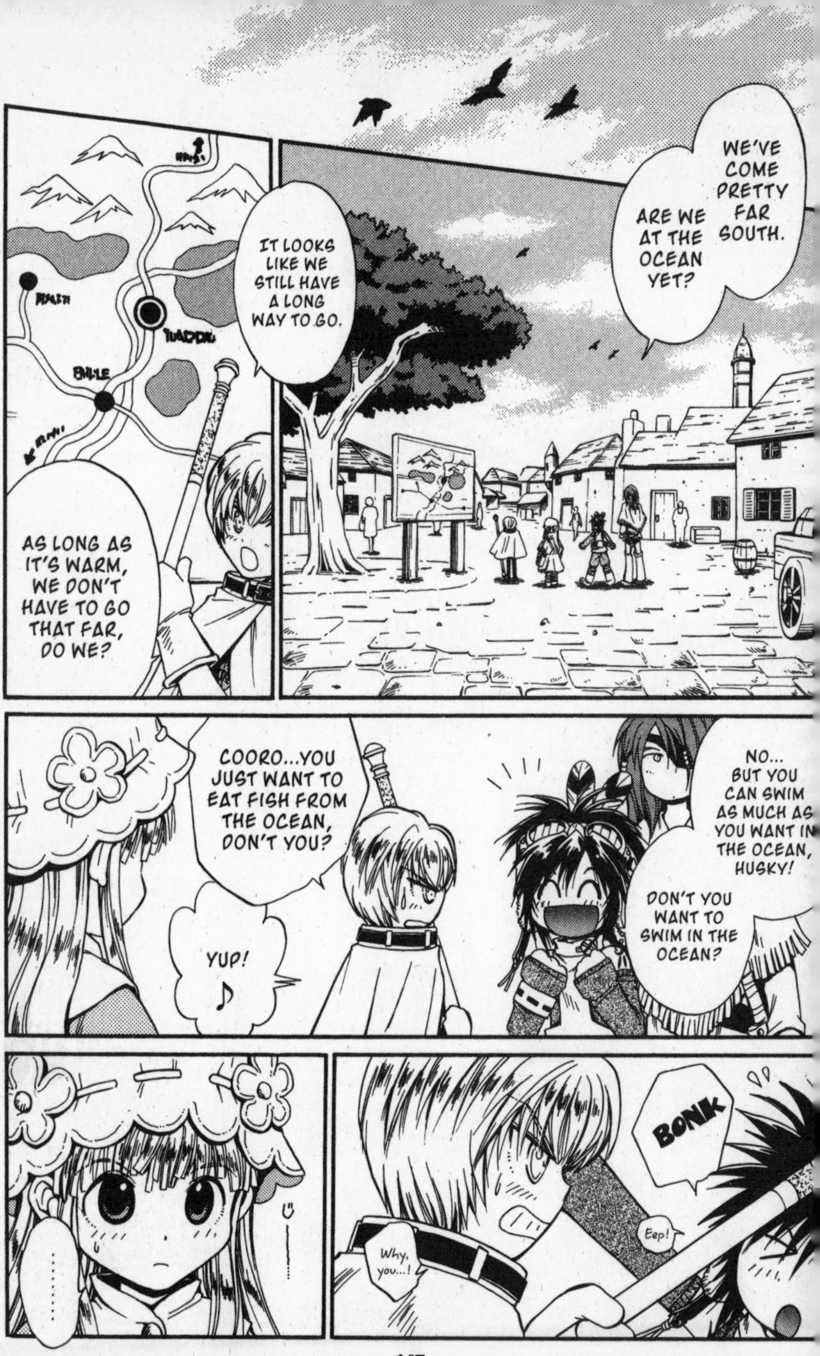
WE'VE COME PRETTY FAR SOUTH.
ARE WE AT THE OCEAN YET?
IT LOOKS LIKE WE STILL HAVE A LONG WAY TO GO.
AS LONG AS IT'S WARM, WE DON'T HAVE TO GO THAT FAR, DO WE?
NO... BUT YOU CAN SWIM AS MUCH AS YOU WANT IN THE OCEAN, HUSKY!
DON'T YOU WANT TO SWIM IN THE OCEAN?
COORO...YOU JUST WANT TO EAT FISH FROM THE OCEAN, DON'T YOU?
YUP! ♪
BONK
Eep!
Why, you...!
......

THE REASON HE NEVER TAKES A BATH WITH ANYONE...

IT REALLY WOULDN'T BE CRAZY TO SAY HE'S A GIRL...!

...IS THAT HE SECRETLY BATHES AT NIGHT SO KNOW ONE WILL FIND OUT HE'S A GIRL!

LET'S MEET BACK HERE LATER.

HEY, THERE ARE A BUNCH OF OPEN SHOPS OVER THERE!

LET'S GO TAKE A LOOK!

SOMETIMES I JUST WANT TIME BY MYSELF...

WHEN THE SUN HAS MADE IT TO THAT TOWER... WE'LL MEET RIGHT HERE, OKAY?

OKAY!

YEAH. SURE.

......

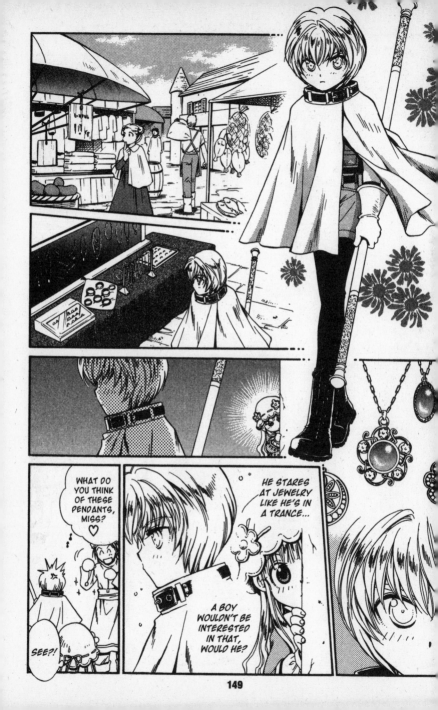

HE STARES AT JEWELRY LIKE HE'S IN A TRANCE...
A BOY WOULDN'T BE INTERESTED IN THAT, WOULD HE?
WHAT DO YOU THINK OF THESE PENDANTS, MISS? ♡
SEE?!

HEE HEE HEE...

WHAT DO YOU WANT, NANA?

AH!

TALK ABOUT CREEPY...

GEEZ...

HUSKY! YOU...

...HAVE A BIG **SECRET**, DON'T YOU?

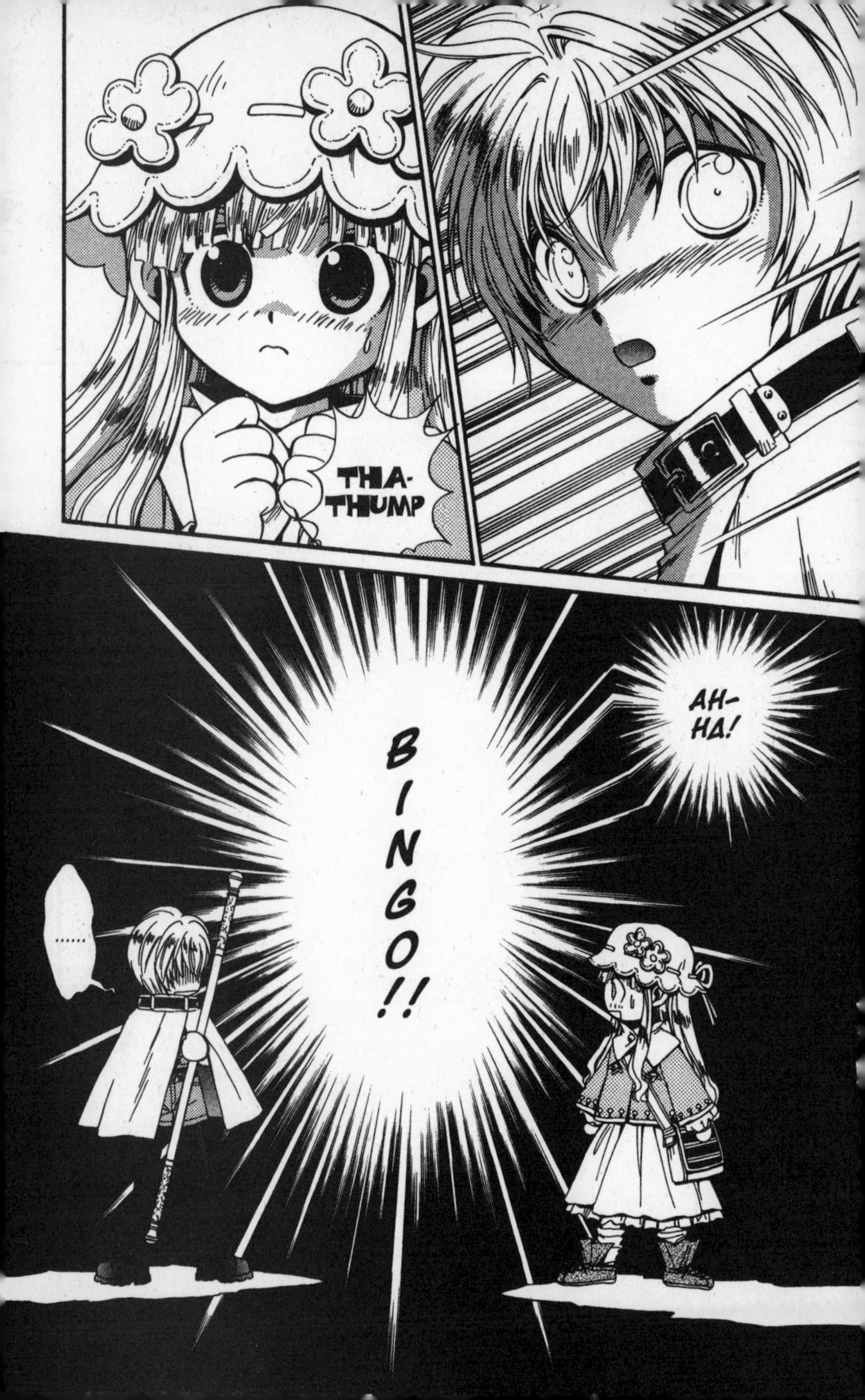
THA-
THUMP
AH-
HA!
BINGO!!
......

YEAH...

R-RIGHT...!

B-BUT...

......

A SECRET...? EVERYBODY HAS SECRETS.

WHAAA?!

OKAY?!

...IF THERE'S SOMETHING YOU CAN'T SAY TO COORO OR SENRI, JUST KNOW YOU CAN TALK TO ME ABOUT IT!

...I'M A GIRL, SO...

OOOH! ♥

THAT COLOR WOULD LOOK GOOD ON YOU, HUSKY!

WH-WHY WOULD I TALK TO A *GIRL* ABOUT ANYTHING?!

AH! HUSKY!

......

WHY DON'T YOU GROW YOUR HAIR OUT, TOO, HUSKY?

I THINK IT WOULD BE PRETTY!

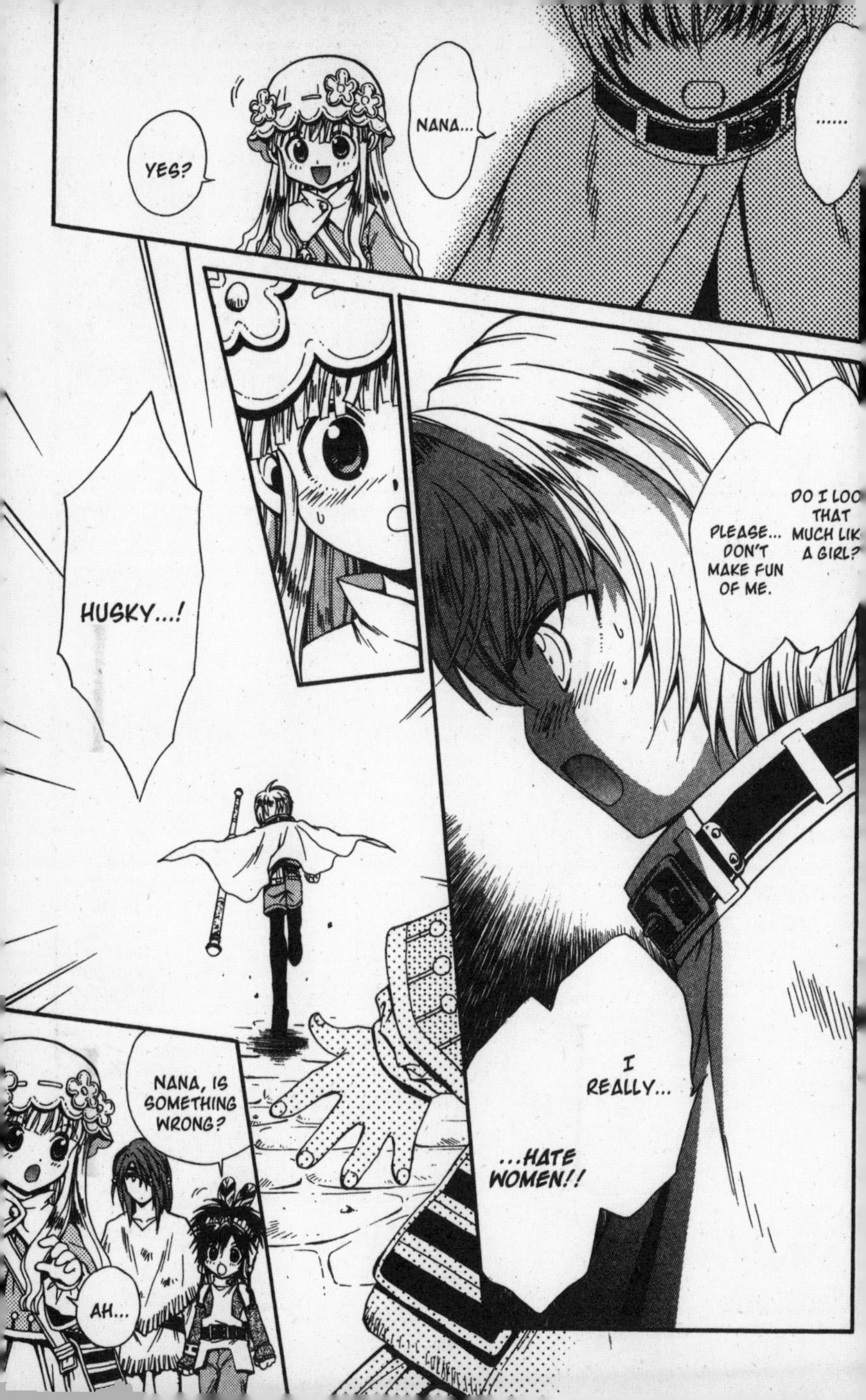
......
NANA...
YES?
DO I LOO THAT MUCH LIK A GIRL?
PLEASE... DON'T MAKE FUN OF ME.
I REALLY...
...HATE WOMEN!!
HUSKY...!
NANA, IS SOMETHING WRONG?
AH...

...TO HIDE THE FACT THAT *HE'S* A GIRL!

I THINK MAYBE HUSKY SAYS HE HATES GIRLS...

HOLY--?!

HUSKY'S A GIRL?!

M-MERMAID PRINCESS?

...HUSKY WAS REALLY PRETTY AS THE LITTLE MERMAID PRINCESS.

COME TO THINK OF IT...

THEN WE'LL JUST HAVE TO *FORCE* IT OUT OF HIM...!

NANA?

SEE? IT'S WEIRD THAT HE'D POINT IT OUT!

RIGHT, SENRI?!

...??

BUT... HUSKY SAID HIMSELF THAT HE'S A BOY.

: : : : : :

IT'S
TRUE...

HIS SKIN IS
SO WHITE,
AND
HE'S SO
SLENDER...

LOOKING
LIKE THAT,
HE'S
VERY...

snicker...

HUSKY IS
SO MUCH
LIKE A
GIRL...

159

......

ARE YOU OKAY, HUSKY?

IT'S OKAY, SENRI. PUT ME DOWN.

HUSKY...

REMEM-
BER
WHEN...

...I TOLD YOU
ABOUT WHEN
I BECAME A
+ANIMA...?

BUT AS
MUCH AS
I WANTED
TO KEEP IT
SECRET...

...I
THOUGHT IT
WOULD FEEL
THAT MUCH
BETTER IF
I TALKED
ABOUT IT.

THAT WAS MY
NUMBER ONE
SECRET.

THAT'S
WHY...

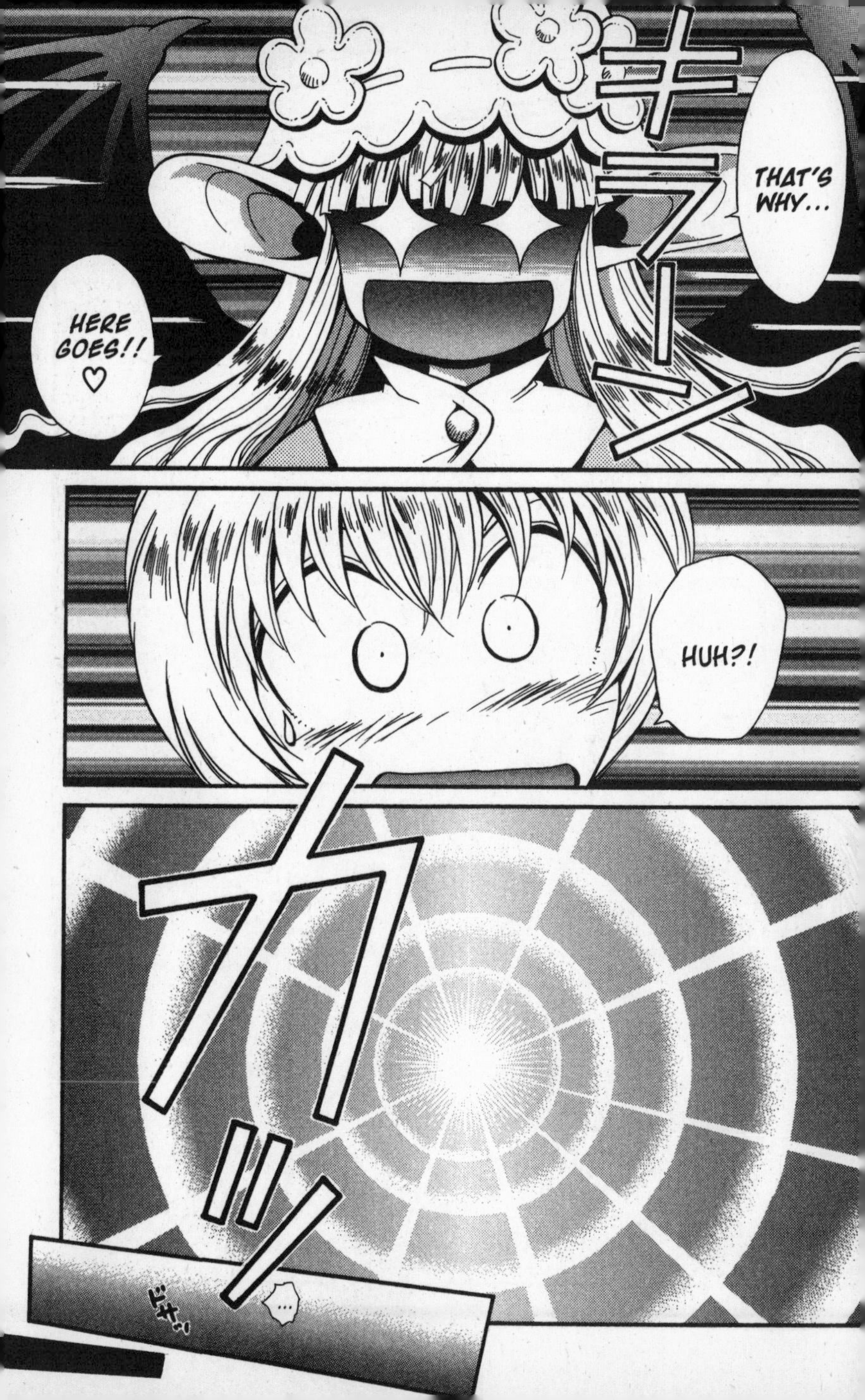
THAT'S WHY...
HERE GOES!! ♡
HUH?!
...

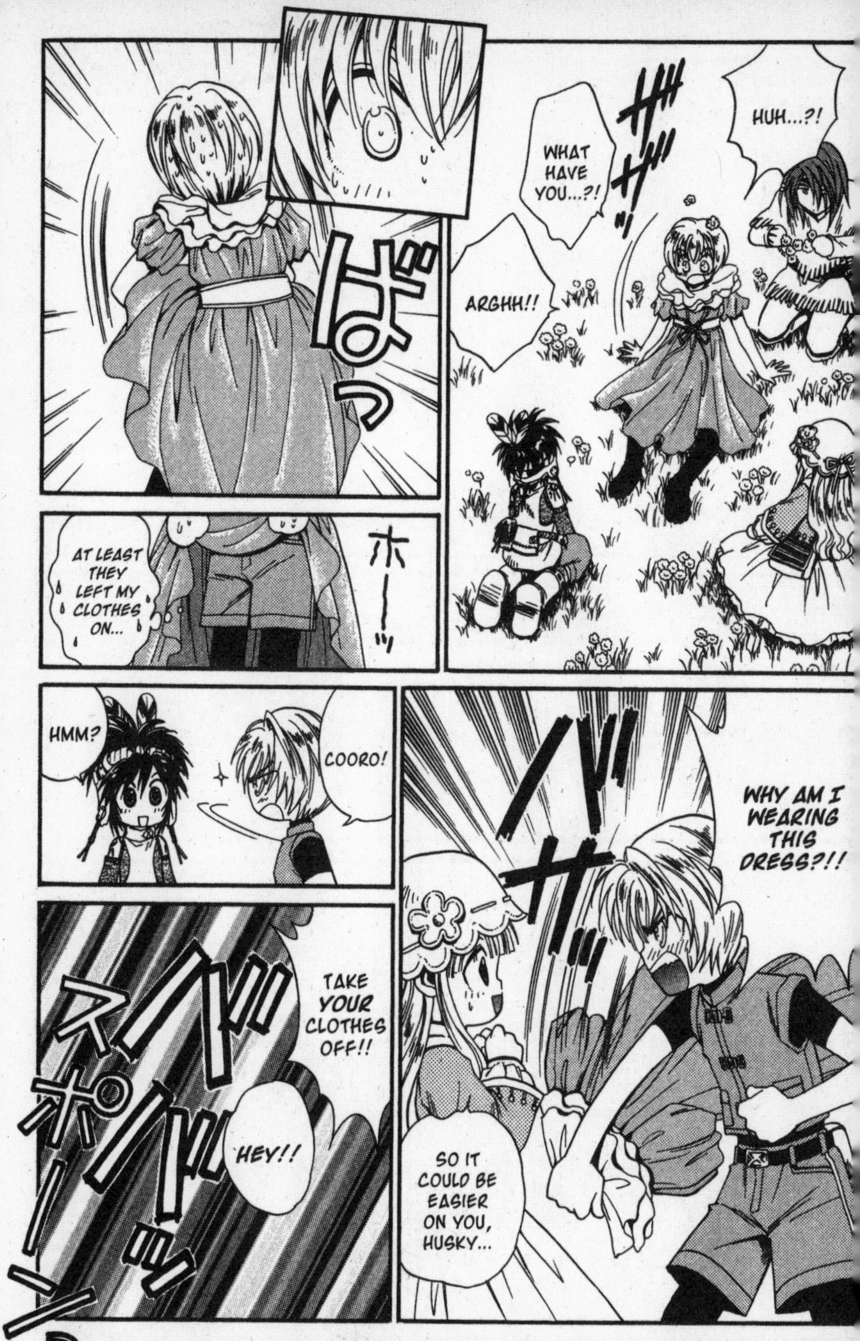
HUH...?!
WHAT HAVE YOU...?!
ARGHH!!
ぱっ
AT LEAST THEY LEFT MY CLOTHES ON...
ホーーッ
WHY AM I WEARING THIS DRESS?!!
SO IT COULD BE EASIER ON YOU, HUSKY...
COORO!
HMM?
TAKE YOUR CLOTHES OFF!!
HEY!!
スポーーンッ

YOU SEE?! YOU GOT IT? I'M A BOY!! B-O-Y!!

Wow, that was fast!

Husky...

GYAAAAH!!

......

'CUZ I'D LOOK BAD IF IT WAS JUST ME!

WHY AM I NAKED, TOO?

YES, IT'S TRUE!

HUSKY, YOU'RE REALLY...

IS... IS IT TRUE?

...A BOY?

THAT'S NOT A SECRET-- IT'S NOT ANYTHING!

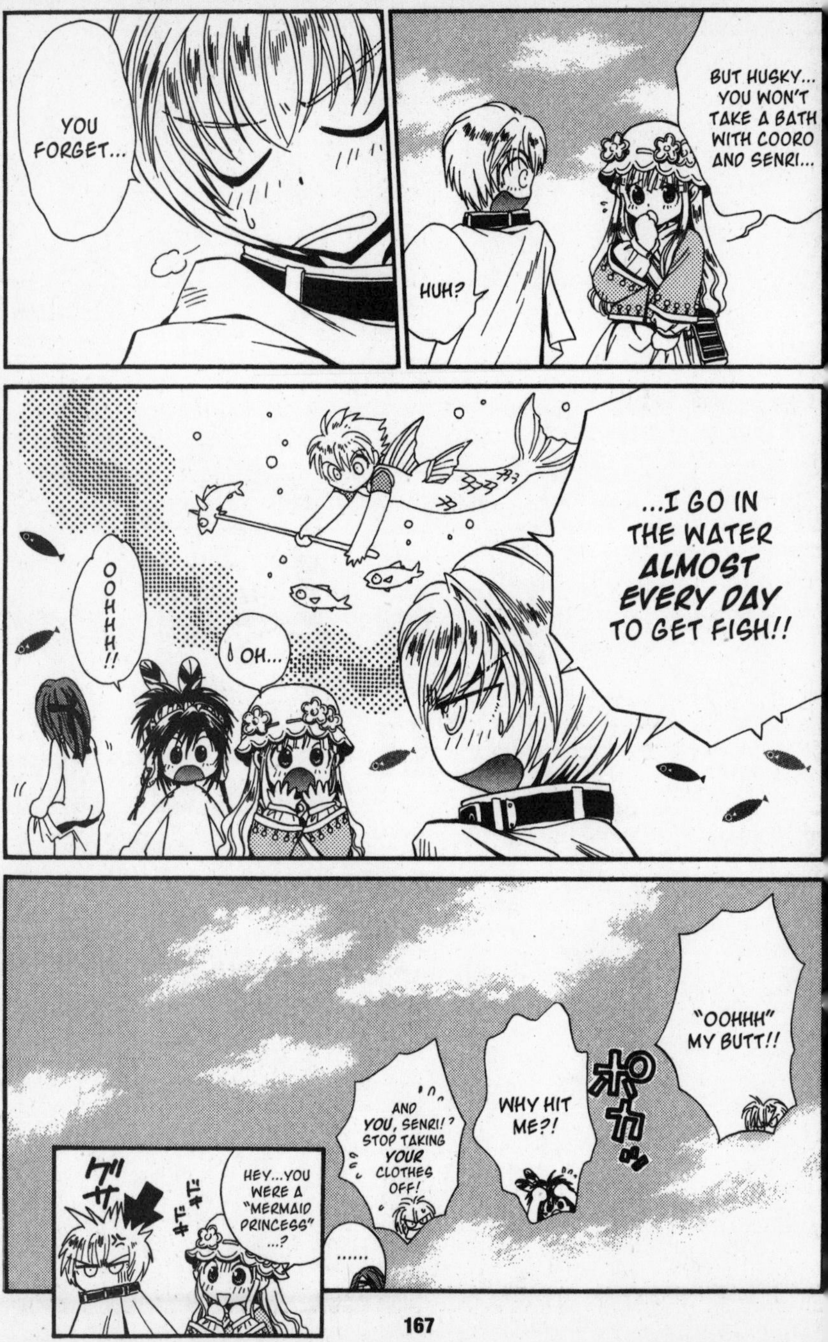
BUT HUSKY... YOU WON'T TAKE A BATH WITH COORO AND SENRI...
HUH?
YOU FORGET...
...I GO IN THE WATER ALMOST EVERY DAY TO GET FISH!!
OH...
OOHHH!!
"OOHHH" MY BUTT!!
ポカッ
WHY HIT ME?!
AND YOU, SENRI! STOP TAKING YOUR CLOTHES OFF!
......
HEY...YOU WERE A "MERMAID PRINCESS" ...?
グサ

He is clever at mimicking.

Chapter 14: Scars

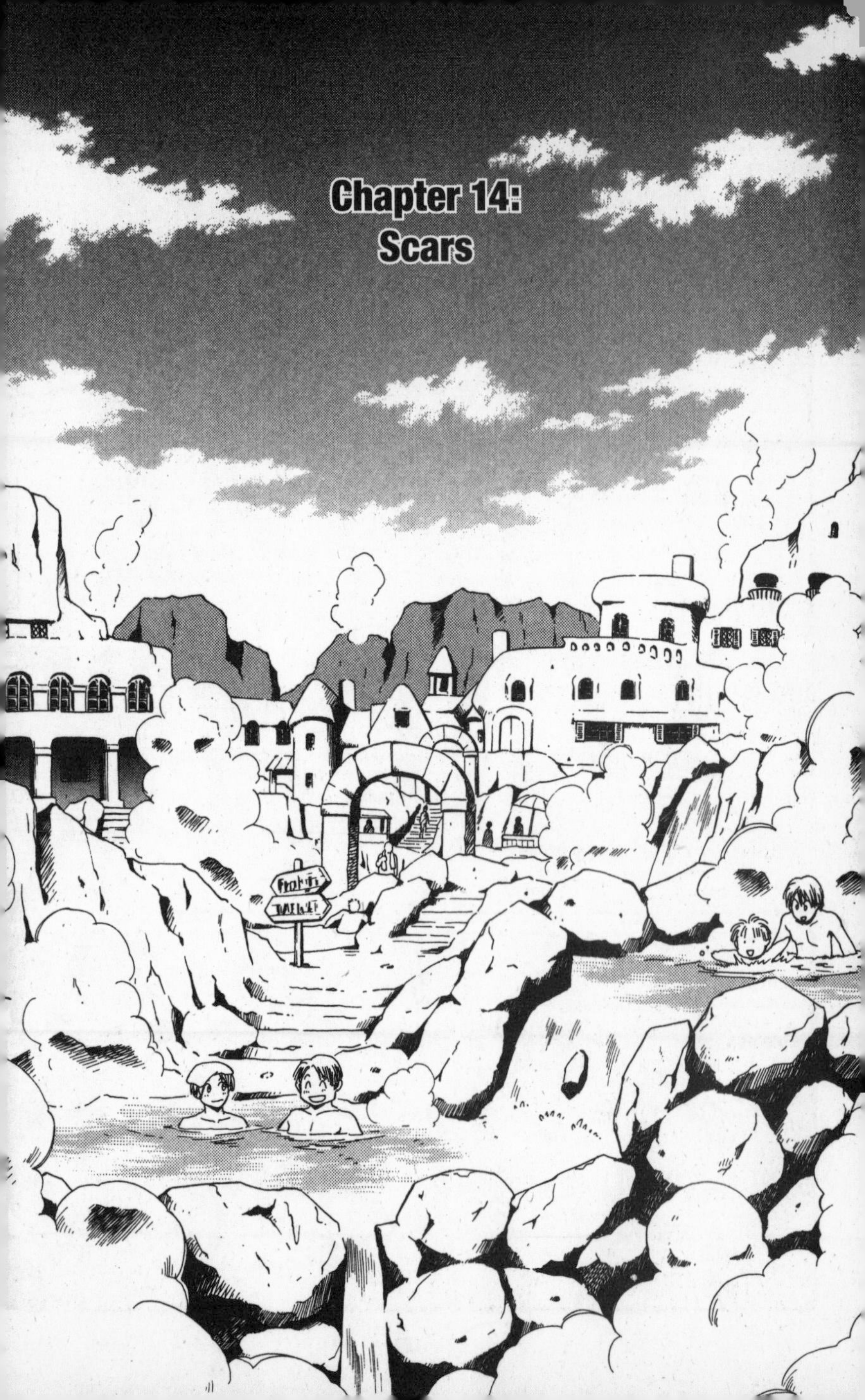

SO IT'S THE HOT SPRINGS TOWN, BUBBLY?

YOUKOSO BUBBLY

HOT SPRINGS?

POOLS FILLED WITH HOT WATER.

IT'S GOOD FOR YOUR BODY TO BATHE IN THEM.

AH...!

BUT WHY, NANA? IT SOUNDS LIKE FUN...!

ON...ON SECOND THOUGHT, I DON'T WANT TO...

ME, TOO!

WOW! I WANT TO TRY THAT!

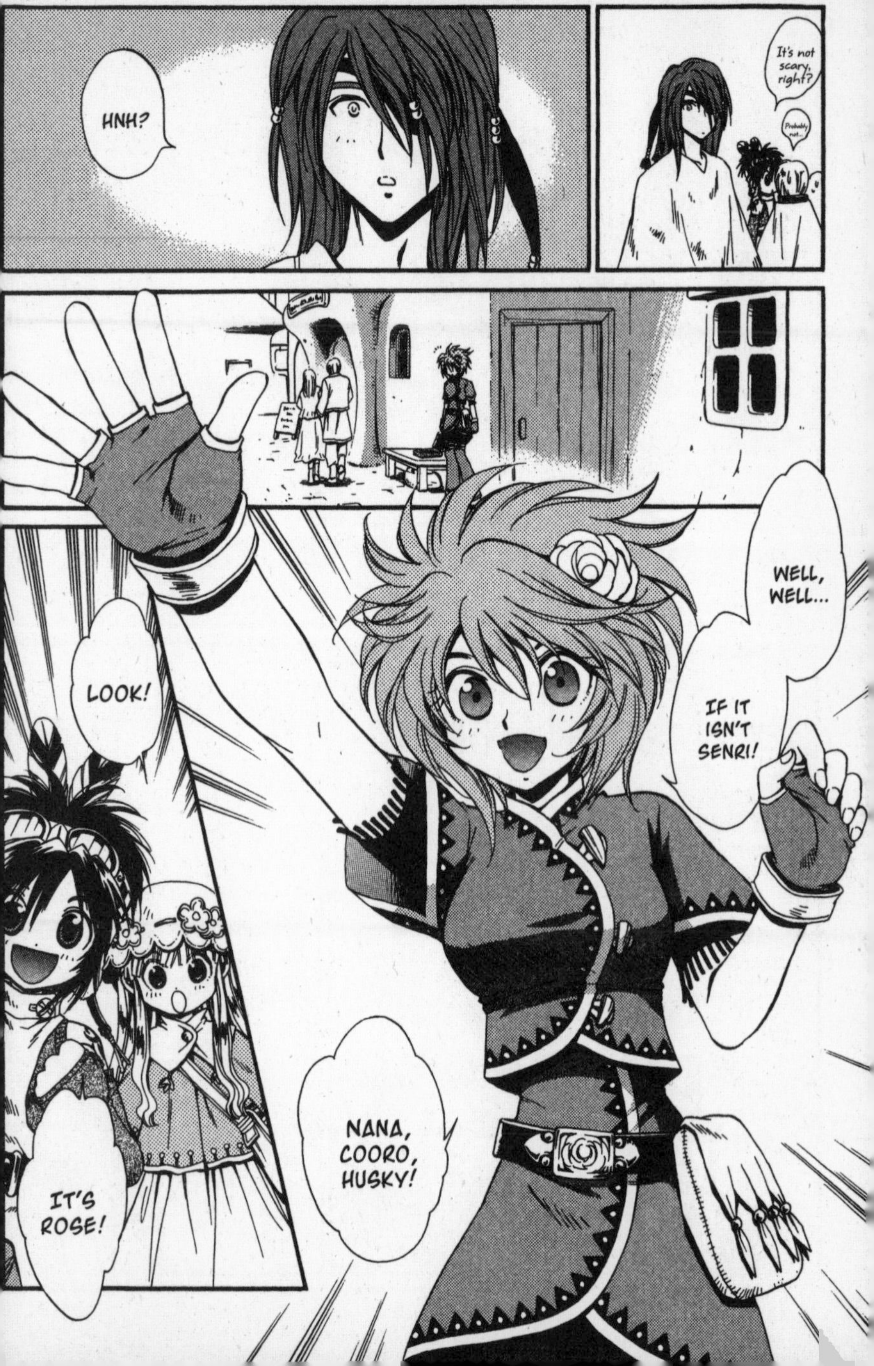
It's not scary, right?
Probably not...
HNH?
WELL, WELL...
IF IT ISN'T SENRI!
LOOK!
NANA, COORO, HUSKY!
IT'S ROSE!

Heh heh! ♡

MAINLY BECAUSE THEY'RE FEELING GOOD AFTER BEING IN THE HOT SPRINGS.

IN A TOWN LIKE THIS, TOURISTS ARE MORE LIKELY TO SPEND FREELY.

THAT'S RIGHT!

YOU'RE PEDDLING IN THIS TOWN?

NO, NOT YET.

HAVE YOU BEEN IN A HOT SPRING, ROSE?

EMPTY, HE SAYS! THAT SOUNDS GOOD. WANNA GO?

THERE'S AN EMPTY HOT SPRING OVER THERE.

UH... UMM...

AND THERE'S AN INN... A REAL GOOD ONE!

ER...

173

174

THAT'S CHEAP.

THAT'S BECAUSE IT'S SO RUN-DOWN.

Y-YOU'LL BE STAYING HERE, RIGHT?

THAT WILL BE AN ADVANCE PAYMENT OF TEN GILLAH PER PERSON, PER NIGHT.

THAT'S RIGHT!

YEAH... BUT OUR HOT SPRING HAS THE BEST "BEAUTY WATER" IN TOWN!

BEAUTY WATER...?!

THEN, WE'LL GO THIS WAY.

NO PEEPING!

YES, I'M GOING IN.

YOU'RE COMING IN TOO, RIGHT HUSKY? EVEN THOUGH IT'S NOT COLD WATER.

THE GIRLS' BATH IS THIS WAY.

THE BOYS' BATH IS THAT WAY.

WHO'D WANT TO?!

Looking at girls... ick!

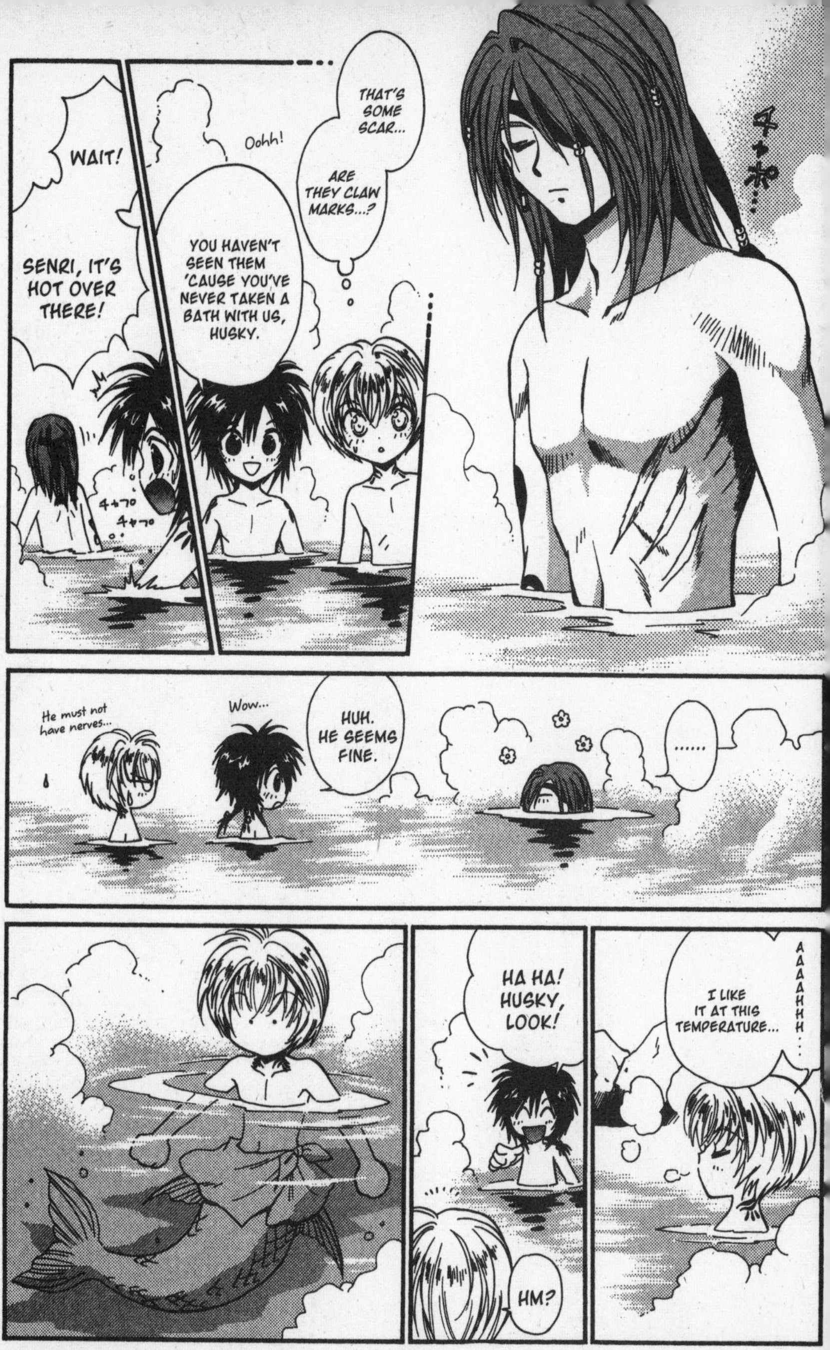
THAT'S SOME SCAR...
ARE THEY CLAW MARKS...?
Oohh!
YOU HAVEN'T SEEN THEM 'CAUSE YOU'VE NEVER TAKEN A BATH WITH US, HUSKY.
WAIT!
SENRI, IT'S HOT OVER THERE!
......
HUH. HE SEEMS FINE.
Wow...
He must not have nerves...
AAAAHHH...
I LIKE IT AT THIS TEMPERATURE...
HA HA! HUSKY, LOOK!
HM?

LET'S JUST SAY YOU CAN GET INTO MANY DANGEROUS SITUATIONS WHEN YOU'RE A +ANIMA.

WHAT...?

THIS...?

MAINLY BECAUSE I'M THE ONLY ONE WHO CAN PROTECT MY LITTLE BROTHER.

...I'M NOT UNHAPPY THAT I BECAME A +ANIMA.

BUT...

IF I KEEP IT THAT WAY, THEN THINGS ARE SETTLED WITHOUT PEOPLE WORRYING MORE THAN THEY HAVE TO.

I TRY NOT TO SHOW THAT I'M A +ANIMA, EITHER.

MY...

...+ANIMA MARKINGS STAND OUT...

...SO I THOUGHT I SHOULDN'T GO TO A HOT SPRING.

REALLY?

I WONDER IF THEY'D UNDER-STAND...

PFFT! TELL THAT TO COORO AND SENRI!

THEY'LL BOTH TRANSFORM AT THE DROP OF A HAT!

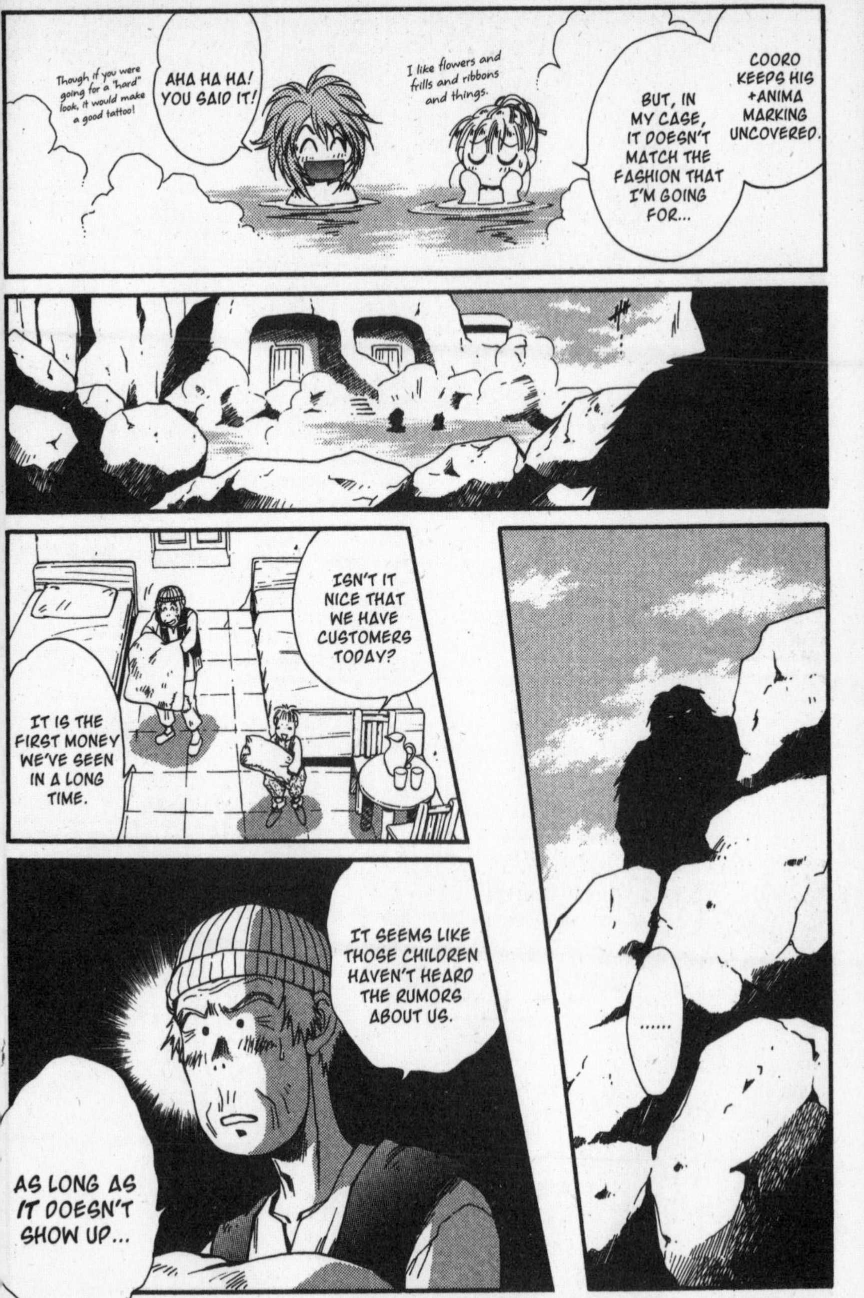
COORO KEEPS HIS +ANIMA MARKING UNCOVERED.
BUT, IN MY CASE, IT DOESN'T MATCH THE FASHION THAT I'M GOING FOR...
I like flowers and frills and ribbons and things.
AHA HA HA! YOU SAID IT!
Though if you were going for a "hard" look, it would make a good tattoo!
......
ISN'T IT NICE THAT WE HAVE CUSTOMERS TODAY?
IT IS THE FIRST MONEY WE'VE SEEN IN A LONG TIME.
IT SEEMS LIKE THOSE CHILDREN HAVEN'T HEARD THE RUMORS ABOUT US.
AS LONG AS IT DOESN'T SHOW UP...

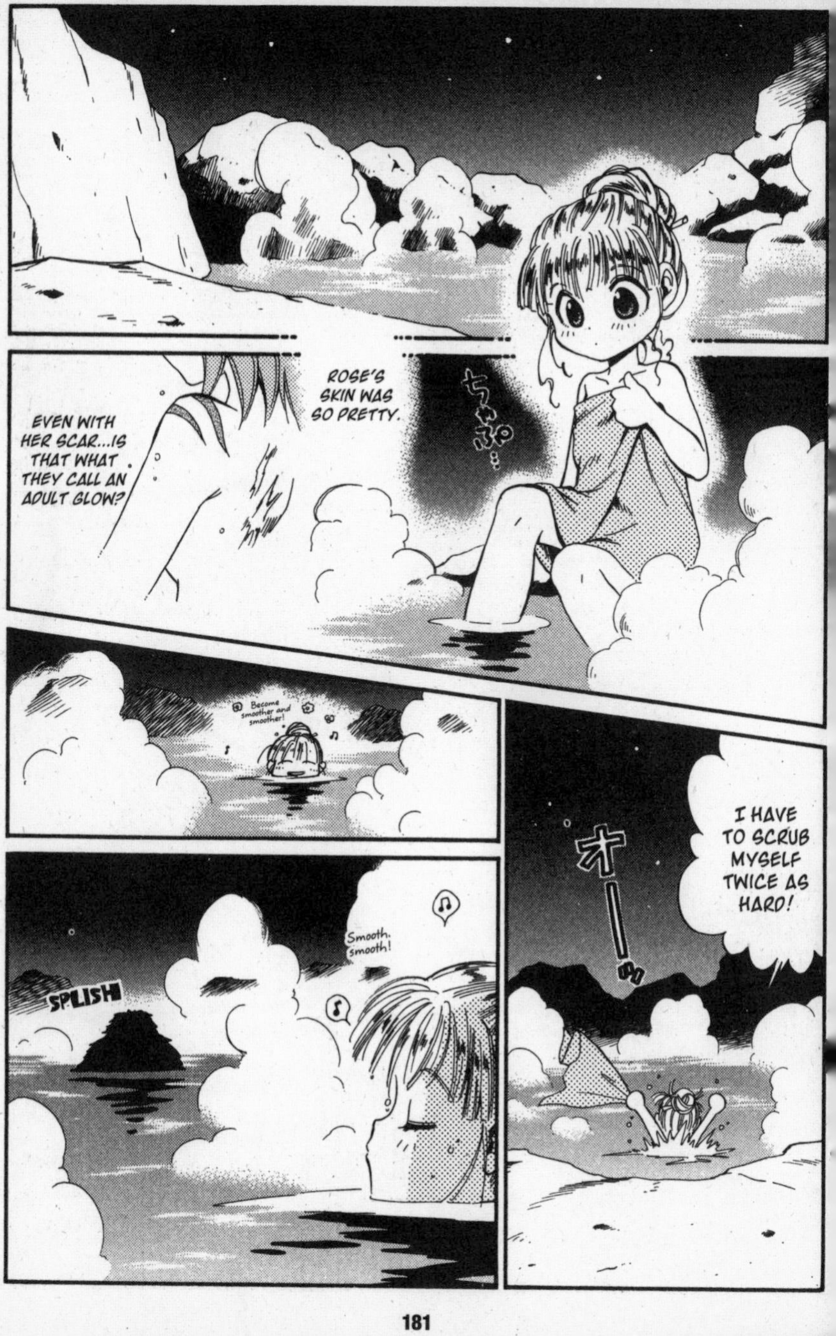
ROSE'S SKIN WAS SO PRETTY.
ちゃぷ…
EVEN WITH HER SCAR...IS THAT WHAT THEY CALL AN ADULT GLOW?
オー
I HAVE TO SCRUB MYSELF TWICE AS HARD!
Become smoother and smoother!
Smooth, smooth!
SPLISH

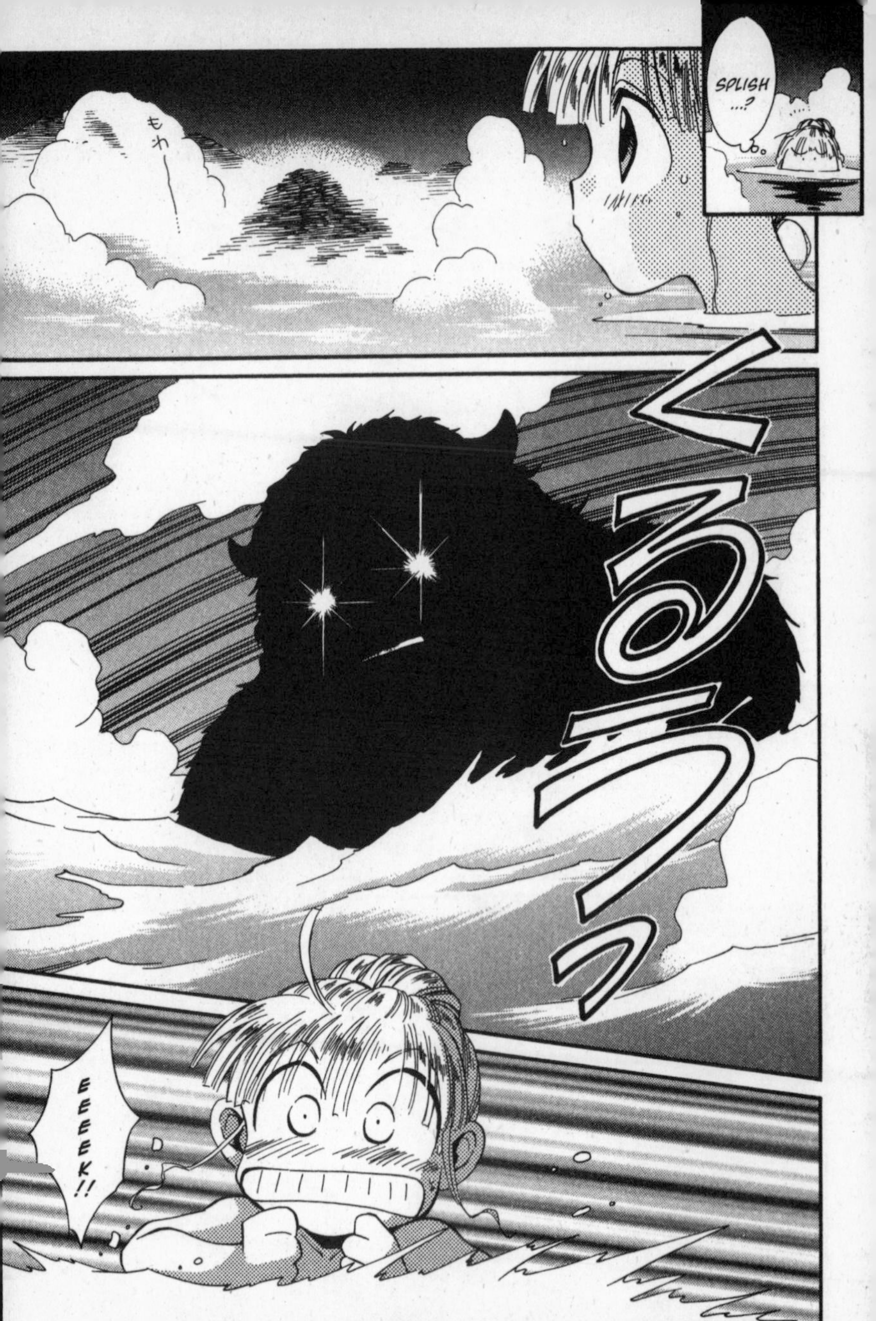
SPLISH ...?
もわ
EEEEK!!

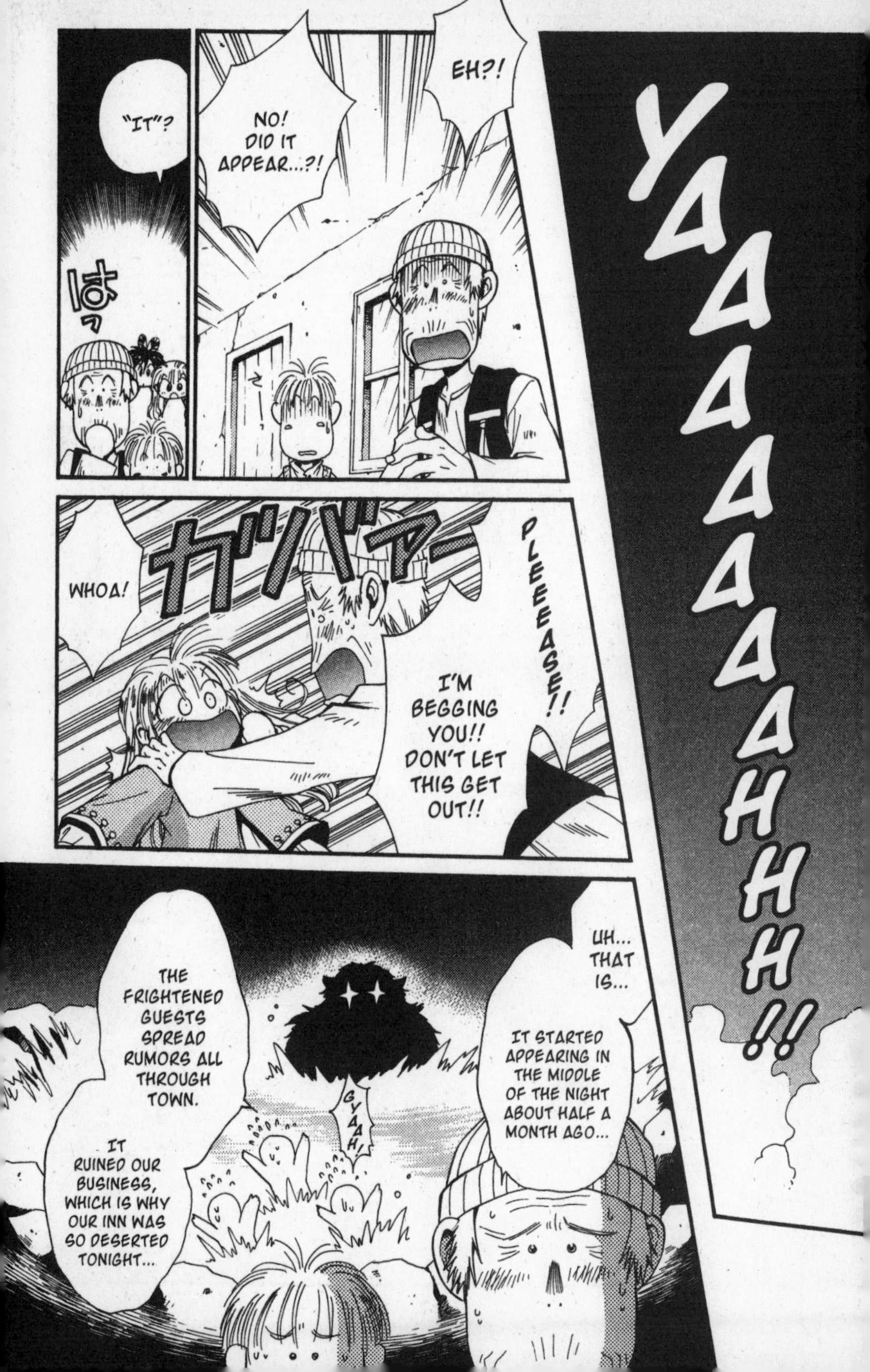
YAAAAAAAAHHHH!!
EH?!
NO! DID IT APPEAR...?!
"IT"?
はっ
PLEEEASE!!
カバァー
I'M BEGGING YOU!! DON'T LET THIS GET OUT!!
WHOA!
UH... THAT IS...
IT STARTED APPEARING IN THE MIDDLE OF THE NIGHT ABOUT HALF A MONTH AGO...
THE FRIGHTENED GUESTS SPREAD RUMORS ALL THROUGH TOWN.
GYAAH!
IT RUINED OUR BUSINESS, WHICH IS WHY OUR INN WAS SO DESERTED TONIGHT...

......

Um, that is...

W-WAIT...! YOU CAN'T!

WHAT?!

WE DON'T HAVE ANY MONEY, BUT THERE'S NOTHING ELSE TO DO.

HMM... IN THAT CASE, WE HAVE NO CHOICE BUT TO HIRE SOMEONE AND GO ON A MOUNTAIN HUNT OR SOMETHING...!

SHOULD WE TRY CHASING IT AWAY?

HEY...

COORO?!

IF WE CAN, WILL YOU GIVE US BACK THE MONEY WE PAID YOU?

Grr!

REALLY?!

M-MONEY?

G-GIVE BACK...?

WELL, ALL RIGHT...

10 x 5 = 50 gillah...

CAN YOU-- WOULD YOU--DO THAT?!

185

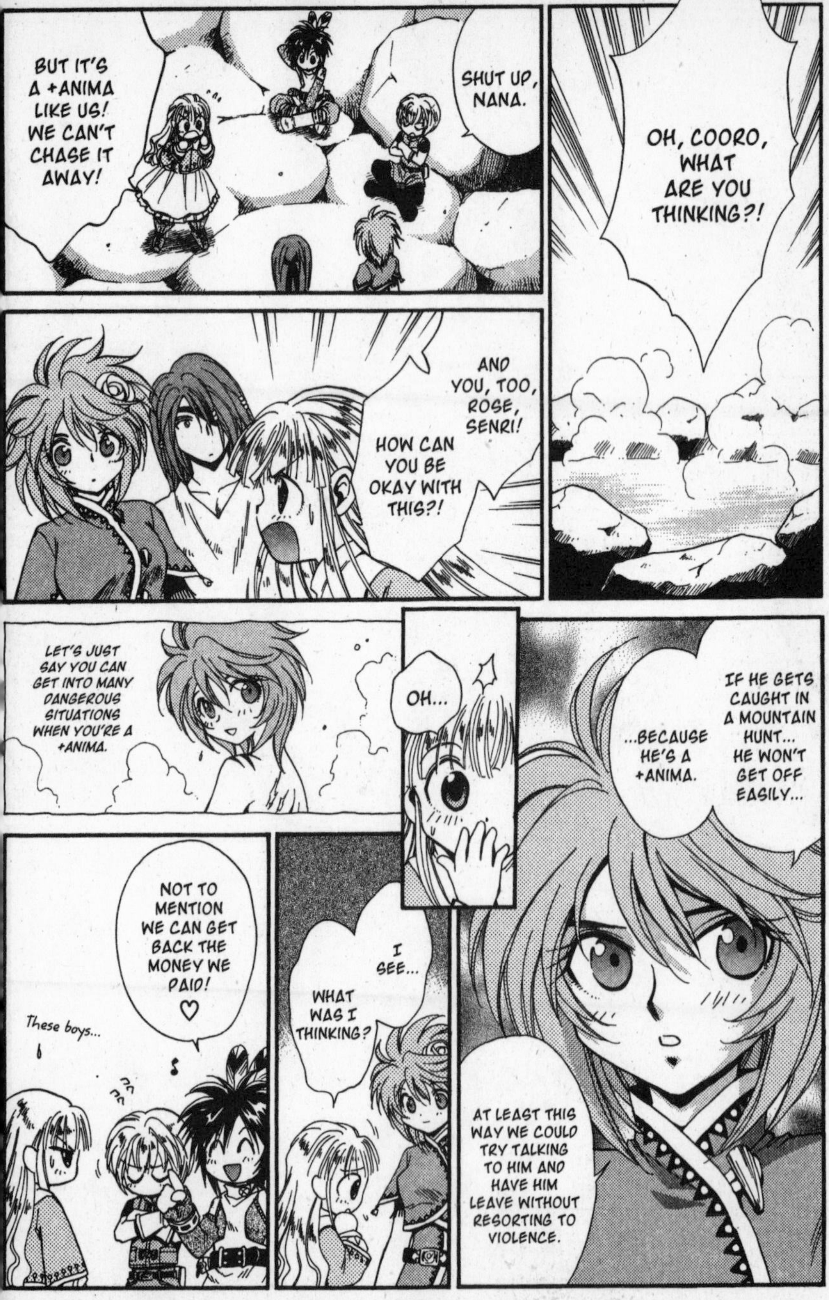
OH, COORO, WHAT ARE YOU THINKING?!
SHUT UP, NANA.
BUT IT'S A +ANIMA LIKE US! WE CAN'T CHASE IT AWAY!
AND YOU, TOO, ROSE, SENRI!
HOW CAN YOU BE OKAY WITH THIS?!
IF HE GETS CAUGHT IN A MOUNTAIN HUNT... HE WON'T GET OFF EASILY...
...BECAUSE HE'S A +ANIMA.
AT LEAST THIS WAY WE COULD TRY TALKING TO HIM AND HAVE HIM LEAVE WITHOUT RESORTING TO VIOLENCE.
OH...
LET'S JUST SAY YOU CAN GET INTO MANY DANGEROUS SITUATIONS WHEN YOU'RE A +ANIMA.
I SEE...
WHAT WAS I THINKING?
NOT TO MENTION WE CAN GET BACK THE MONEY WE PAID! ♡
These boys...

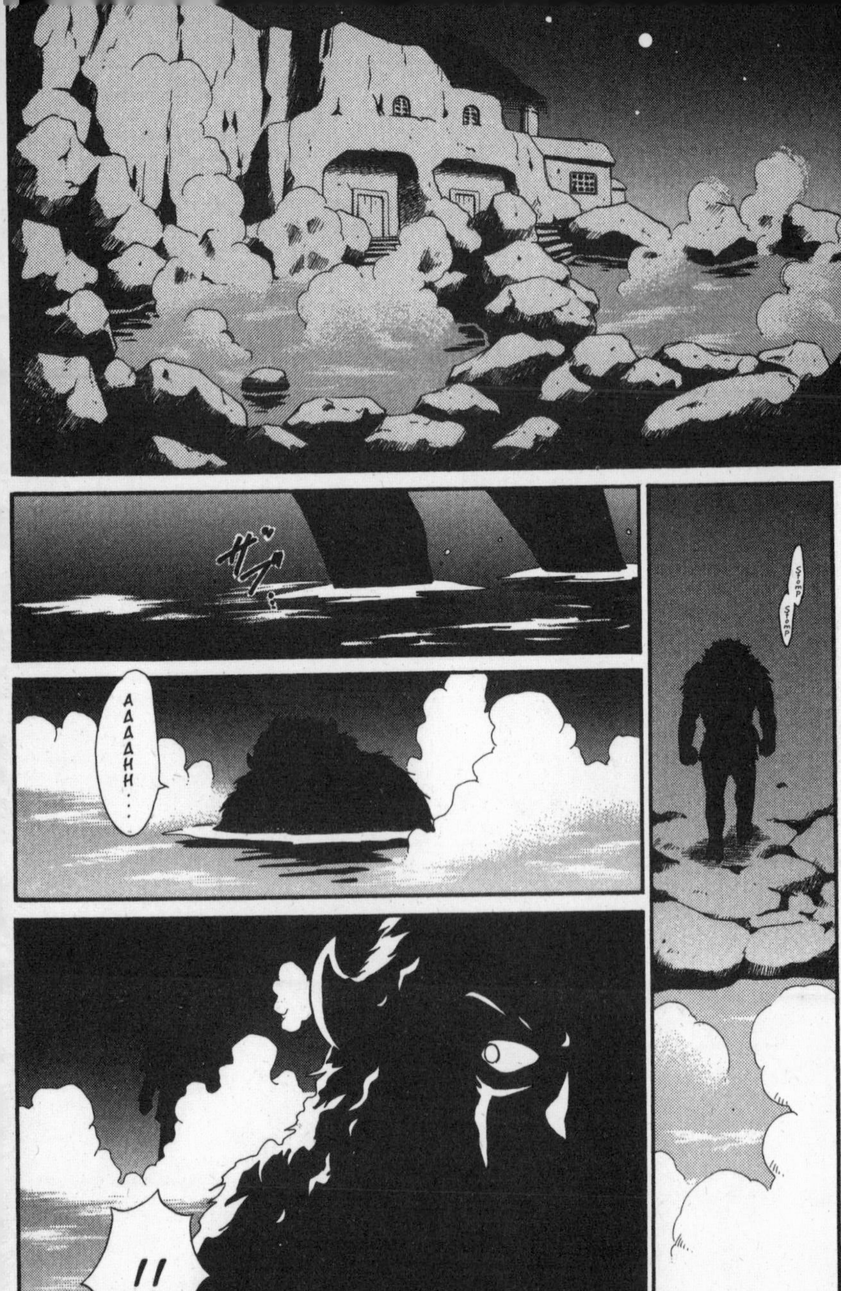
STOMP STOMP
AAAAHH...
!!

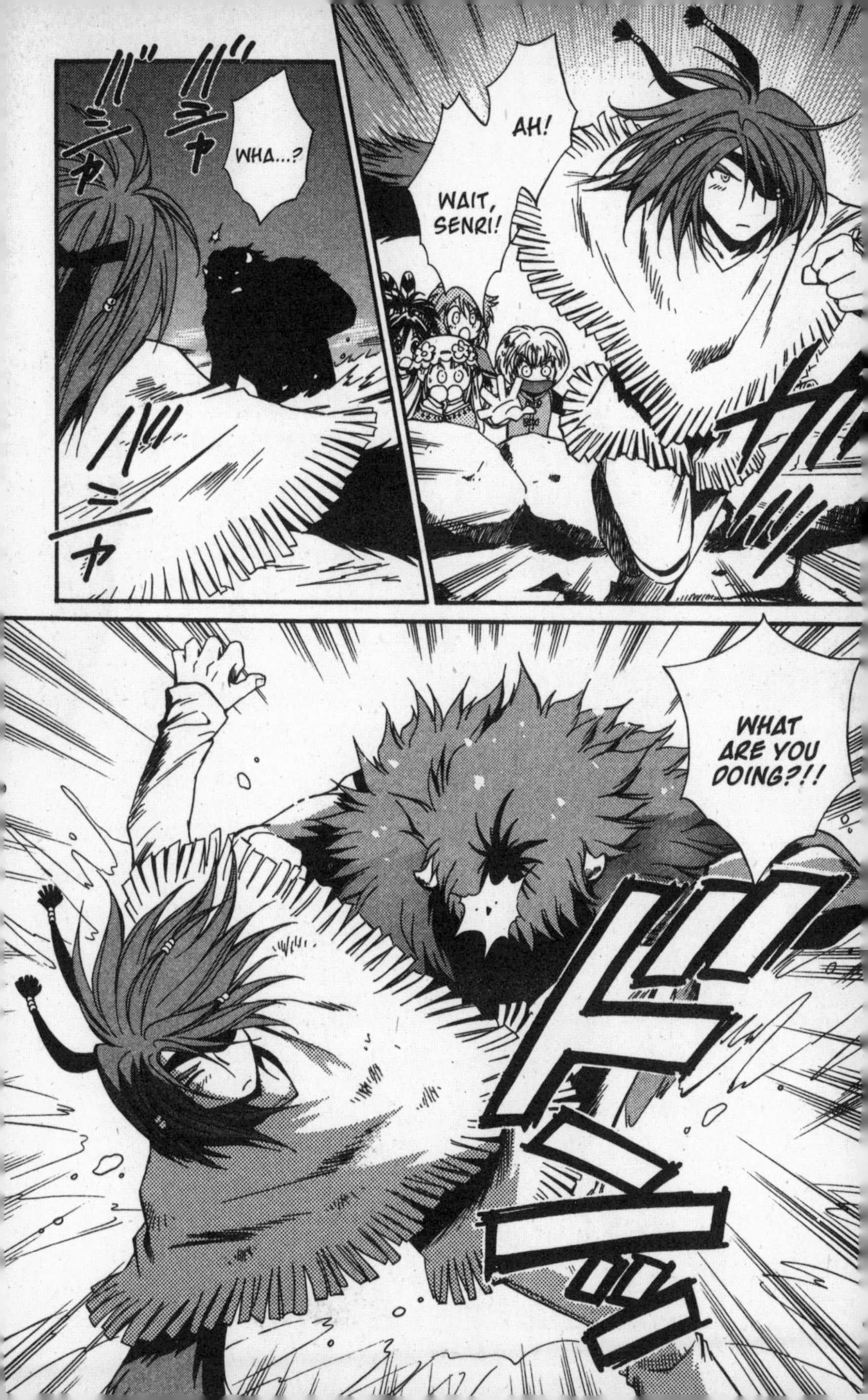
AH!
WAIT, SENRI!
WHA...?
WHAT ARE YOU DOING?!!

WARGH!!

WAH!!

WELL IT AIN'T GONNA HAPPEN!

YOU'RE PLANNING TO CHASE ME OFF, AREN'T YOU?

I HAVE A RIGHT TO USE THE HOT SPRING, TOO!!

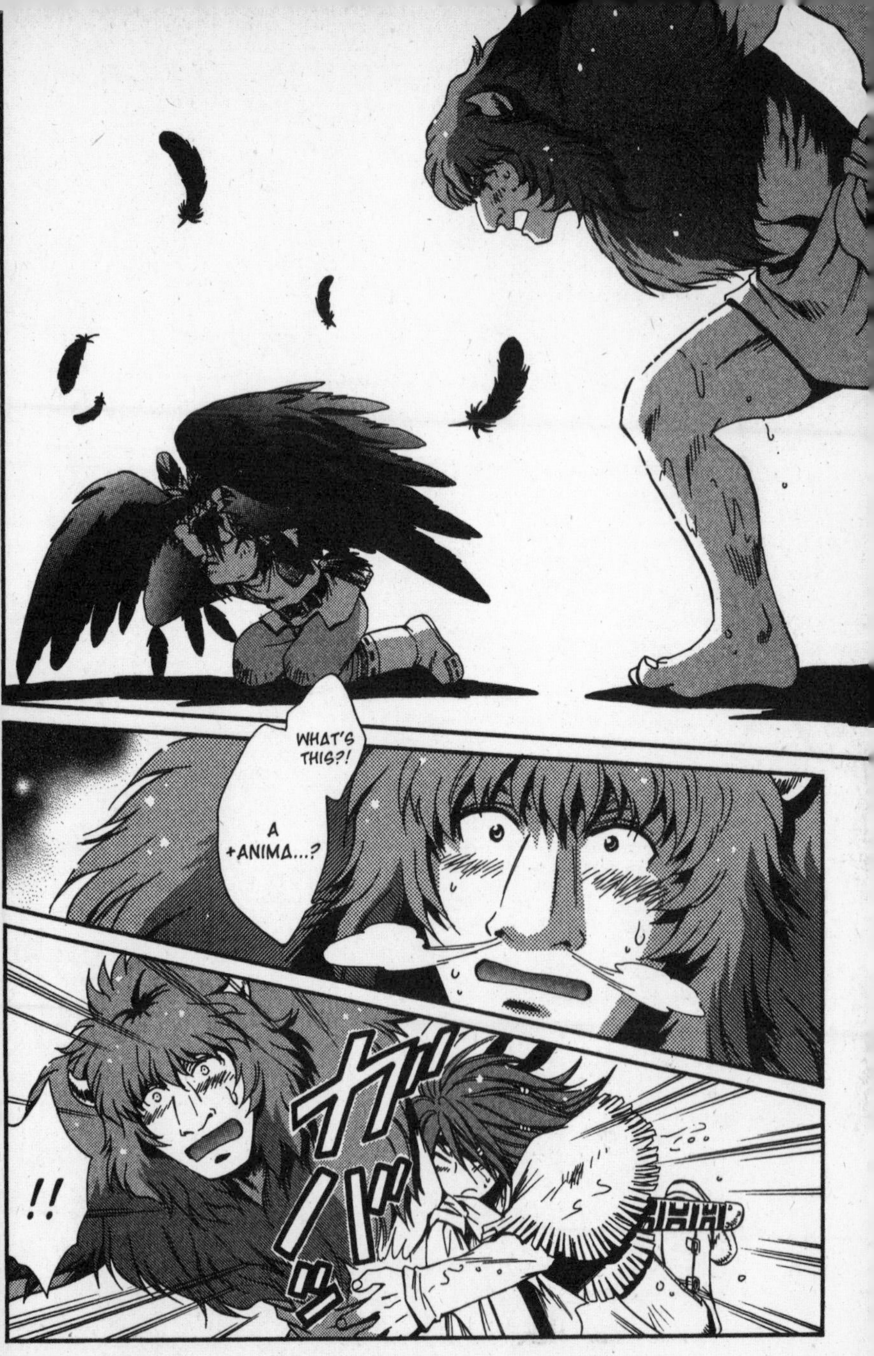
WHAT'S THIS?!
A +ANIMA...?
!!

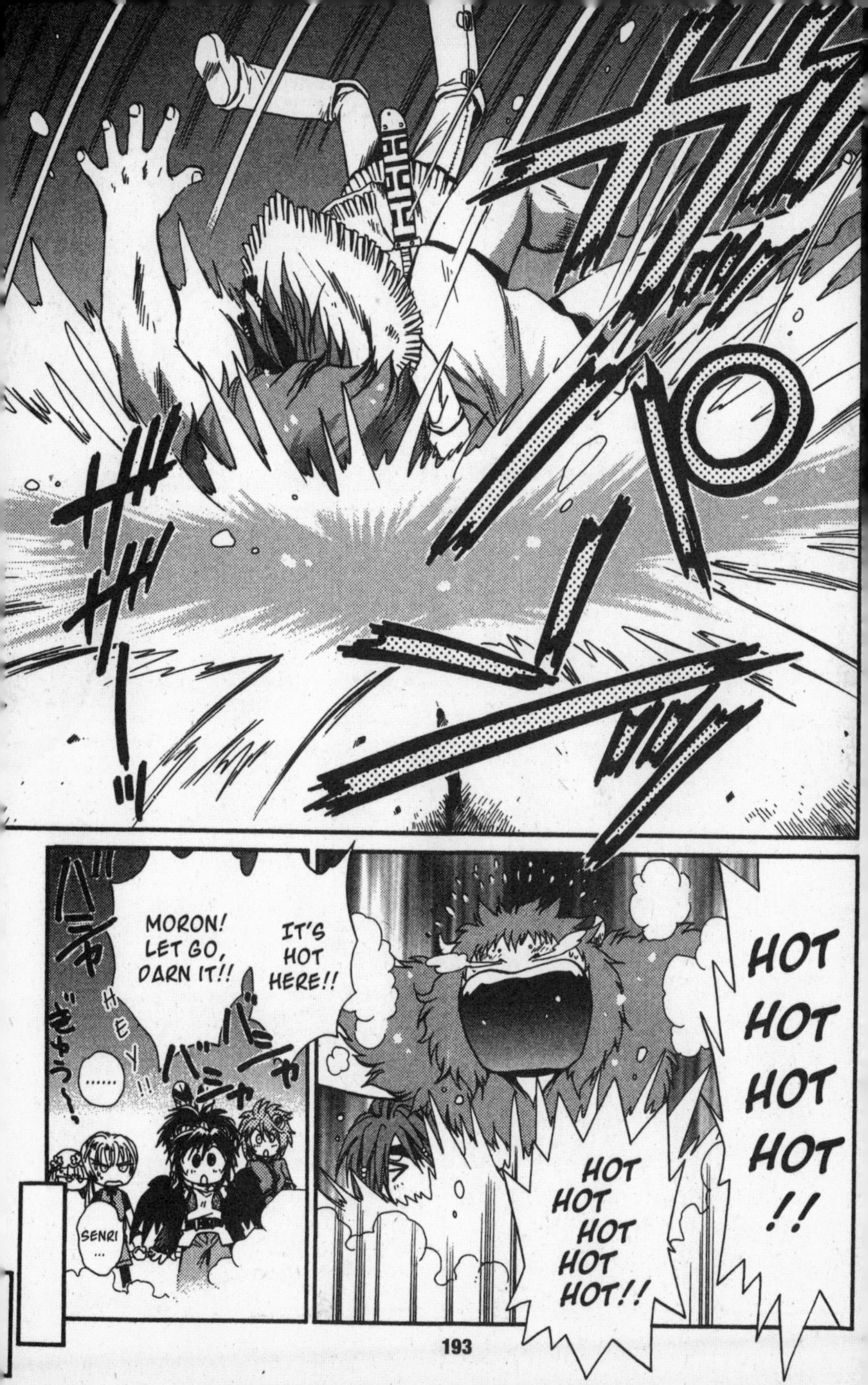

HOT HOT HOT HOT HOT!!
HOT HOT HOT HOT HOT!!
IT'S HOT HERE!!
MORON! LET GO, DARN IT!!
HEY!!
......
SENRI ...

OH, THIS?

IT HAPPENED WHEN I WAS IN +ANIMA FORM.

WOUNDS HEAL EASIER IN THE FORM YOU WERE IN WHEN YOU GOT THEM.

THE HOT SPRING HERE WORKED REALLY WELL.

UM...

SO DID THE OWNER OF THIS PLACE ASK YOU TO STAND GUARD HERE?

MISTER, YOU GOTTA RUN AWAY!

HE WAS SAYING THEY'D START A MOUNTAIN HUNT FOR YOU!

195

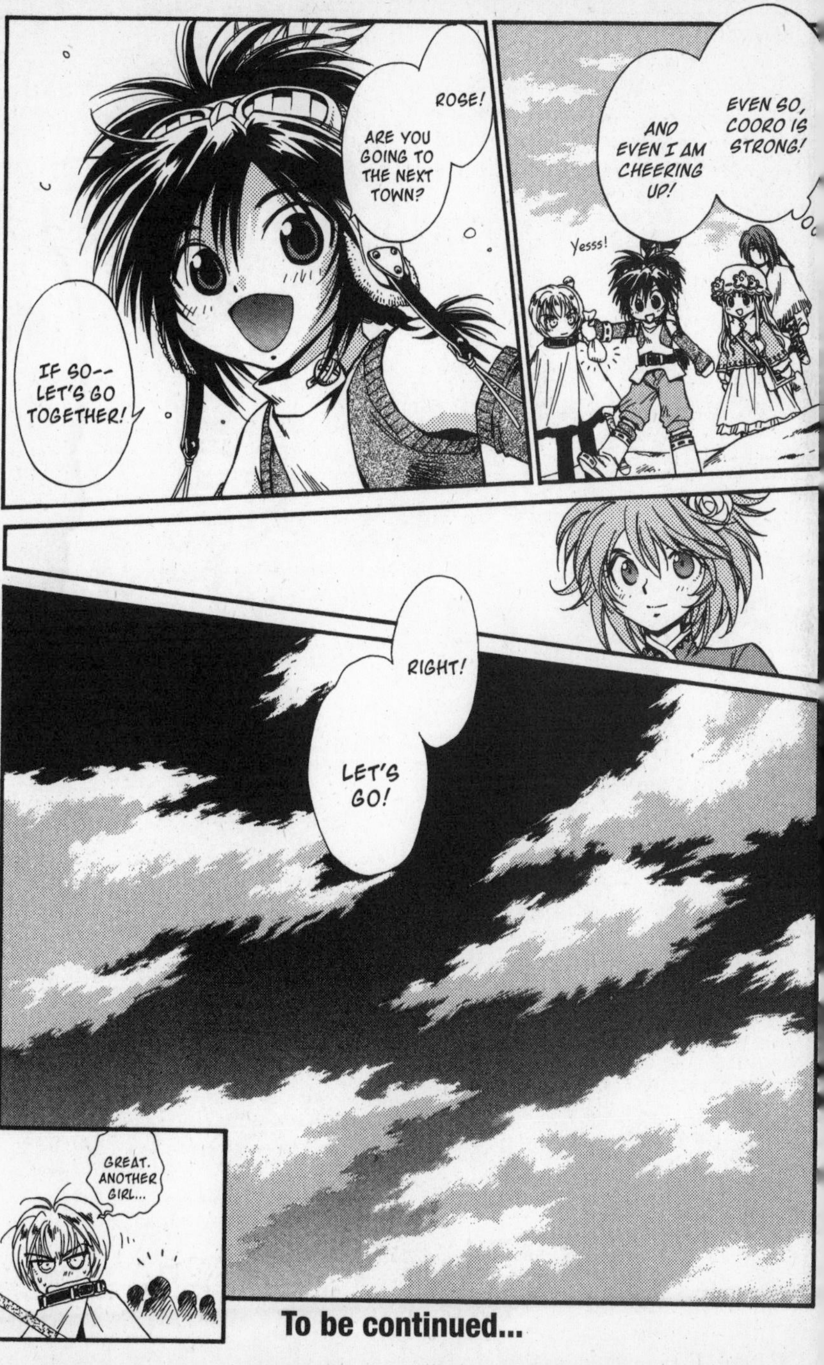
EVEN SO, COORO IS STRONG!
AND EVEN I AM CHEERING UP!
Yesss!
ROSE!
ARE YOU GOING TO THE NEXT TOWN?
IF SO-- LET'S GO TOGETHER!
RIGHT!
LET'S GO!
GREAT. ANOTHER GIRL...

To be continued...

Cooro's favorite food is apples!
It's a common, simple red fruit, and its
round shape invites a feeling of fullness--
so it fits Cooro perfectly. Apple pie, baked
apples, bread covered in apple jam, and
of course raw apples!
Well...Cooro will eat anything, except he
doesn't like bitter things because he's a
little kid.

Favorite Foods

Apple pie.♡
He likes it jam-
packed with filling.

← Dried fish

Husky makes me wonder if he has a
favorite food. I get the feeling that he
doesn't care whether food tastes good.
He'd probably say, "When I'm hungry, it
doesn't matter what I eat, as long as I
get some nourishment." If I had to pick
something, I'd guess he'd like clean, fresh
food. He wouldn't like greasy or sweet foods
as much, and he prefers fish to red meat.
That makes me think, "Isn't that like
cannibalism?" (teasing Husky)

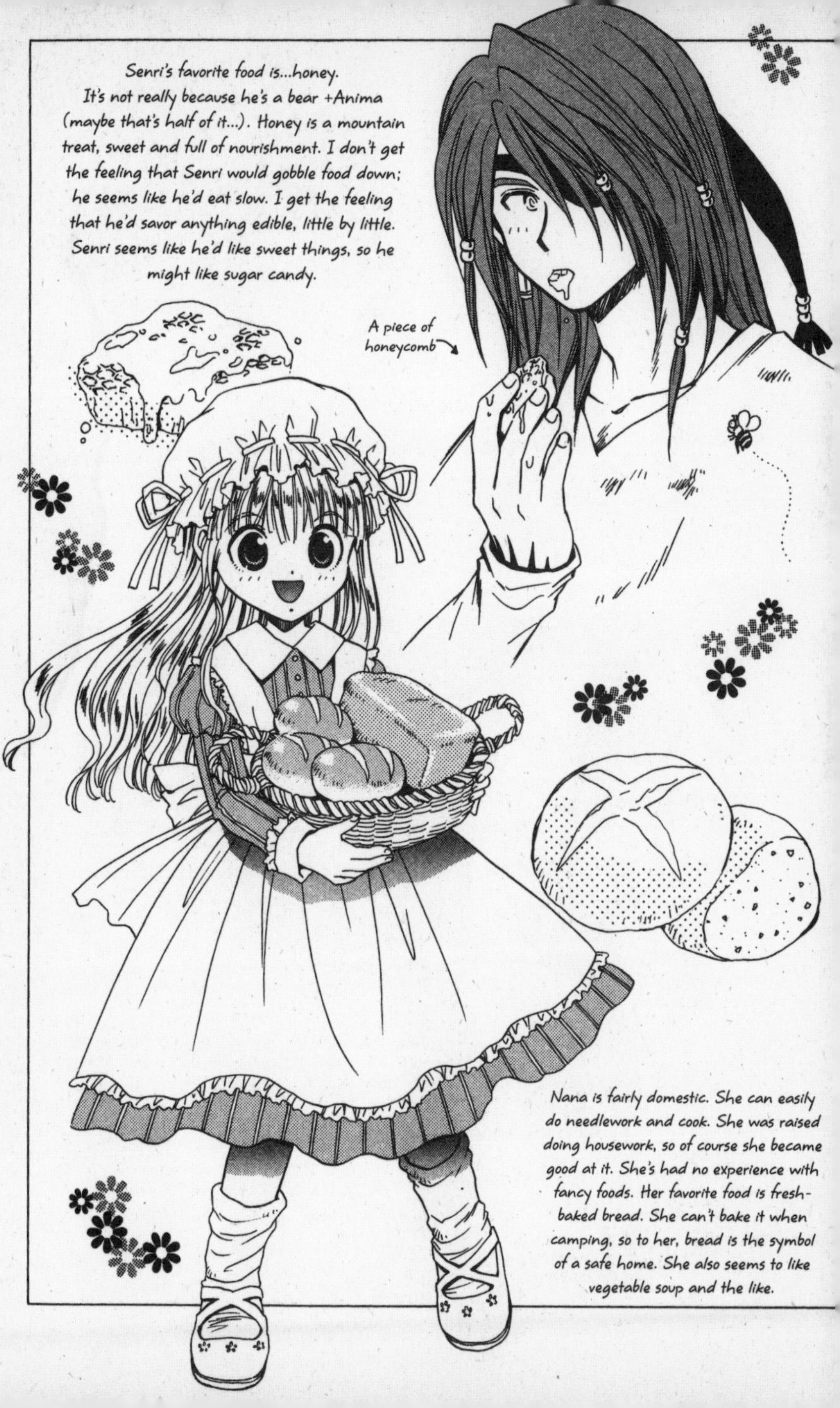
Senri's favorite food is...honey. It's not really because he's a bear +Anima (maybe that's half of it...). Honey is a mountain treat, sweet and full of nourishment. I don't get the feeling that Senri would gobble food down; he seems like he'd eat slow. I get the feeling that he'd savor anything edible, little by little. Senri seems like he'd like sweet things, so he might like sugar candy.
A piece of honeycomb
Nana is fairly domestic. She can easily do needlework and cook. She was raised doing housework, so of course she became good at it. She's had no experience with fancy foods. Her favorite food is fresh-baked bread. She can't bake it when camping, so to her, bread is the symbol of a safe home. She also seems to like vegetable soup and the like.

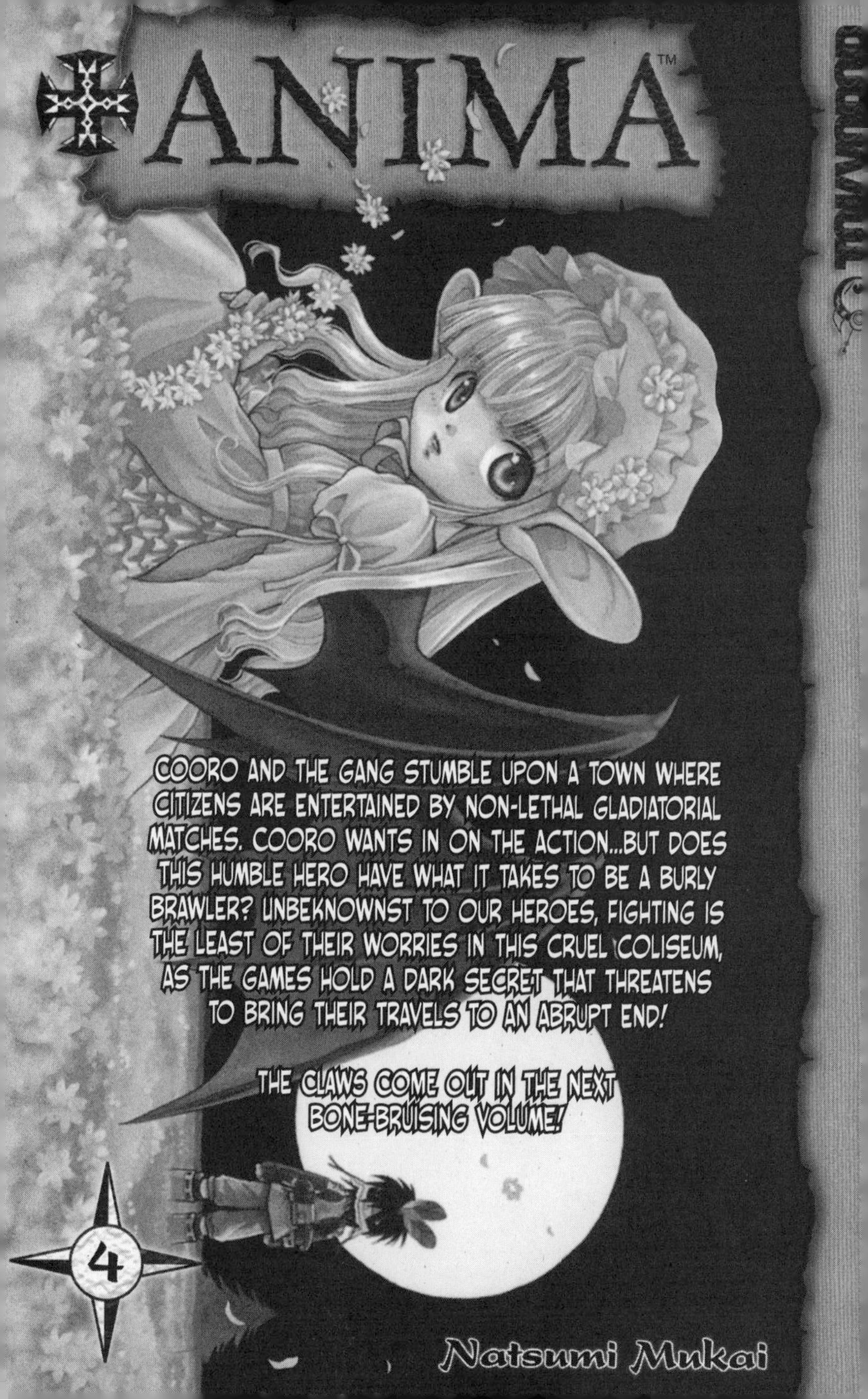

+ANIMA™
TOKYOPOP
COORO AND THE GANG STUMBLE UPON A TOWN WHERE CITIZENS ARE ENTERTAINED BY NON-LETHAL GLADIATORIAL MATCHES. COORO WANTS IN ON THE ACTION...BUT DOES THIS HUMBLE HERO HAVE WHAT IT TAKES TO BE A BURLY BRAWLER? UNBEKNOWNST TO OUR HEROES, FIGHTING IS THE LEAST OF THEIR WORRIES IN THIS CRUEL COLISEUM, AS THE GAMES HOLD A DARK SECRET THAT THREATENS TO BRING THEIR TRAVELS TO AN ABRUPT END!
THE CLAWS COME OUT IN THE NEXT BONE-BRUISING VOLUME!
4
Natsumi Mukai

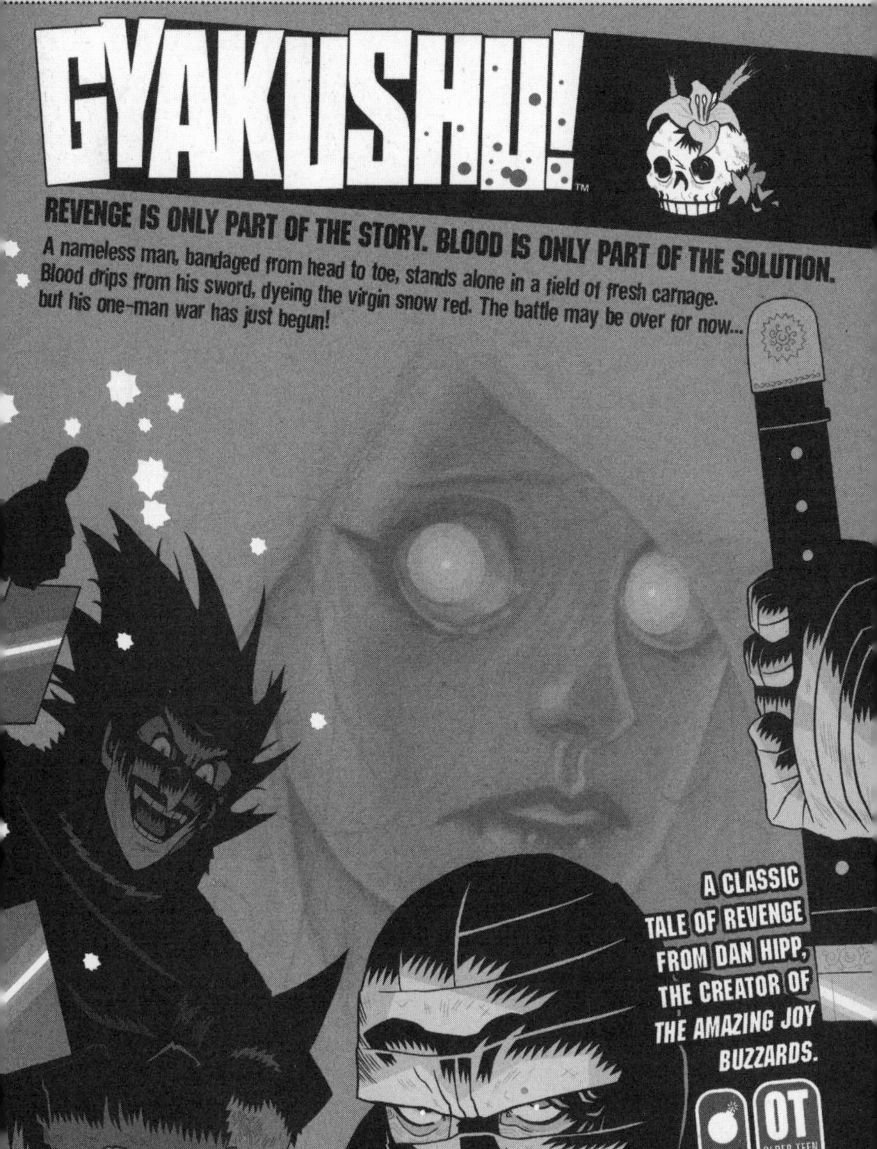
GYAKUSHU!™
REVENGE IS ONLY PART OF THE STORY. BLOOD IS ONLY PART OF THE SOLUTION.
A nameless man, bandaged from head to toe, stands alone in a field of fresh carnage. Blood drips from his sword, dyeing the virgin snow red. The battle may be over for now... but his one-man war has just begun!
A CLASSIC TALE OF REVENGE FROM DAN HIPP, THE CREATOR OF THE AMAZING JOY BUZZARDS.
ACTION
OT OLDER TEEN AGE 16+
© Daniel Hipp and TOKYOPOP Inc.